THE POLITICAL ECONOMY OF THE PUBLIC BUDGET IN THE AMERICAS

The Political Economy of the Public Budget in the Americas

Edited by
Diego Sánchez-Ancochea
and Iwan Morgan

INSTITUTE FOR THE STUDY OF THE
AMERICAS

UNIVERSITY OF LONDON · SCHOOL OF ADVANCED STUDY

British Library Cataloguing-in-Publication Data
A catalogue record for this book is available from the British Library

ISBN 978 1 900039 94 9

INSTITUTE FOR THE STUDY OF THE
AMERICAS
UNIVERSITY OF LONDON · SCHOOL OF ADVANCED STUDY

Institute for the Study of the Americas
University of London
Senate House
Malet Street
London
WC1E 7HU

Telephone: 020 7862 8870
Fax: 020 7862 8886

Email: americas@sas.ac.uk
Web: www.americas.sas.ac.uk

CONTENTS

TABLES AND FIGURES

Tables

Figures

NOTES ON CONTRIBUTORS

Manuel R. Agosin is Professor of Economics at the University of Chile, Santiago, and a former economist for the Inter-American Development Bank. He has published an extensive array of journal articles and working papers in his main field of interest. These include development issues, the effect of financial liberalisation on developing economies,and Chile's economic performance. He is also co-editor of a recently published book, *Solving the Riddle of Globalization and Development* (2008).

Edmund Amann is Reader in Economic Studies at the University of Manchester, Jorge Lemann Visiting Professor at the University of Illinois and Professorial Lecturer at the Paul H. Nitze School for Advanced International Studies (SAIS), Johns Hopkins University. His research interests centre on the economics of emerging market countries, especially those of Latin America. He is especially interested in the role that technology can play in assisting emerging market countries to redefine their place in the international division of labour. His publications include *Regulating Development: Evidence from Africa and Latin America* (Edward Elgar, 2007) and *Economic Liberalisation and Industrial Performance in Brazil* (Oxford University Press, 2000).

Werner Baer is the Jorge Lemann Professor of Economics at the University of Illinois. His research interests include industrialisation and privatisation in Latin America and he has written extensively on the Brazilian economy. Professor Baer has also been a consultant for the World Bank, Ford Foundation, Brazilian Planning Ministry, US Information Agency, and US State Department and a visiting scholar in several Latin American and European countries. Recent publications include *Equity and Distortions in Regional Resource Allocation in Brazil* (The Haworth Press, 2007) (co-edited with Geoffrey Hewings) and the sixth edition of *The Brazilian Economy: Growth and Development* (Lynne Rienner, 2007) as well as several articles in international journals.

Dennis S. Ippolito is the Eugene McElvaney Professor of Political Science and chairman of the Department of Political Science at Southern Methodist University. Prior to joining the faculty at SMU in 1982, he taught at the University of Virginia and at Emory University. Professor Ippolito's research focuses on federal budget policy and fiscal policy. His books include *Why Budgets Matter: Budget Policy and American Politics*, *Budget Policy and the Future of Defense* and *Uncertain Legacies: Federal Budget Policy from Roosevelt through Reagan*. Other books on budget policy have analysed spending and deficit-control, federal credit programs and contingent liabilities, and constitutional restrictions on fiscal policy.

Colin M. Lewis is Professor in Latin American Economic History at the London School of Economics & Political Science and an Associate Fellow of the Institute for the Study of the Americas, University of London. His main research interests are in economic and social policy, the political economy of state formation and business history. His recent publications include: *Argentina: a short history* (2002) and, edited with Christopher Abel, *Exclusion & Engagement: social policy in Latin America* (2002). He is currently completing a study of British business in the Argentine, and editing a volume on social policy reform, citizenship and state action in Latin America.

Roberto Machado is currently Economic Affairs Officer and Coordinator of the Economic Development Unit at the UN Economic Commission for Latin America and the Caribbean Subregional Headquarters for the Caribbean in Port of Spain. His research interests include economic growth, fiscal policies, and Foreign Direct Investment, especially in Latin America and the Caribbean. His recent publications are 'Openness and the International Allocation of Foreign Direct Investment', *Journal of Development Studies*, October 2007 (with Manuel R. Agosin) and 'Aid and Fiscal Policy in Nicaragua: A Fiscal Response Analysis', *Journal of International Development*, forthcoming.

Andrew H. Mitchell is Postdoctoral Fellow in Economics at the UCLA Center for Economic History. He has worked extensively on the comparative fiscal history of Argentina and Australia, the subject of his doctoral thesis. He is currently working on a project that explores the links between progressive taxation and development.

Iwan Morgan is Professor of US Studies and Head of US Programmes at the Institute for the Study of the Americas, University of London. He has written extensively on US political economy, including *Eisenhower versus 'The Spenders'* (1990) and *Deficit Government* (1995). His most recent publication (co-edited with Philip Davies) is *Right On? Political Change and Continuity in George W. Bush's America* (2006) and he is presently working on a study of US presidents and the budget deficit.

Diego Sánchez-Ancochea is University Lecturer in Political Economy at the University of Oxford and Fellow of St Antony's College. He was previously Senior Lecturer in Economics at the Institute for the Study of the Americas (University of London). His research concentrates on state-society interactions, income inequality and public policy in small Latin American countries. Recent publications include the co-edited volumes *Responding to Globalization: The Political Economy of Hemispheric Integration in the Americas* (Palgrave Macmillan, 2008) (with Kenneth Shadlen) and *Transnational Corporations and Development Policy* (Palgrave Macmillan, forthcoming, 2008) (with Eric

Rugraff and Andrew Sumner) as well as a forthcoming special issue on Latin America's model of capitalism in *Economy and Society*.

Aaron Schneider is Assistant Professor of Political Science and Latin American Studies at Tulane University. He was previously a Fellow in Governance at the Institute for Development Studies at the University of Sussex. His research concentrates on the politics of public finance in developing countries, with particular attention to the way governments respond to fiscal pressures that result from insertion in the international economy. Recently published works include 'After the Washington Consensus: International Assistance and Governance', *Revista Debates*, 2:1: 15-31, 2008 and 'Corruption and the World Bank' in Leonardo Avritzer ed. *Dictionary of Political Corruption*, (forthcoming, UFMG Press).

Carlos E. Schonerwald is Professor in Economics at the Universidade do Vale do Rio dos Sinos (UNISINOS) and Researcher of the Economic Commission for Latin America and the Caribbean (ECLAC). He was previously adjunct instructor in Economics at the Weber State University and instructor at the University of Utah. His research concentrates on economic growth and development, international economics and industrial organisation. Recent papers include 'Institutions, Geography, and Terms of Trade in Latin America: A Longitudinal Econometric Analysis' which will be presented at the American Economic Association meeting, 2009.

Matías Vernengo is Assistant Professor of Economics at the University of Utah, where he teaches macroeconomics, Latin American economic history and the history of economic thought. He has been a consultant for ECLAC, ILO and UNDP on development issues. His research is focused on the macroeconomic aspects of economic development in Latin America, in particular Argentina and Brazil. He is the co-editor of *Ideas, Policies, and Economic Development in the Americas* (Routledge, 2007) and author of several (too many!) articles. He would rather have more time to read.

PART I
INTRODUCTION

INTRODUCTION: THE POLITICAL ECONOMY OF THE BUDGETS IN COMPARATIVE PERSPECTIVE

Diego Sánchez-Ancochea and Iwan Morgan

Introduction

Despite their significant differences in regards to ideology, social values and levels of state intervention, the United States and Latin America share some characteristics in their public budgets.[1] In comparison to Western Europe in particular, the Americas should be regarded as a region of small 'fiscal states'. Our use of this term applies to states with relatively low taxes and consequently limited fiscal resources available for social spending and infrastructure investment.[2]

For a large body of literature in politics and economics, low taxes are a public good. A small government is supposed to free resources for the private sector, enhance individual incentives and expand savings. Low taxes minimise market distortions and expand savings and efforts. A low-tax equilibrium, however, is problematic — particularly in countries with high levels of inequality, because the state is unable to expand social spending and implement an active redistributive policy. This is particularly evident in the United States and in most Latin American countries, where high levels of inequality coexist with low redistributive social spending and relatively low levels of taxation. Given growing social demands for health, education and other public services, a small fiscal state may also face high public deficits and periodic fiscal crises.

This book, the result of a conference organised by the Institute for the Study of the Americas with support from Chatham House in November 2006, explores some of these problems and risks, highlighting the differences and similarities between the United States and various Latin American countries. Our comparative analysis is based on three fundamental claims. First, the region as a whole is characterised by small fiscal states, which face some common problems to secure high levels of public investment in infrastructure, and especially contribute to more equitable distributional structures. Second, a preferential access to foreign capital loosens the fiscal constraints in the United States much more than in Latin America. In fact, the United States has hitherto been able to maintain high levels of public and trade deficits with total support from global financial markets — something that become clear with the approval of the US$700 billion Troubled Asset Relief Program in September 2008. Meanwhile, Latin American countries have suffered the 'disciplining' force of these same markets, which have pressured them to maintain low public deficits. Third, this situation may no longer be sustainable in the context of high trade imbalances and the escalating fiscal deficit resulting from the public response to one of the worst financial crises in the last century. Consequently, even the United States may not be spared the necessity to expand tax revenues to meet future challenges for much longer.

In the remainder of this introductory chapter, we develop these three claims with more detail based on the evidence from the different contributors to the volume. We start with a discussion of the size of the fiscal state in the Americas. The next section highlights the differing degrees of freedom to implement fiscal policies in the United States and Latin America, which are caused by different access to foreign funds. The final section explores key policy issues, including the likelihood of fiscal reforms that can contribute to reduce inequality and promote competitiveness in the Americas.

We should at the outset emphasise that the volume does not aim to provide final answers, but should rather be seen as an attempt to encourage further research on public policy, the size of the state and political economy from a comparative perspective within the Americas. The United States and Latin America are obviously very different in levels of development and in their position in the global economy. At the same time, they present striking similarities in patterns of inequality (particularly with high concentration of income at the top) and in the characteristics of the fiscal state that merit further exploration. We hope this set of papers from specialists on the United States and Latin American political economies will encourage new work on the subject — something particularly urgent given the current global financial circumstances.

A Commonality Within the Americas: The Smallness of the Fiscal State

While taxes and public spending have some unique determinants (Campbell, 1993; Campbell and Allen, 1994), they are ultimately closely linked. Since governments do not have unlimited access to credit, their ability to generate revenues constitutes an upward limit on public spending. On the other hand, the demand for public services can pressure governments to increase taxes to finance them. It is therefore useful to consider both components of the budget simultaneously when discussing the size of the fiscal state in the Americas.

Countries in the Americas generate lower tax revenues than countries elsewhere with similar characteristics (measured in terms of income per capita, income inequality and other economic variables). According to data for 2002, the share of total taxes (national and local) in gross domestic product (GDP) in the United States was just 26.4 per cent — the second lowest among OECD countries (just above Mexico) and well below the European Union (EU) average (40.3 per cent).[3] Chile is the only Latin American country with a tax burden comparable with similar countries (Sánchez-Ancochea, this volume, Chapter 10).[4] Raising revenues equivalent to only 9.5 per cent of GDP in 2005, Guatemala has one of the smallest tax burdens of any country in the world (Agosín et al., this volume, Chapter 7).

The divergence between the Americas and other parts of the world in terms of taxation began during the twentieth century, and was directly linked to differences in the development of the welfare state. According to data from Sokoloff and Zolt (2007), national tax revenues as a percentage of GDP around 1870 were higher in the United States than in England, Germany, Sweden, Norway and Switzerland, but lower than in Argentina and Brazil.[5] By 1970, however, total taxes (including state and local ones) were 35.7 per cent in Belgium, 40.4 per cent in Denmark, 32.5 per cent in Finland, 32.9 per cent in Germany, 39.8 per cent in Sweden and only 27.7 per cent in the United States (Campbell, 2005 from OECD original data). The differences were even larger at the beginning of the twenty-first century, as discussed in Sánchez-Ancochea's contribution to this volume (Chapter 10).

In the case of the United States, low taxes constrained the growth of social programmes and public infrastructure during the second half of the twentieth century, and resulted in what Galbraith (1999) called the 'social imbalance' between private affluence and public scarcity, particularly when combined with high levels of military spending.[6] Ippolito (this volume, Chapter 9) offers a detailed account of tax and spending policy during this period. Tax cuts prompted by neo-Keynesian doctrine in the 1960s and supply-side doctrine in the 1980s were subsequently frozen or reversed in the name of fiscal prudence and balanced budgets. In 1964–66, for example, the Johnson administration cut taxes and increased social spending and the aegis of the Great Society, but had to levy a tax sub-charge in 1968 because of concerns that a growing deficit was generating inflation. The Reagan tax cuts of 1981, which undermined public revenues in contravention of 'Laffer-curve' expectations, were also followed by tax increases in 1982, 1984 and 1990 to tackle the growing budget deficit. The end result of all these policy shifts was that both taxes and public spending remained relatively stable during the period 1948–2006, with no real upward trend.[7]

In Latin America, the share of public revenues in GDP experienced an upward trend during the second half of the twentieth century, but the expansion was slow (see Table 1.1). In fact, the bulk of the growth took place in the 1970s (when the tax share in relation to GDP jumped by more than four percentage points) and the expansion of the tax burden has slowed down significantly in more recent times. Many countries in the region faced difficulties in introducing successful tax reforms, and some experienced policy reversals. The case of Argentina, as discussed by Lewis and Mitchell (this volume), is illustrative. While warning about different methodological problems with the data, they show how central government receipts in Argentina fluctuated between 8 per cent and 14 per cent of GDP during most years between 1945 and 2000, with no clear upward trend. During this period, the Argentine state failed to introduce reforms that could have broadened the tax base and diversified public revenues. At the same time, pressures to expand public services grew and the public sector became more active. By the early 1970s, social spending as a percentage of GDP was above 16 per cent, and public companies were present in many economic sectors, notably railways, telecommunications, electricity, large banks and food processing (Filgueira, 2005; Lewis and Mitchell, this volume, Chapter 2).

Why are taxes and public spending relatively low in the Americas? Are the roots of the small fiscal state similar in the United States and Latin America? While the literature on the determinants of the size of the state (particularly in relation to social spending) is vast, there are few systematic comparisons between the United States and Latin America. Some influential recent literature on the

Table 1.1: Latin America — Public Revenues as Percentage of GDP, 1950–2000

	Five-year Moving Average
1950	10.98
1960	11.90
1970	12.13
1980	16.57
1990	17.86
2000	19.46

Note: Calculated as the non-weighted average of 12 countries (1950) and 17 countries (for the rest of the period).

Source: Own calculations with data from Oxford Latin America Economic History database.

subject emphasises the historical differences between these two parts of the Americas in terms of initial endowments and income distribution (Engerman and Sokoloff, 1997; Engerman, Mariscal and Sokoloff, 2002; Sokoloff and Zolt, 2007), but does not systematically explore the contemporary situation or recognise some striking similarities between the United States and Latin America.

The current volume constitutes an invitation for future research on the size and characteristics of the fiscal state in the Americas. A number of its contributors identify key variables that can inform future inquiries. Some variables — for example, state credibility or the long-term ideological divisions between political parties — are apparently unique to either Latin America or the United States. Lewis and Mitchell (this volume, Chapter 2), for example, highlight the lack of state credibility in the Latin American context — that is, states have been unable to implement the fiscal and monetary policies required to 'devise sustainable taxation and borrowing strategies that facilitate the provision of tangible public goods'. This lack of credibility has a double dimension: citizens are unwilling to contribute to the expansion of the state, while investors (both domestic and foreign) are reluctant to acquire public debt.[8] The result is a vicious cycle: fiscal institutions that lack credibility are unable to secure enough tax revenues and public credit and consequently lack the capacity and resources to provide an optimum level of public goods — further weakening state credibility.

In the United States, fiscal institutions are stronger and, despite conservative criticisms of the public sector, the state does not face problems of credibility. Americans are, for example, highly motivated to pay taxes. In a study of tax morale — that is, the intrinsic motivation to pay taxes — Alm and Torgler (2004, p. 15) find that 'the individuals in the United States have the highest tax morale across all countries, followed by those in Austria and Switzerland', and they speculate that this may be the result of an electoral system that promotes closer relations between legislators and the electorate than in other countries.

Political preferences and ideology may in turn be more important in the United States than in Latin America when accounting for the level of public revenues and spending. According to Ippolito's analysis of tax policy in the United States, 'the budget policy battles of the past several decades make very clear the debate over the size of government is a serious one in the United States, and we can expect tax policy to remain at the heart of that debate for a very long time'. The different behaviours of the last Democrat and Republican administrations clearly illustrate this point (Ippolito, this volume, Chapter 3). In 1993, Bill Clinton raised top marginal rates for income tax (from 31 per cent to 39.6 per cent) and the Medicare payroll taxes, and levied additional taxes on social security benefits. Eighty per cent of these changes, which aimed to safeguard social entitlements and simultaneously reduce the public deficit, targeted high-income taxpayers. George W. Bush, on the other hand, reversed this trend and introduced sweeping tax cuts, particularly for the very rich, in 2001 and 2003. The reforms included a reduction in income tax rates and the estate tax — which also was to be repealed by 2010 — as well as a lowering of dividend and capital gain taxes to just 15 per cent. In conjunction with the effects of economic recession, Bush's tax cuts wiped out the revenue gains of the 1990s. The share of tax revenues in GDP, which had increased from 18 per cent in 1990 to 20.9 per cent in 2000, declined to 17.9 per cent in 2002 and just 16.3 per cent in 2004.

Until recently, the struggle between political parties about the size of the state has been less intense in Latin America than in the United States, due to a set of interrelated factors. First, the prevalence of authoritarian regimes over much of the twentieth century curtailed many of the debates about key economic issues. Right-wing governments in Chile and Central America were particularly effective in maintaining a low tax base and controlling social spending. Second, left-wing parties have had limited access to power in many Latin American countries (Huber et al., 2006). Third, Latin American political parties have historically been characterised by weak levels of institutionalisation and links with voters that are more personalistic than programmatic (Mainwaring and Torcal, 2006). As a result, debates about key economic policy issues are more volatile, and sharp shifts in policy discourses more common. Fourth, Latin American countries have also faced significant external pressures to limit progressive taxation and adopt reformist policies. According to Huber (2002: 15), 'time and again, overt and covert interventions were directed against reformist political actors and left repressive authoritarian regimes in their wake'.

Given the dramatic asymmetries in levels of development between the United States and Latin America, this accent on differences is not surprising. Nevertheless, when thinking about a future comparative research agenda, it may also be useful to explore some common structural variables. By way of illustration, we will briefly discuss two that have been emphasised in the political economy literature: access to political power and race fractionalisation.[9]

Latin America and the United States are both characterised by asymmetric access to political power — some individuals and corporations have privileged influence on the political process, while trade unions and other social movements are generally weak. According to the World Bank (2004, p. 3), the political systems in Latin America suffer from 'high degrees of inequality of influence, with disproportionate influence over the state by wealthy individuals or corporations while poorer groups typically interact with the state through vertical relations of patronage, or are excluded'. Trade unions have historically been weak, and represented only a small share of the labour force. Unionisation rates vary significantly within the region, but no country has a rate above 30 per cent of the labour force, and small countries tend to have negligible levels (McGuire, 1999; Schneider and Karcher, 2007). Relations between trade unions and governments have also been either antagonistic or paternalistic, and workers have found themselves with little influence on the characteristics and level of public programmes (Huber, 2002). Weak trade unions have also been a significant factor behind the limited success of social-democratic parties in the region, which generally have been unable to pressure for larger fiscal states (Huber, 2005).

Much of the literature on the size of the fiscal state in the United States emphasises similar variables (Campbell and Allan, 1994; Campbell, 2005; Esping-Andersen, 1990; Korpi, 2006). Despite business fragmentation (Martin, 1991), the importance of lobbying and the private financing of political campaigns in the United States have been instrumental in expanding the influence of large firms and rich donors. According to the Center for Responsive Politics, a non-partisan think tank, corporations spent 15 times more than trade unions in the various elections in 2000. In particular, the top 82 US companies contributed an estimated US$33 million to political action committees, excluding soft money donations (Anderson and Cavanagh, 2000). Given their focus in radical innovation and competition through costs, US business firms are generally more supportive of low taxation and a small welfare state than their counterparts in Continental Europe (Hall and Soskice, 2001; Iversen and Soskice, 2006).

Trade unions have been weaker in the United States than in many other developed countries, particularly in Western Europe, during the twentieth century. In 1970, the United States had a unionisation rate of 25 per cent compared with 33 per cent in Germany, 45 per cent in the United Kingdom and well above 50 per cent in Austria, Norway and the Scandinavian countries. US trade unions have been particularly weakened since the late 1970s, at a time when the progressivity of taxation greatly diminished (more than in other countries), the tax burden stagnated and social programmes generally became less generous (Coates, 2000; Campbell, 2005; Levy and Temin, 2007).

The consequences of the asymmetric access to policy-making in terms of the level of taxes and public spending, particularly in social programmes, is evident in both Latin America and the United States, and has been highlighted by the comparative literature on developed countries. According to Campbell (2005: 407), for example, 'countries where the labor movement is centralized and strong politically tend to have higher tax rates than countries where labor is more decentralized and weak politically'. In the Latin American context, the asymmetric class structure affects not just the level but also the structure of the tax system, which is over-reliant on regressive indirect taxation. In Central America, for example, value-added and excise taxes generate between 50 per cent and 60 per cent of total tax revenues, while income taxes suffer from multiple exceptions (Agosin et al., this volume, Chapter 7). Political inequality is also evident in the distribution of many public services (including health and education), which are highly concentrated in the largest cities and favoured high-income groups.

Race has also been mentioned as a key variable to explain the size of the state and the limited provision of redistributive social services — a large component of public spending in any country — in different parts of the Americas. In a sample of 55 developed and developing countries (including several in Latin America), Alesina et al. (2001) find a strong correlation between race fractionalisation and the share of social spending in GDP — which is in turn directly linked to the level of taxes. In Latin America, race has played a double role in explaining the small size of the state. Racial heterogeneity reinforced the difficulties of creating a political base to pressure for higher taxes and public spending (World Bank, 2004). At the same time, racial discrimination has also reduced the willingness of the elite to support an expansion of public services for the poor.

There is a growing, parallel literature that highlights the importance of race in explaining the small size of the welfare state — which, we must repeat, accounts for a large share of total public spending — in the United States. In a detailed comparison of the factors behind differences in (redistributive) social spending, Alesina and Glaeser (2004, p. 134) conclude that 'about 50 per cent of the gap between the United States and Europe may be due to race fractionalization'.[10] In an excellent revision of the literature on inequality and redistribution, McCarty and Pontusson (2008) discuss the various mechanisms that link race and welfare spending. Race fractionalisation in the United States may weaken social solidarity and thus reduce the willingness of the middle class and the rich to pay taxes. Identity politics may also reduce the importance of material interests when making decisions — a point brilliantly explained by Krugman (2007) in a recent popular book on the politics of inequality in the United States. Racism is partly the result of the development of negative stereotypes regarding the behaviour of the black population and its effective use by conservative politicians.

In concluding this subsection, it is useful to reiterate two basic ideas from the previous discussion. Despite their sharp differences in economic and institutional structures, the United States and Latin America both have small fiscal states. Yet relatively little research has so far been undertaken to systematically compare the factors that explain low public taxes and spending in each case, and explore how they interact with different levels of socio-economic and institutional development across the Americas.

Low Public Spending and the Consequences of Small Fiscal States

Conservative observers and some neoclassical economists welcome small fiscal states. According to Daniel Mitchell, of the Heritage Foundation, government intervention is so costly and inefficient that 'reducing the size of government would lead to higher incomes and improve America's competitiveness' (Mitchell, 2005, p. 5). Comparing the fiscal state in Europe and the United States, Mitchell also argues that the United States has performed better than 'old' Europe because it has a small state — a point often made by conservative observers who criticise European sclerosis. Some studies have even tried to estimate the optimum spending level in the United States, placing it at around 17.5 per cent of GDP (e.g. Veder and Gallaway, 1998).

Glen Hubbard, chair of George Bush's Council of Economic Advisers in 2001–02, extended this conclusion to Latin American countries. In his view, 'excessive state control limits the ability of the private sector to develop the financial capacity for growth, leading to larger-than-necessary public sector spending and thus the need to raise corresponding revenues. The problem for growth is that most taxes distort economic activity and thus impinge on growth.' (Hubbard, 2002: 3) Some econometric studies have also highlighted the negative relationship between public consumption and economic growth (see, for example, Barro, 1991; Sala-i-Marti, 1997).

Yet a detailed comparison of different countries within the developed world signals little relationship between the size of the fiscal state and economic efficiency (Freeman, 2000; Hall and Soskice, 2001: Korpi, 1996; Pontusson, 2005). In fact, between 1960 and 2004, real GDP per capita in local currency grew at exactly the same rate (2.2 per cent per year) in Sweden and the United States, despite sharp differences in the size of the public sector. Finland (2.9 per cent) and Norway (3.1 per cent) were two of the best performers within developed countries, while maintaining high levels of taxes and government spending (see Table 1.2).

While the size of the fiscal state arguably has limited influence on economic growth and efficiency, certain types of government expenditures have great significance for some socio-economic variables such as income distribution. In particular, and as discussed in detail in Sánchez-Ancochea's contribution to this volume (Chapter 10), high social spending increases the redistributive impact of the state. Korpi and Palme (1998), for example, show that countries with large redistributive budgets and universal social programmes have higher levels of redistribution (defined as the difference between the Gini coefficient before and after tax and transfers) than those with low social spending and focus on targeted problems — like that of the United States. The low redistributive power of the US budget — which is directly linked to its small size, to the concentration of social spending in contributory programmes like social

Table 1.2: Annual average rates of economic growth for selected developed countries, GDP in constant local currency, 1960–2004

	1960–70	1970–80	1980–90	1990–2004	1960–2004
Denmark	3.71	1.53	1.54	1.69	2.07
Finland	4.39	3.30	2.61	1.65	2.86
France	4.46	2.70	1.94	1.36	2.49
Germany	–	3.66	2.15	1.27	2.18
Japan	9.32	3.29	3.36	1.18	3.96
Korea, Republic of	5.59	5.35	7.46	4.79	5.70
Norway	3.36	4.24	2.24	2.62	3.07
Sweden	3.88	1.62	1.89	1.65	2.20
United Kingdom	2.22	1.84	2.42	2.13	2.15
United States	2.53	2.20	2.28	1.90	2.20

Source: Own calculations with data from the World Development Indicators database.

security and to high levels of military spending — is also acknowledged by Alesina et al. (2001), Pontusson (2005), Stephens (2002) and many others.

This finding is particularly worrisome because of the high levels of inequality before taxes and transfers that the United States has historically had. In the early 1980s, the Gini coefficient for gross income (i.e. before tax and transfers) was significantly higher in the United States (35.6) than in Germany (28.5) and all the Nordic countries (where it was between 28.4 and 30.8) (data from Pontusson, 2005, p. 40). In recent times, inequality has increased rapidly, particularly due to the concentration of income at the top of the distributional structure. The income share of the richest 1 per cent in the United States (excluding capital gains) has increased from 7.7 per cent in 1973 to almost 20 per cent in 2005 (Piketty and Saenz, 2006 and 2008).

The implications of this finding for Latin America are profound.[11] If the region is serious about reducing inequality and expanding the redistributive power of the state, it should not attempt to follow the US liberal model based on a small fiscal state and target social programmes. This is a particularly important comparative finding at a time when conditional cash transfers based on targeting principles are spreading in the region, and universal principles have been abandoned (Huber, 2002; Mkandawire, 2006; Sánchez-Ancochea, this volume, Chapter 10).

The lack of public revenues in the Americas may also be especially problematic for the sustainability of the public deficits in the long run. In the case of the United States, in particular, the current level of taxes may be insufficient to finance the uncontrollable share of government spending — a point discussed in detail by Ippolito in Chapter 3. Currently, nearly 65 per cent of federal outlays are devoted to payments to individuals — notably under Social Security, Medicare and Medicaid entitlements — and another 10 per cent goes on interest payments. Entitlement spending involves fixed commitments over which the government has no or little control, and these will grow steadily in the future as a result of demographic factors. In fact, according to some estimations, combined spending for Social Security, Medicare and Medicaid will alone be around 20 per cent of GDP by 2050, surpassing the current level of all federal taxes (Ippolito, Chapter 3). The United States thus faces difficult political decisions in the next few decades that directly result from the small revenue capacity of its federal government. Future policy-makers could try to modify the terms of the programmes (an option that Ippolito sees as inevitable) but, given their popularity, this will face strong opposition from large segments of the population. They may also rely on growing public debt, but this will have problematic effects on the current account and the the value of the dollar (Morgan, this volume, Chapter 4). The future growth of the public debt will also be constrained by its rapid expansion in the last months of 2008 — likely to continue in 2009 — as a result of the sharp financial crisis and the subsequent recession. Or the United States can face up to the necessity of undertaking a significant expansion of the fiscal state.

While most Latin American countries do not face the same demographic pressures on public spending, they have insufficient revenues to meet its various long-term demands for several reasons. First, interest payments as a proportion of total public expenditure in many Latin American countries are higher than in the United States. According to Table 1.3 (which does not include data for countries like Brazil and Ecuador), only four Latin American countries have a lower interest burden than the United States. In countries like Argentina (26 per cent), Colombia (19.4 per cent) and Costa Rica (18.2 per cent), the share of interests on the government budget is almost twice as high as in the United States.[12] If we add payments of the principal, the differences may be even larger, although comparative data are hard to obtain.[13]

Second, Latin America's competitive challenges are significantly larger than those of the United States. In particular, the region must improve its public infrastructure if it is to compete with China and other developing countries in the near future. According to a World Bank report, 'the region is spending less than 2 per cent of GDP on infrastructure — but 4–6 per cent per annum is needed if it is to catch up or keep up with countries that once trailed it, such as Korea or China' (Fay and Morrison, 2005, p. i). If these countries are to attract foreign investment and create new knowledge-based assets, Latin American governments will also need to increase expenditure in education, training, research and development, as well as subsidies to domestic firms (Paus, 2005).

Third, the region must increase its redistributive spending (particularly universal pensions, child allowances and health), while simultaneously

Table 1.3: Various countries in the Americas. Interest payments and military spending (% total public spending), 2005

	Interest payments	*Military spending*
Argentina	26.31	5.87
Bolivia	10.03	7.13
Chile	4.58	20.20
Colombia	19.39	11.90
Costa Rica	18.19	–
Dominican Republic	9.57	3.26
El Salvador	12.47	3.52
Guatemala	10.76	3.75
Mexico	13.33	3.34
Nicaragua	9.04	3.27
Panama	21.46	4.51
Paraguay	7.13	–
Peru	10.85	7.24
Uruguay	15.90	4.99
Venezuela, RB	11.73	4.40
United States	9.61	19.26

Note: Data for Mexico is from 2000, for Panama from 2001 and for Argentina and the Dominican Republic from 2004.

Source: World Development Indicators database (last accessed 9 April 2008).

improving the quality of its service and the management of all public resources (Huber, 2002). Although there were significant advances in the expansion of social spending during the 1990s, there is still a need for further expansion of social spending in health, education and social support, particularly in low-income countries. According to the Economic Commission for Latin America and the Caribbean (ECLAC), 'public social expenditure remains subject to strong budgetary constraints and in many cases is associated with small tax burdens. As a result, the level of such expenditure is too low in a number of countries, particularly since there are signs that the international assistance and borrowings that used to provide countries with some sort of margin may cease to be available' (ECLAC, 2007, p. 24).

Some of these demands should undoubtedly be met through a reallocation of public resources. Many social programmes in Latin America are highly regressive: in Brazil, for example, 46 per cent of public payments to individuals go to the richest decile, mainly in the form of pensions (Amann and Baer, this volume, Chapter 6). Yet the restructuring of these services, while urgent, will be politically laborious and insufficient to meet all social needs. Additionally, most Latin American countries cannot reduce unproductive military spending in any significant way, as it is already moderate. As Table 1.3 indicates, the share of military expenditures in the total public budget in all Latin American countries (with the exception of Chile) is lower than in the United States and only exceeds 7 per cent in four countries. Like the United States, therefore, Latin America may have to recognise the need to gradually expand public revenues as a share of GDP if it is to meet all its social, economic and financial needs.

A Big Difference: External Conditions and Degrees of Freedom

Taxes are not the only way to finance public expenditure — at least in the short run. Countries can also resort to public debt to support both public consumption and investment, thus allowing them to run public deficits. Public credit-financed deficits can also be an excellent anti-cyclical Keynesian policy, and have been used by political parties of different persuasions.

The level of public debt and public deficits varies significantly among different countries in the Americas. Table 1.4 compares the cash public balance as a percentage of GDP across the Americas in 2004. The United States has a higher public deficit (–3.6 per cent) than Argentina (–0.46 per cent) or Chile (2.11 per cent), but lower than Bolivia (–5.39 per cent) or Colombia (–5.52 per cent). The United States does not seem to enjoy any particular advantage in this area or be any different from the rest of the Americas. Yet a more detailed analysis reveals significant asymmetries between Latin America and the United States — a point emphasised by various contributors to the volume.

In Latin America, most countries currently face restrictions to run high public deficits on a sustainable and secure basis. Public debt denominated in local currency is constrained by a relative lack of demand. The number of domestic investors willing and able to hold domestic public bonds is small, and foreign investors are reluctant to acquire them for fears of currency devaluation. A few countries have been able to issue significant quantities of debt in these conditions — in Costa Rica, for example, around 70 per cent of public debt is denominated in colones — but the terms are relatively costly.

As a result, all Latin American countries have borrowed in foreign currency — particularly in US dollars — and have faced major long-term risks. This is not something new in any way, since the region has been borrowing in the external markets since the nineteenth century. In 1890, for example, almost 100 per cent of Argentinean public debt and 75 per cent of Brazilian debt was denominated in hard currency (Bordo and Meissner, 2007). More recently, during the 1970s, excess liquidity in the international markets as a result of the dollar recycling allowed Latin American countries to borrow heavily and run high public deficits.

Table 1.4: Selected countries in the Americas. Cash surplus/deficit (%GDP), 2004

Country	% GDP
United States	−3.64
Argentina	−0.46
Bolivia	−5.39
Chile	2.11
Colombia	−5.52
Costa Rica	−1.33
Dominican Republic	−0.65
El Salvador	−3.28
Guatemala	−0.92
Mexico[1]	−1.17
Nicaragua	−1.06
Paraguay[2]	1.08
Peru	−1.19
Uruguay	−2.51
Venezuela, RB	−1.30

Notes: [1]Data from 2000.
         [2]Data from 2005.

Source: World Development Indicators electronic database (last accessed April 8, 2008).

The debt crisis of the early 1980s, however, revealed the dependent position of Latin American countries. The Federal Reserve's decision to increase interest rates in 1981–82 resulted in a rapid expansion of the debt service payments outside the country. The US prime rate in real terms went from −1.7 per cent in 1977 to 3.0 per cent in 1980 and 8.1 per cent in 1981, and Latin America's debt servicing as a share of total exports jumped from 38.3 per cent in 1980 to 59.0 per cent in 1982 (Bulmer-Thomas, 2003). The large expansion of public debt payments forced governments to adopt painful budgetary decisions, reducing social spending and sharply expanding public revenues.

By saddling Latin American countries with high debt shares and reducing their credibility in international markets, the debt crisis imposed new constraints on fiscal management that left governments facing difficult dilemmas. The example of Lula's government in Brazil — discussed by Amann and Baer in this volume (Chapter 6) — is particularly illustrative. President Lula arrived in power in 2003 with the clear mandate of reducing income inequality and improving the conditions of both the middle class and the poor. His supporters expected a radical departure from the economic policies of Fernando Henrique Cardoso's preceding regime, including a debt-financed expansion of public spending and the implementation of more ambitious social programmes. Yet Lula's administration adopted orthodox policies that included an overly cautious approach to public budgets. The primary public surplus (i.e. balance before interest payments) as a percentage of GDP increased from 3.5 per cent in 2002 to 3.9 per cent in 2003 and 4.3 per cent in 2005, and even exceeded the levels agreed with the International Monetary Fund (IMF).[14] This approach to fiscal policy limited the expansion of social policy. In fact, in 2006 the government spent just 0.5 per cent of GDP (2.5 per cent of the public budget) on Bolsa Famila — its star social programme based on cash transfers to the poor — compared with 3.6 per cent for debt servicing (18 per cent of the budget).

For Amman and Baer, this policy approach was contradictory. As they put it, 'the sequencing adopted may create difficulties. An initial period of economic orthodoxy, because of its effects on growth, might make it very difficult to allow for a subsequent large dose of policies aimed at greater socio-economic equity.' In their view, the Lula administration could have tackled the inequality and growth agendas simultaneously, implementing both a more expansionary fiscal policy and more ambitious structural reforms (particularly to limit the influence of interest rates in the allocation of the public budget). This would have resulted in larger advances in social indicators than the administration achieved both in the short and long run.

Although it is true that Brazil has consistently failed to maximise its degrees of freedom during the last 15 years, and could have set more heterodox fiscal targets, one should not forget the external constraints that the country has faced. The Lula administration was partly responding to international pressures when it adopted its ultra-orthodox policy approach. As Amann and Baer themselves show in this volume, and in previous work, the interest rate spread between Brazilian and US bonds widened significantly in the run-up to the election of President Lula in 2002, thus exerting an upward pressure on public finances. More heterodox policies would have been penalised by foreign investors and international financial institutions, and resulted in new difficulties for the public budget.

Schonerwald da Silva and Vernengo's contribution to this volume (Chapter 5) further explores the negative effect that externally conditioned orthodox budgetary policies have in most Latin American countries. Based on a simple macroeconomic model inspired by Lener, Domar and Pasinetti, they show that a combination of high primary surpluses, high interest rates and an over-valued exchange rate may lead to an artificial reduction in the dollar-denominated public debt to GDP ratio (thanks to the over-valuation of the currency), but will have negative effects on the long-term evolution of the economy. In particular, according to their account, this type of macroeconomic policy — which has been actively promoted by international organisations and indirectly supported by international financial markets — may result in: (1) low economic growth due to insufficient public investment in infrastructure; (2) an increase in inequality as wealth is transferred to rich bond-holders; and (3) the risk of financial crises, as the overall fiscal position can change rapidly as a result of a currency devaluation. In Schonerwald da Silva and Vernengo's view, Latin American countries should be willing to adopt expansionary fiscal policies since 'deficits and growing debt, when sustainable, may boost economic growth and be a blessing'. Whether economic conditions and the ideological bias of financial markets allow countries in the region to adopt this type of policy is another matter.

The United States could not have faced more different conditions to manage its budgetary policy since the early 1980s, if not before. Between the FY1982 and 1986, for example, the federal deficit averaged 5 per cent of GDP as a result of the expansion of military spending and a huge personal tax cut. At the same time, the current account deficit increased and the United States became dependent upon (and was successful in attracting) foreign savings to finance it (Morgan, this volume, Chapter 4). While the Clinton administration succeeded in securing budget surpluses in 1998–2000, the situation reversed rapidly after George W. Bush expanded military spending and introduced (regressive) tax cuts. Between 2000 and 2005, the public balance as a share of GDP moved from +2.4 per cent to –2.5 per cent (Ippolitto, this volume, Chapter 9). Higher public deficits contributed to a sustained expansion of the current account deficit (in what is traditionally called the 'twin deficits'): in 2006, the US current account was equivalent to 6.5 per cent of GDP, a level that had been unsustainable in many other countries (Morgan, this volume, Chapter 4). Yet the United States did not have to deal with any real negative response from external financial markets.

The ability of the United States to accumulate public (and private) foreign debt without significant risks and pressures when compared with Latin America may have relatively little to do with the underlying macroeconomic conditions. In particular, the saving rate is even lower in the United States than in most Latin American countries. In 2004, gross domestic savings as a percentage of GDP was only 13.9 per cent in the United States, compared with 26.2 per cent in Argentina, 21.0 per cent in Brazil, 29.2 per cent in Chile and 20.0 per cent in Mexico.[15] Instead, one has to look at differences in institutional structures and external conditions among various countries in the Americas. Three differences may be particularly important. First, the US government benefits from higher levels of credibility than any Latin American country. As Lewis and Mitchell (this volume, Chapter 2) point out, state credibility has a positive effect not only on tax revenues but also in the state's capacity to borrow.

Second, the United States is unique in its ability to issue bonds in its own currency, and 95 per cent of its debt is denominated in dollars. This circumstance minimises the effect that a depreciation of the currency — which has proven dramatic for many Latin American countries — has on public debt and the management of the budget. Moreover, as dollar-denominated assets in the rest of the world increase, the likelihood of a dramatic run against the dollar is reduced since dollar-holders would be the first to lose (Morgan, this volume, Chapter 4). The role of the dollar as the most important global currency and of the US bonds as the preferred asset in times of instability became clear during the second part of 2008. Despite a deep financial crisis that affected some of the largest US banks, the depreciation of the dollar was negligible. A similar crisis in any Latin American country, on the other hand, would have triggered a massive run away from the local currency.

Third, with 27 per cent of global GDP in current dollars, the United States is the largest market in the world and the main buyer of manufacturing goods from many countries, particularly in Asia. As a result, the United States has built a relationship of mutual interdependence with them, purchasing foreign goods and receiving financial inflows to finance the public deficit and private consumption. As Morgan highlights when referring to the previous period of the 1980s, 'foreign governments have a crucial interest in maintaining the wellbeing of the American economy as the engine of global growth'.

The impact of differences in borrowing capacity on public policy in different parts of the Americas is unquestionable. While Latin American countries like Brazil cannot increase public spending in social programmes and infrastructure unless they simultaneously raise new taxes, the United States can over-spend when it desires to do so. More importantly, the United States has been able to implement counter-cyclical fiscal policies when faced with a recessionary environment, while Latin America has actually been forced to adopt pro-cyclical fiscal policies since the mid-1980s (Ffrench-Davis, 2005). Wibbels (2006) explores this asymmetry between OECD and Latin American countries in some detail. Based on an econometric analysis of the relationship between volatility, economic growth and fiscal policy, he concludes that 'in the global North, governments can respond to … shocks by borrowing on capital markets and spending counter-cyclically on social programmes. No such opportunity exists for most governments in the developing world that have limited access to capital markets in tough times.' (2006, p. 435).

Yet Iwan Morgan's contribution to this volume (Chapter 4) warns that even the United States faces foreign constraints to accumulate public (and private) debt. In particular, the US reliance on Asian central banks' accumulation of debt may have reached its limits in the last few years. According to some estimates, by 2004 Asian governments led by China held 60 per cent of the global reserves, much of it in dollars. These countries had a growing interest in diversifying their foreign holdings — and in fact began doing so in 2005.

While the Bush administration supported a depreciation of the US dollar as the best way to reduce the current account deficit and thus the dependence on foreign lenders, Morgan believes that this strategy has always been both risky and difficult to implement. On the one hand, China has been reluctant to accept an appreciation of the renminbi. Between 1 April 2007 and 8 April 2008, the dollar depreciated by 17 per cent in relation to the euro, but by only 10 per cent in relation to the Chinese currency. On the other hand, an appreciation of the renminbi would increase US prices, and could even expand the current account deficit in the short run. In Morgan's view, it could also 'encourage the Chinese to go on a shopping expedition for U.S. assets that were now going relatively cheap [and] … ordinary Americans would find it difficult to retain belief in their nation's economic sovereignty'.

Instead, Morgan believes that a significant reduction of the US public deficit is necessary to secure a 'soft' landing and control the level of foreign debt. A public surplus — which could primarily be secured by allowing Bush's tax cuts to expire as scheduled — would increase the US saving rate and expand the degrees of freedom of fiscal policy when needed. Yet more recent events in the private side of the American economy may have rendered this solution insufficient. The housing crisis and its reverberating consequences on the financial markets since mid 2007 have moved the US economy into recession and may result in a hard adjustment of its current account. Whether the United States can sustain its unique ability to operate a counter-cyclical fiscal policy through massive borrowing in the new environment remains to be seen and constitutes an additional troublesome element of the current financial crisis.[16]

Towards a Stronger Fiscal State: Exploring the Political Challenge

Given these changing external circumstances, together with more permanent demographic and socio-economic trends, building stronger fiscal states with more revenue-raising capacity may be urgent both in the United States and in Latin America. In the United States, as already discussed, the ageing of the population will result in growing demands for spending in Social Security and Medicare. In Latin America, a significant expansion of investment in infrastructure is necessary to compete in the global economy (Agosín et al., this volume, Chapter 7; Fay and Morrison, 2005). Given high levels of inequality, a larger redistributive budget is also important all across the Americas.

How do you build stronger fiscal states? From a technical viewpoint, the answer is clear and well known: countries must expand tax revenues while trying to minimise efficiency losses. In Chapter 7 of this volume, for example, Agosin, Machado and Schneider propose a workable tax reform agenda for countries in Central America — a region in dire need of public revenue expansion. These small economies should not increase tax rates, but instead concentrate on broadening the tax base by eliminating unjustified exemptions. In particular, Central American governments should expand the definition of taxable income in the personal income tax (including financial income and capital income); tax worldwide income; eliminate most exemptions in the corporate income tax (including those that favour export processing zones); and leave exemptions in the value-added tax only for basic goods. All these measures would help to expand the share of taxes in GDP by three or four percentage points, placing Central America closer to the world average for countries with similar income.

In his discussion of inequality and redistribution in Latin America (Chapter 10), Sánchez-Ancochea echoes these recommendations, while also insisting on the importance of expanding taxes on the rich. This may require a small expansion in the top marginal rates in personal income tax, which have been reduced excessively in the last three decades. Sánchez-Ancochea also proposes the creation of more ambitious property taxes. Property taxes are still very low in Latin America (just 0.3 per cent of GDP), but have a large revenue potential given the high land concentration and the difficulties of taxing mobile factors of production like capital.

In the United States, much of the recent debate on tax policy has also focused on the level of direct taxes on the rich, and particularly on the fate of the tax cuts that the Bush administration introduced in 2001 and 2003. In his chapter on taxation (Chapter 9), Ippolito acknowledges the criticisms that the tax cuts have received (due to their impact on income inequality and the public deficit), but argues that the record has been mixed. In his view, 'revenue levels ... have been in line with long-term revenue trends, despite tax cuts. Progressivity has increased significantly for most income groups, again despite tax cuts.'[17] What is clear, however, is that tax cuts have been partly responsible for the increase in the public deficit the United States experienced during the Bush administration, and that allowing them to expire would be the easiest way to improve the public accounts in the short run (Morgan, Chapter 4). In the long run, an expansion of payroll and income taxes, particularly for high-income groups, may be absolutely necessary if the country wants to avoid painful cuts in popular and successful programmes like Social Security and Medicare, and will likely constitute one of the objectives of the Obama administration after stabilising the economy.

The answer to how to strengthen the fiscal state is thus not technical, but political — a point discussed by different contributors to this volume. While it is impossible to explore here the vast literature on the politics of tax reform, it may be useful to draw on Schneider's discussion of the Central American case in this volume to highlight some key factors for successful reform implementation. In particular, he stresses the importance of building credible social consensus around tax policy, and offers a roadmap to determine how likely this is to happen in different countries.[18]

The expansion of taxes in many unequal developing countries will only succeed if new social contracts supported by different classes are created. In particular, the elite (especially the emerging groups that are benefiting from globalisation) must be 'wrapped into coalitions with underprivileged and marginalized groups, creating a balance in which rising elites accept their responsibility to pay for the privilege of prosperity' (Schneider, this volume, Chapter 8; see also World Bank, 2004).

To determine how likely this consensus is to emerge in different countries, Schneider analyses the characteristics of the party system as a tool to understand deeper political confrontations and as a determinant of the structural constraints for a tax reform agenda in different socio-economic contexts. He underscores two key dimensions of the political debate in Central America: the level of commitment to liberal citizenship (e.g. concerns about corruption, human rights and democratic participation) and the degree of identification with a market orientation in economic affairs. In countries like El Salvador, where there is intensive polarisation about the role of the market and a weak support for liberal citizenship, tax reforms may be harder to achieve than in countries with more consensual political systems, like Honduras. More importantly, the strategy that reformers should implement to secure an expansion of tax revenues greatly depends on the nature of political interactions.

Debates about the nature of liberal democracy and the characteristics of the economic system are not unique to Central America, but dominate political conflict across the Americas — even if some countries have additional political cleavage (e.g. around regional politics in Ecuador, ethnicity in Bolivia or race in the United States). In many countries, these debates — especially regarding the size of the state and the relationship between state and markets — have become increasingly polarised. In the United States, in particular, increasing differences between political parties over economic and political issues reflect the increasingly unequal socio-economic structure (McCarty et al., 2006). The Republican Party's embrace of a conservative creed of small government, together with the support it receives from the economic elite, may have worsened the chances of strengthening the fiscal state in the last three decades (Hecker and Pierson, 2005). In Latin America, the situation is more fluid and political parties are more unstable — as discussed in the initial section — but there are still sharp divisions regarding the size and character of the state.

The political challenge to strengthen the fiscal state is thus immense, particularly when one also considers the need to link tax reforms with the allocation of public spending and its impact on inequality and growth. In the United States, for example, the expansion of Social Security and Medicaid for the elderly, while important and popular, is already crowding out programmes with more long-term redistributive power such as affordable primary, secondary and college education, training and childcare support for working or single parents. Latin American countries, on the other hand, must find a difficult balance between infrastructure investment and various redistributive programmes. Yet all these discussions will be unavoidable in the near future if countries are to secure the long-term sustainability of public budgets and achieve a more equitable distribution of economic benefits.

Conclusions

In their historical comparative research of Latin America and the United States, the influential economic historians Stanley Engerman and Kenneth Sokoloff stressed the differences between the two regions in economic structures and development outcomes (e.g. Engerman and Sokoloff, 1997; Sokoloff and Zolt, 2007). In their view — which has influenced other historians — the United States' higher economic growth and more modern institutional structure were partly a result of deep differences in geography and the distribution of income.

The emphasis on the differences between various Latin American countries and the United States is hardly surprising. While the United States is the world's largest economy in terms of being a sole superpower, Latin America has had a disappointing economic performance and suffers from weak institutions and little influence in the global economy.

This introductory chapter, however, has emphasised that there are also striking similarities between the contemporary political economy of both regions. All countries in the Americas are characterised by high levels of market income inequality, which are not significantly reduced by government intervention. The United States and most countries in Latin America also have weak fiscal states — that is, government revenues and spending are relatively low by international standards.

Why do both sets of countries have relatively weak fiscal states? Can we find some common explanations despite the asymmetric level of development in the United States and Latin America? How does inequality relate to the small fiscal states? How do international conditions (particularly access to foreign sources of funds) affect each region? Can the United States be a model for Latin America in terms of budgetary policy — as some proponents of the Washington Consensus seemed to believe? By studying different dimensions of the fiscal state in various countries of the Americas, this volume can offer some preliminary answers to these questions. More than that, the volume is primarily an invitation to explore some of these issues in the future — an objective that has become particularly pressing after the historic crisis that exploded in the second half of 2008.

References

A. Alesina, E. Glaeser and B. Sacerdote (2001) 'Why Doesn't the United States Have a European-Style Welfare State?' *Brookings Papers on Economic Activity*, no. 2, pp. 187–254.

A. Alesina and E. Glaeser (2004) *Fighting Poverty in the US and Europe: A World of Difference* (Oxford: Oxford University Press).

J. Alm and B. Torgler (2004) 'Culture Differences and Tax Morale in the United States and Europe', *AYPS Working Paper*, May, Atlanta.

S. Anderson and J. Cavanagh (2000) Top 200: The Rise of Corporate Global Power Institute for Policy Studies, December. Available from www.corpwatch.org/article.php?id=377#power (accessed 2 April 2008).

R. Barro (1991) 'Economic Growth in a Cross Section of Countries', *Quarterly Journal of Economics*, vol. 106, no. 2, pp. 407–43.

M. Bordo and C. Meissner (2007) 'Financial Crises, 1880–1913: The Role of Foreign Currency Debt' in S. Edwards et al. (eds.), *The Decline of Latin American Economies: Growth, Institutions and Crises* (Chicago: The University of Chicago Press), pp. 139–94.

V. Bulmer-Thomas (2003) *The Economic History of Latin America Since Independence* 2nd ed. (Cambridge, UK: Cambridge University Press).

L. Burman (2007) 'Tax Fairness, the 2001–2006 Tax Cuts, and the AMT', Statement Before the Committee on Ways and Means, US Congress, 6 September.

J. Campbell (1993) 'The State and Fiscal Sociology', *Annual Review of Sociology*, vol. 19, pp. 163–85.

J. Campbell (2005) 'Fiscal Sociology in an Age of Globalization: Comparing Tax Regimes in Advanced Capitalist Countries', in V. Nee and R. Swedberg (eds), *The Economic Sociology of Capitalism* (Princeton: Princeton University Press), pp. 391–419.

J. Campbell and M. Allen (1994) 'The Political Economy of Revenue Extraction in the Modern State: A Time-Series Analysis of U.S. Income Taxes, 1916–1986', *Social Forces*, vol. 72, no. 3, pp. 643–69.

Coates, D. (2000) *Models of Capitalism: Growth and Stagnation in the Modern Era* (Cambridge: Polity Press).

ECLAC (2007) *Social Panorama of Latin America and the Caribbean. Preliminary Summary* (Santiago: Economic Commission for Latin America and the Caribbean).

S. Engerman and K. Sokoloff (1997) 'Factor Endowments, Institutions and Differential Paths of Growth Among New World Economies: A View from Economic Historians of the United States', in S. Haber (ed.), *How Latin America Fell Behind: Essays on the Economic Histories of Brazil and Mexico, 1800–1914* (Stanford: Stanford University Press).

S. Engerman, E. Mariscal and K. Sokoloff (2002) 'The Evolution of Schooling Institutions in the Americas, 1880–1945', unpublished Working Paper, UCLA Department of Economics.

G. Esping-Andersen (1990) *The Three Worlds of Welfare Capitalism* (London: Polity Press).

M. Fay and M. Morrison (2005) *Infrastructure in Latin America and the Caribbean: Recent Developments and Key Challenges* (Washington, DC: World Bank Group).

R. Ffrench-Davis, R. (2005) *Reformas para América Latina. Después del Fundamentalismo Neoliberal* (Buenos Aires, Argentina: Siglo XXI Editores).

F. Filgueira (2005) 'Welfare and Democracy in Latin America: The Development, Crises and Aftermath of Universal, Dual and Exclusionary Social States', paper prepared for the UNRISD Project on Social Policy and Democratization, Geneva.

R. Freeman (2000) 'Single Peaked vs. Diversified Capitalism: The Relation Between Economic Institutions And Outcomes', NBER Working Paper 7556.

J.K. Galbraith (1999 [1958]) *The Affluent Society*, 5th ed. (London: Penguin).

W. Gale, P. Orszag and I. Shapiro, 'Distributional Effects of the 2001 and 2003 Tax Cuts and Their Financing', *Tax Notes*, vol. 103, no. 12, pp. 1539–48.

J. Hacker and P. Pierson (2005) 'Abandoning the Middle: The Bush Tax Cuts and the Limits of Democratic Control', *Perspectives on Politics*, no. 3, pp. 33–53.

P. Hall and D. Soskice (2001) 'An Introduction to Varieties of Capitalism', in P. Hall, and D. Soskice (eds.), *Varieties of Capitalism: The Institutional Foundations of Competitiveness* (Oxford: Oxford University Press).

G. Hubbard (2002) 'A Pro-Growth Agenda for Latin America', presentation at the Foreign Policy Association, New York, October.

E. Huber (2002) 'Conclusions: Actors, Institutions, and Policies', in E. Huber (ed.), *Models of Capitalism. Lessons for Latin America* (University Park, PA: Pennsylvania State University Press).

E. Huber (2005) 'Inequality and the State in Latin America', paper prepared for the Conference of the APSA Task Force on Difference and Inequality in the Developing World, University of Virginia, 22–23 April.

E. Huber, F. Nielsen, J. Pribble and J. Stephens (2006) 'Politics and Inequality in Latin America and the Caribbean', *American Sociological Review*, vol. 71, no. 14, pp. 943–63.

E. Huber and J. Stephens (2001) *Development and the Crisis of the Welfare State. Parties and Policies in Global Markets* (Chicago: University of Chicago Press).

T. Iversen and D. Soskice (2006) 'Distribution and Redistribution: The Shadow of the Nineteenth Century' (mimeo).

W. Korpi (1996) 'Eurosclerosis and the Sclerosis of Objectivity: On the Role of Values Among Economic Policy', *The Economic Journal*, vol. 106, no. 439, pp. 1727–46.

W. Korpi (2006) 'Power Resources and Employer-Centered Approaches in Explanations of Welfare States and Varieties of Capitalism. Protagonists, Consenters, and Antagonists', *World Politics*, vol. 58, pp. 167–206.

W. Korpi and J. Palme (1998) 'The Paradox of Redistribution and Strategies of Equality: Welfare State Institutions, Inequality, and Poverty in the Western Countries' *American Sociological Review*, vol. 63, no. 5, pp. 661–87.

P. Krugman (2007) *The Conscience of a Liberal* (New York: Norton).

F. Levy and P. Temin (2007) 'Inequality and Institutions in 20th Century America', Economics Department Working Papers, 07-14, Massachusetts Institute of Technology.

S. Mainwaring and M. Torcal (2006) 'Party System Institutionalization and Party System Theory after the Third Wave of Democratization', in R. Katz and W. Crotty (ed.), *Handbook of Party Politics* (London: Sage).

J. Martin (1991) *Shifting the Burden: the Struggle over Growth and Corporate Taxation* (Chicago: University of Chicago Press).

J. Martínez (2006) 'Regímenes de bienestar en América Latina: consideraciones generales y trayectorias regionales', *Revista Centroamericana de Ciencias Sociales*, vol. II, no. 2, pp. 45–79.

N. McCarty and J. Pontusson (2008) 'The Political Economy of Inequality and Redistribution', Princeton University, manuscript in progress.

N. McCarty, K. Poole and H. Rosenthal (2006) *Polarized America. The Dance of Ideology and Unequal Riches* (Cambridge: MIT Press).

J. McGuire (1999) 'Labor Union Strength and Human Development in East Asia and Latin America', *Studies in Comparative International Development*, vol. 33, no. 4, pp. 3–34.

D. Mitchell (2005) 'The Impact of Government Spending on Economic Growth', *Executive Summary Backgrounder*, no. 1831 (31 March), Heritage Foundation.

T. Mkandawire (2006) 'Targeting and Universalism in Poverty Reduction', UNRISD Social Policy and Development Programme Paper no. 23, Geneva.

OECD (2007) *Latin American Economic Outlook 2007* (Paris: OECD).

E. Paus (2005) *Foreign Investment, Development and Globalization: Can Costa Rica Become Ireland?* (New York: Palgrave).

T. Piketty and E. Saenz (2006) 'The Evolution of Top Incomes: A Historical and International Perspective' NBER Working Paper 11955, Cambridge.

T. Piketty and E. Saenz (2008) The Evolution of Top Incomes Database. Updated version at http://elsa.berkeley.edu/~saez (accessed 31 March 2008).

J. Pontusson (2005) *Inequality and Prosperity: Social Europe vs. Liberal America* (Ithaca: Cornell University Press).

X. Sala-i-Marti (1997) 'I Just Ran Four Million Regressions', Universitat Pompeu Fabra Economics Working Paper 2001.

B. Schneider and S. Karcher (2007) 'Labor Markets in Latin America: Inflexibility, Informality, and Other Complementarities', unpublished manuscript.

K. Sokoloff and E. Zolt (2007) 'Inequality and the Evolution of Institutions of Taxation', in S. Edwards et al. (eds.), *The Decline of Latin American Economies. Growth, Institutions and Crises* (Chicago: University of Chicago Press).

D. Soskice (2007) 'Inequality, Varieties of Capitalism and Political Systems', paper presented at the International Conference 'Social policy, economic development and income inequality: Latin America in comparative perspective', Institute for the Study of the Americas and University of Costa Rica, London.

J. Stephens (2002) 'European Welfare State Regimes: Configurations, Outcomes, Transformations' in E. Huber (ed.), *Models of Capitalism. Lessons for Latin America* (University Park: Pennsylvania State University Press).

R. Veder and L. Gallaway (1998) 'Government Size and Economic Growth', paper prepared for Joint Economic Committee, US Congress.

E. Wibbels (2006) 'Dependency Revisited: International Markets, Business Cycles, and Social Spending in the Developing World', *International Organization*, vol. 60, no. 2, pp. 433–68.

World Bank (2004) *Inequality in Latin American and the Caribbean: Breaking with History?* (Washington, DC: World Bank Annual Research Study on Latin America and the Caribbean).

Notes

[1]   In this introductory chapter and in several contributions to this volume (particularly in Chapters 5 and 10), Latin America is treated as an homogeneous entity. This is not without its problems, given the differences in the size of the government and in the characteristics and generosity of the welfare state (Filgueira, 2005; Martínez, 2007). Nevertheless, there is ample evidence that the region has common socio-economic and political similarities (e.g. income inequality, inefficient allocation of public spending, insufficient taxes, especially on personal and corporate income) that make its comparison with the United States fruitful.

[2]   Our use of the term 'Americas' excludes Canada, whose fiscal condition is different.

[3]   The federal government raises even less in taxes. As Ippolito's contributions to this volume show, the share of federal revenues in GDP has averaged slightly more than 18% since the 1950s, with no clear growing long-term trend.

[4]   According to a similar exercise done by the World Bank (2004), Nicaragua and Uruguay are the two countries with higher tax revenues as GDP than expected by their income level. When all taxes (including social security contributions) are considered, we should also add Brazil to this list, since its revenue level according to Amann and Baer (this volume, Chapter 6) is 36% of GDP. (World Bank estimations for Brazil are significantly lower.)

[5]   With regard to the United States, and when compared with Western Europe, the form of taxation was of critical significance. High tax revenues in the late nineteenth century reflected high tariff rates, which the Republican Party

supported as a means to promote industrial policy, and the Democrats opposed. The party position on taxes reversed as income tax grew in significance in the twentieth century.

[6] According to Ippolito (Chapter 3), 'during the 1950s, for example, defence spending accounted for well over half the budget; defence-GDP levels remained above 10% through the latter part of that decade'. The share of military spending in the budget decreased by half in the 1970s, increasing slightly during the Reagan administration.

[7] According to Ippolito's data, federal taxes have always been in the 17–20% range during this period, while federal public spending have been in the 17.5–22.5% range.

[8] According to a report of OECD (2007) using Latinobarometro data, just 27% of citizens in Chile (the first country in the ranking), 18% of those in Brazil, 17% of those in Argentina, 9% of those in Mexico and 7% of those in Ecuador (the last country in the ranking) believe that tax revenues are well spent.

[9] Recent literature also focuses on the importance of institutions to explain differences in public spending and taxes, with some similarities and some differences between Latin America and the United States. Although a detailed discussion of these theories is beyond the scope of this introduction, it is important to mention that federal governments, majority political systems (as opposed to proportional ones) and strong division of power all contribute to lower the level of taxes and social spending. For interesting reviews, see Alesina and Glaeser (2004), Campbell (2005) and Huber and Stephens (2001). For an innovative attempt to compare Latin America with the United States and other liberal market economies, see Soskice (2007).

[10] According to their calculations, the probability that two people chosen randomly will be from different races — their definition of race fractionalisation — is 49% in the United States, but only 10% in the United Kingdom and 6% or less in most other European countries including Germany and the Scandinavian countries.

[11] Income inequality in Latin America is characterised by high concentration at the top of the distribution structure with the rich receiving a larger share of total income than in any other region of the world (Sánchez-Ancochea, this volume, Chapter 10; World Bank, 2004). According to data from 1992, the richest decile in Latin America received 48% of total income in that year, 1.7 times more than in OECD countries. While inequality has decreased slightly in some Latin American countries like Brazil, this general pattern still prevails.

[12] Some of these data under-estimate the burden of interest payments in some Latin American countries because they do not include the quasi-fiscal debt of the Central America (which is large in some countries like the Dominican Republic). We should also remember that interest payments in Latin America

are more volatile than in the United States because they depend on many factors outside government's control (e.g. devaluation of the currency and changes in US monetary policy).

[13] Amann and Baer (this volume, Chapter 6) estimate that the Brazilian government spends around 40% of public expenditures in amortisation refinancing.

[14] This conservative approach to fiscal policy was accompanied by a tight monetary policy based on high interest rates. The Central Bank also maintained its commitment to inflation targeting, thus subordinating all policy goals (including inequality and poverty reduction) to the control of inflation.

[15] Data from the World Development Indicators electronic database (accessed 8 April 2008). The data on the net saving rate, which exclude consumption of fixed capital and are a more adequate representation of financing needs, were significantly lower in all countries. In the United States, the data have even turned negative in recent times.

[16] This is already happening with its monetary policy. Between December 2007 and March 2008, the Federal Reserve reduced interest rates by half (from 5% to only 2.5%), something few other countries could have sustained without worrying about the devaluation of their currency and the health of the public sector.

[17] There is, however, no agreement on the distributional effect of the 2001 and 2003 tax cuts, and many critics argue that it will have a regressive impact on income distribution. See, for example, Burman (2007), Gale et al. (2004), Hacker and Pierson (2005) and Krugman (2007).

[18] Schneider's chapter also stresses the need to understand the type of obstacles that different reforms are likely to face. He identifies four different types of potential obstacles to successful reform based on the specific characteristics of the measures implemented: existence of a strong and concentrated opposition, problems of collective action, lack of information regarding the success of the reforms and existence of high transaction costs. Different problems call for different strategies, going from a 'big bang' to more gradual and incremental approach.

PART II
PUBLIC BUDGETS: INTERNAL AND
EXTERNAL DETERMINANTS

2

FISCAL CREDIBILITY, PUBLIC GOOD AND THE BUDGET: THE STRUGGLE OVER FEDERAL TAXING AND SPENDING IN THE ARGENTINE DURING THE LATE TWENTIETH CENTURY

Colin M. Lewis and Andrew H. Mitchell

> *It is enough to consider the construction ... of roads and bridges ... telegraphs and ports ... the improvement of rivers ... the building of schools ... the construction of towns ... or infrastructure projects in the new national territories ... to reflect on the enormous importance that the material presence ... the (late nineteenth century) state began to have in this crucial, formative phase of Argentinian society.*
> (Oszlak 1982, pp. 151–52)

> *A major reason for these failures is that the set of market-based policies — the so-called Washington consensus — that underpinned the ... Latin American experiments has a fatal flaw: it assumes that it is possible to carry out economic reforms to create efficient markets without a concomitant reform in the political institutions that limit government and guarantee property rights and individual liberty. The reason this assumption is flawed is that there is no such thing as a 'free market' independent of politics ... In point of fact, world history offers us no case of a well-developed market system that was not embedded into a well-developed political system.*
> (Haber, North and Weingast, 2002, pp. 1–2)

Introduction

The opening quotations illustrate that historians, political sociologists and economists have long acknowledged the role played by public goods in the formation of states and markets. Expanding the supply of public goods was fundamental to the creation of a 'national market', a 'national society' and a 'nation-state' in the Argentine during the decades after 1860. The creation and reproduction of political order entails economic and social costs. It also involves choices, as well as challenges and opportunities. The language of the discourse may vary: historians of the nineteenth century tend to refer to 'progress' while students of late twentieth century market-based models favour 'reform'. Yet all acknowledge that understanding how change does (or does not) become embedded entails appraising costs and choices: who pays for the cost of progress; who benefits from reform. In part, the answer to these questions revolves around the supply of public goods and access to them. As was argued in the 1990s, monetary stability was an important public good. Possibly, after decades of monetary 'disorder' including several bouts of hyperinflation, many in the Argentine regarded it as *the* most important public good. Establishing fiscal order, and formulating a new budgetary regime, was critical to the maintenance of monetary stability — as events were to demonstrate.

This chapter explores interconnections among taxation, the provision of public goods and state credibility in order to explain budgetary pressures in the Argentine during the late twentieth century. It opens with a short review of the literature on credibility. The second section offers a stylised survey of modern Argentinian fiscal history. The third focuses on fiscal options during the 1990s, a period when the country appeared to be moving away from the monetary and budgetary chaos that had characterised most of the post-World War II decades. The chapter closes with an appraisal of fiscal credibility and budgetary equity. In focusing narrowly on budgetary and fiscal aspects of the period, the paper does not purport to offer a critique of the Menem-Cavallo Convertibility Plan, though obviously the Plan provides the background against which tax performance is assessed.

State Credibility and Macroeconomic Stability

Recent contributions to the literature offer insights into analyses of the financing and provisioning of public goods. Two concepts, deriving from new institutional economics and mainstream economic history, are particularly useful: 'credible commitment' and the 'trilemma'. North (1994, pp. 8, 17–21; North and Thomas, 1973, pp. 66–67, 99, 120, 138–40) emphasises the importance of the rule of law for economic growth. Credible state commitment is critical in areas such as taxation and borrowing. The emergence of the fiscal state, based on 'sustainable taxation' and 'responsible borrowing', facilitates the thickening of capital markets and the proliferation of financial instruments, institutions and mechanisms usually regarded as essential for growth. The growth and success of public credit allows an expansion of financial intermediation, the development of financial institutions and the consolidation of a stock market

(Capie 2001, pp. 39–40, 48–50). Responsible borrowing and capital market deepening connects with the trilemma — namely, the trade-off among stable exchange rates, open capital accounts and an active monetary policy attuned to domestic requirements, or domestic control of money supply and interest rates (Obstfeld, Shambaugh and Taylor, 2004, pp. 1–2). While all three policy objectives may be critical for growth, history demonstrates that credible states may apply any two of these desired policies, but not all three.

Taxation and borrowing finance the provision of public goods, the supply of which is crucial to state credibility and the ability of the state to tax and to borrow. This is not so much a tautology as a virtuous circle. Public credit feeds back into state credibility via the flexibility of solvency and the ability of the state to provide such public goods as order and stability. A means of building credibility is the provision of public goods that promote development. If such public goods succeed in fostering growth, they enhance fiscal institutions via potentially greater fiscal revenues (and hence a greater ability to repay public borrowing). A means of viewing the relationships and feedbacks between public credit and state credibility is path dependency. An illustration of a positive path dependency among government credit, public goods and state credibility is shown in Figure 2.1(a). An illustration of a negative path dependency of public credit is shown in Figure 2.1(b).

It follows that monetary and fiscal policies determine the capacity of a state to devise sustainable taxation and borrowing strategies that facilitate the provision of tangible public goods. An ability to implement sustainable fiscal and budgetary policies which obviate recourse to deficit finance is equally of paramount importance for the delivery of that illusive public good, monetary

Figure 2.1: Fiscal Institutions and State Credibility

a)

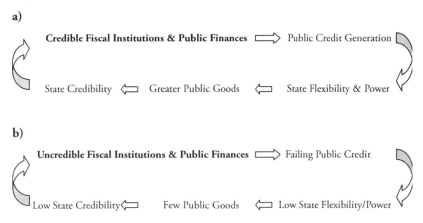

stability. The maintenance of monetary order is the hallmark of the modern 'fiscal state'.

One way of depicting the links between the state, fiscal institutions, credibility and public goods is to view the state as a firm. In this view, the state provides society (taxpayers cum shareholders cum citizens) with public goods in return for taxation. The state represents the broadest potential for societal collective action. It is uniquely capable of overcoming the problem of collective action: free-riding. Yet the state-as-firm view is limited by who controls the state. Olson (1993) illustrates this succinctly: the Hobbesian anarchy of 'roving bandits' destroys all incentives to invest and produce; 'stationary bandits' or dictators are an improvement as they begin to provide public goods, particularly peaceful order; and democracy best engenders development by increasing the incentives to invest and produce via greater public goods provision. For the state-as-firm approach to be useful, there is an implicit assumption that control of the state significantly depends upon the support of substantial segments of society. The state-as-firm view means the state must provide society with a return on taxation if fiscal institutions are to become, and remain, a substantial resource.

If the state provides a high level of desired public goods, it can achieve something of a virtuous circle, as many public goods foster the development ultimately necessary to expand both the tax base and state credibility. Taxpayers are likely to recognise the return on taxation implied by development through greater cooperation. As Sokoloff and Zolt (2006) argue, tax systems are the oldest and most fundamental of institutions, and an indicator of state capacity. The technical efficiency to the tax system reflects on state competence, and determines how the cost of public goods and services is borne by different segments of society. Individuals and groups will be more willing to support government if anticipated benefits from financing the state match or exceed the incidence of taxation — and distribution of the fiscal burden is considered to be broadly equitable. This facilitates fiscal solidarity. How societies raise fiscal revenue is related to the authority of the state, and control over public expenditure generally follows the power to tax (Sokoloff and Zolt, 2006, pp. 1–2).

In one sense, the state always provides goods for somebody. It would have no reason to exist otherwise. The question is: what type of goods and for whom? A distinction can be made between public and collective goods. Collective goods are provided for powerful groups within society, whereas public goods are provided for society in general. The same good can be a collective good in one society and a public good in another. For instance, property rights might be accessible only to members of powerful groups in one society, making them a collective good. Where property rights — like stable currency — are widely accessible, they are public goods. All states usually provide a mix of public and collective goods. States lacking credibility typically provide few if any public goods, whereas credible states provide a significant level of public goods.

Fiscal institutions in themselves do not determine whether a significant and sufficient level of public goods will be achieved, but they do determine state solvency and potential to deliver public goods. Several forms of funding are available to governments: taxation, borrowing and printing money. These mechanisms are not mutually exclusive. At various times, many governments have resorted to all three simultaneously. However, as the so-called Oliveira-Tanzi effect shows, persistent, high rates of inflation are usually associated with monetary expansion, which limits the effectiveness of the state's other financing mechanisms. Inflation negatively affects tax yields as the time lag between fixing liabilities and the receipt of payments means that the real value of tax revenues is eroded. Hence the vicious circle emerges: the monetisation of budget deficits triggers inflation, inflation reduces real tax yields, declining receipts lead to a widening fiscal gap which in turn results in further monetisation of the deficit, and so the inflationary spiral continues. Inflation also raises the real cost of borrowing — at home and abroad — exerting further pressure on the budget. Public sector deficits undermine the confidence of creditors and taxpayers — and, following Figure 2.1, the credibility of the state. As is widely observed, the use of monetisation to finance persistent fiscal deficits has been one of the principal problems of the Argentine during the second half of the twentieth century. Indeed, Tanzi's early research was based on the Argentine.

Echoing Adam Smith ('Little else is requisite to carry a state to the highest degree of opulence from the lowest barbarism, but peace, easy taxes and a tolerable administration of justice; all the rest being brought about by the natural course of things.'), North and Thomas (1973) explore the origins of the fiscal state. They identify Holland and England — notably post-1688 England — as successful examples of efforts to establish property rights, fiscal extraction by consent and sustainable indebtedness. Spain and France are identified as failures (North and Thomas, 1973).[1] Defining the fiscal state as one that is able to translate a flow of tax revenue into manageable borrowing, Daunton (2001) dates the appearance of the modern state somewhat later. In 1815 Europe, only Britain was a fiscal state. According to Daunton's definition, della Paolera, Irigoin and Bózzoli (2003) may be depicted as presenting the emergence of a fiscal state in the Argentine as a fitful, discontinuous process. Indeed, it is questionable whether the modern Argentinian state has ever achieved the requisite degree or depth of 'fiscality'. As a number of scholars acknowledge, for much of the nineteenth and twentieth centuries there was serious disorder in the public accounts with large budgetary deficits. Although, during the course of the nineteenth century, expenditure gradually evolved to fulfil minimal state functions — the administration of justice, maintenance of public security and national defence and the conduct of external relations — rarely was revenue sufficient (Comín and Díaz Fuentes, 2006). This tended to generate large public debts that placed further strains on the budget, particularly during the latter part of the twentieth century. Indeed, only for relatively limited periods have Argentinian administrations achieved the capacity to borrow long in the domestic currency, re-emphasising the failure to develop a viable fiscal and monetary system. To quote della Paolera, Irigoin and Bózzoli (2003):

> 'For more than half a century governments made frequent recourse either to printing money or to trying other, more sophisticated means of expanding the money supply to resolve fiscal deficits … All such policies resulted in high levels of inflation. Moreover, positive rates of inflation persisted every year from 1940. This process reached a dramatic peak during the hyperinflation of 1989–90 when inflation rates reached nearly 200 percent per month.' (2003, p. 74)

Some Stylised History: Argentinian Fiscal Institutions and State Capacity

An indicator of state credibility is the size of fiscal institutions relative to the economy. Weiss and Hobson (1995, pp. 4–5) find that an index for state strength (or capacity) is the ability to tax, *not the ability to spend*. They link state strength to the consolidation of infrastructural power — that is, an ability to penetrate and extract resources from society, and allocate them to desired ends. Moreover, state capacity correlates with state credibility: a strong state is defined as one that possesses the ability to extract high amounts of taxation relative to non-tax revenues: 'extractive power' marks the difference between strong and weak states (Hobson, 1997, p. 234; Snider, 1987, p. 325). The proportion of fiscal revenue to GDP may be taken as an indicator of state capacity and, broadly, state credibility. An increase in the ratio should point to an increase in state capacity and credibility. It is important to qualify the historical value of fiscal revenue to GDP, as both the nature and the standard of state interaction in the economy have changed over time. For instance, in the late twentieth century strong/developed states increasingly chose to interact more indirectly with the economy via regulation. This is especially true since 1970, a period when state strength has been assessed in terms of ability to 'govern the market'. State power is now measured not so much by the ratio of fiscal revenue to GDP as qualitative engagement with the market — a capacity to pick and choose when and how to intervene in the market (Weiss and Hobson, 1995, pp. 4–7; Snider, 1987, pp. 321–22). Nevertheless, for much of the twentieth century, the tax/GDP ratio remains a meaningful indicator of state credibility.

There appears to be an emerging consensus in the fiscal political economy literature that modern low-income developing economies effect a tax-revenue:GDP ratio of around 12–16 per cent. Medium-income developing economies operate a ratio of 17–20 per cent. High-income developing economies manage to achieve approximately 25–27 per cent. The OECD ratio was 38 per cent in the mid 1990s (Snider, 1987, p. 325; Tanzi 1987, 2000; Tanzi and Zee 2000; Sokoloff and Zolt, 2006, p. 35). What can be learnt by applying this categorisation to the Argentine, not least during the early part of the twentieth century when the country might be presented as a 'high-income developing economy', with levels of per capita income that exceeded those of most Western European countries?

Figure 2.2 shows federal government tax receipts as a percentage of GDP. The data presented offer an incomplete picture of government revenue, and consequently only an approximate indicator of state fiscal depth or capacity. A number of methodological problems are encountered when attempting to assess the extent of Argentinian federal revenue. For much of the period covered, there were no consolidated national accounts.[2] State corporations were usually 'off the books', some government firms occasionally generated surpluses. However — and especially during the latter part of the twentieth century — state-owned enterprises featured in official accounts on the 'expenditure' side rather than the revenue side, meaning that they ran massive

Figure 2.2: The Argentine Central Government Tax Receipts as a Percentage of GDP, 1900–2000

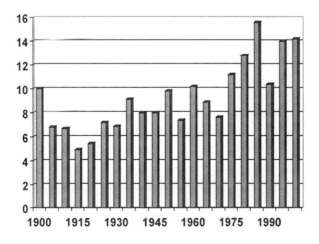

Source: OxLAD

deficits, not modest surpluses. Another problem relates to social insurance. Although treated as revenue, until fairly recently pensions contributions were not listed under government income. With the extension of social security coverage in the early 1920s, and in the late 1940s and early 1950s (periods when various insurance funds were in the black), the pensions system yielded substantial surpluses. Nevertheless, for much of the 1940s, and the last third of the twentieth century, the social insurance system was in deficit (e.g. see Lewis, 1993; Lewis and Lloyd-Sherlock 2002; Arza, 2004). Hence, this item also featured principally on the 'expenditure' side of the budget rather than under 'revenue'. Consequently, federal tax receipts may under-reflect total national government income at various points during the period covered by Figure 2.2. However, they serve as a reasonable long-run proxy.

Several characteristics of the federal tax regime are captured by Figure 2.2. First, for most of the twentieth century, tax revenue rarely exceeded 10 per cent of GDP. Second, in terms of volatility, there is little evidence of a trend. While the ratio of federal tax income to GDP appears to rise from around 1915 to about 1950, the 'trend' was hardly sustained, with volatility returning in the last decades of the century. Third, and consistent with overall volatility, sharp spikes in the graph are invariably followed by precipitous declines in the fiscal take. For example, the recovery around 1935 is followed by slippage. Further recoveries in 1950 and 1960 are similarly followed by decline in the ratio of federal tax receipts to GDP. Some sort of trend may be observed during the years of the *proceso* (the bloody 1976–83 military regime), but again this is not sustained. Observations for 1995 and 2000 point to a plateau, rather than an upward trend in federal tax receipts, and, as is widely known, fiscal receipts

Figure 2.3: The Argentine, Chile and Mexico Central Government Tax Receipts as a Percentage of GDP, 1940–2000

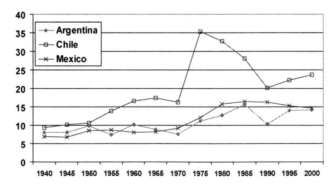

Source: OxLAD

collapsed in the immediate aftermath of the 2001–02 panic, as much due to a collective withdrawal of consent to be taxed as to the economic crisis.

If Figure 2.2 demonstrates the long-run position of Argentinian federal government tax receipts, Figure 2.3 offers comparisons with Chile and Mexico.

While there are similar methodological problems with the sources, OxLAD data at least facilitates approximate comparisons with Chile and Mexico.[3] The graph illustrates the divergence that occurred during the second half of the twentieth century, even if the trend is particularly pronounced in the case of Chile. A notable feature of the Chile data is the rising trend in the fiscal take a generation or so before the Pinochet *putsch* of 1973, even if the trend becomes particularly distinct thereafter. While the Mexico curve does not rise relative to the Argentine until after 1970, and the gap between the two lines is considerably less than between those for Chile and the Argentine, it demonstrates considerably less volatility. Between 1980 and 2000, the Mexico curve is steady and stands above that of the Argentine, notwithstanding the crises that beset both countries — and other emerging market economies — at this point. Perhaps the proximity of all three curves before 1950 is as remarkable as the divergence thereafter.

Though Argentinian revenue flows proved sticky across the twentieth century, expenditure demands rose, especially after the 1930s. Increased government spending was associated with (often hesitant) democratisation and a change in the prevailing economic ideology — the shift from liberal orthodoxy to Keynesianism, a tendency that was not peculiar to the Argentine. There was a marked expansion in government expenditure during the 1916–30 Radical ascendancy. While critics of UCR administrations tended to emphasise bureaucratisation — a growth in state sector employment associated with the extension of political patronage to the middle classes — there was also substantial (not always unremunerative) investment in economic infrastructure. In real terms, government expenditure almost doubled between 1916 and 1930 (Rock, 1975; Rapoport, 2000, pp. 149–51; Hora, 2001, pp. 155–56; Gerschunoff and Llach, 2003, pp. 64–67). Yet it was only after 1930 that the state assumed a much larger and more direct economic role. The number of public works undertaken in the 1930s and early 1940s increased as government initiatives substituted for a decline in private investment. State action between 1930 and 1943 included a massive programme of road construction and the formation of a merchant marine (Herschel and Itzcovich, 1957, p. 109; Veganzones and Winogra, 1997, pp. 146–47). Notwithstanding a broadly Keynesian approach to current and capital expenditure during the period, according to Rapoport there was also a fairly successful struggle to diversify and expand the fiscal base (Rapoport, 2000, pp. 253–55).

The scope and direction of state expenditure was subject to further change in the 1950s. First, the content of economic goods provision moved steadily from 'infrastructure' to production, and the range of public goods expanded to embrace a range of social services. During the first Perón presidencies, most public utilities were nationalised, the government assumed responsibility for the administration of the pensions system (private companies were banned), and state initiatives in the fields of education, health and housing grew. Designed to be redistributive, the weight of expenditure also shifted from capital/investment funding towards the current. Labour costs came to assume a very high proportion of disbursements of virtually all branches of government, including state-owned enterprises and services (Vitelli, 1990; Veganzones and Winograd, 1997, p. 129; Lewis and Lloyd-Sherlock, 2002; Gerschunoff and Llach, 2003, pp. 177–84). By the late 1960s, the state monopolised large sectors of the economy, including railways, telecommunications, electricity, gas, coal, large banks, oil, and food processing (Veganzones and Winograd, 1997, p 149). The tendency for the size of the state sector to grow, and for the range of goods and services provided by the state to increase, continued until the 1980s, including the years of the *proceso*, notwithstanding the avowed commitment of the regime to economic liberalism (Veganzones and Winograd, 1997; Rapoport, 2000, pp. 789–800; Romero, 2001, pp. 212–20; Gerschunoff and Llach, 2003, pp. 352–57). Poor management of state enterprises, inadequate economic planning and lack of investment led to a quantitative and qualitative deterioration of state services and an increase in production costs.

Proliferation of the quantity and diversity of state enterprises in the Argentine over the post-World War II period was comparable only to that observed in

Figure 2.4: The Argentine Central Government Expenditure as a Percentage of GDP, 1950–1990

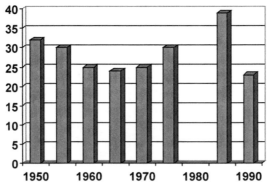

Source: INDEC

Italy, India and the socialist economies of Eastern Europe. The increase in public goods provision should have enhanced state credibility. It did not. This was due to a failure to devise an efficient means of financing the growth in state outreach and because government enterprises contributed little to overall macroeconomic efficiency. On the contrary, the expansion of the state, and the operations of state-owned enterprises, drove the fiscal deficit.

As Figure 2.4 shows, unlike the revenue ratio, federal expenditure as a proportion of GDP often approximated that of developed fiscal states. The 'problem' lay on the revenue side. Despite periodic efforts to control government spending, the figure confirms a failure to close the gap between state revenue and expenditure. For most of the third quarter of the twentieth century, the gap was wide and widening, culminating in bouts of hyperinflation in the late 1980s. Instability resulting from a failure to equalise revenue and spending is captured by the gap between government income and expenditure, and by violent swings in the size of the public sector deficit. Indeed, as early as the 1950s, Prebisch had warned that the country faced stark choices: healthy money or uncontrolled inflation (República Argentine, 1956).

One reason for the increase in expenditure was a lack of financial control over state-owned enterprises. From the 1940s onwards, government firms made a huge, often unknown and unknowable, contribution to the public deficit. This was due to gross inefficiency greatly encouraged by lack of adequate supervision. Lack of supervision was so extensive that state enterprises did not even furnish accounts to the government. From the 1960s, the financial condition of state enterprises was particularly poor. They were often responsible for over 80 per cent of the total public deficit (Veganzones and Winograd, 1997, pp. 151–52).

Figure 2.5: The Argentine Public Sector Deficit as a Percentage of GDP, 1950–1990

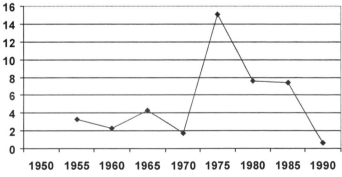

Source: INDEC and Min Econ

Uncontrolled expenditures undermined public finances. The size and volatility of the public sector deficit, and the apparent inability of government to bring spending under control, demonstrated the weakness of fiscal institutions and eroded confidence in the state itself.

Several scholars have noted that finessing the gap between revenue and expenditure was hardly a late twentieth century phenomenon. Comín and Díaz Fuentes observe that between 1865 and 1939, on average, revenue barely financed 80 per cent of government expenditure (Comín and Díaz Fuentes, 2006, p. 9; see also della Parlera, Irigoin and Bózzoli, 2003, pp. 69–72). The root of the problem, however, arose from the decline in state credibility. For fairly long periods during the late nineteenth and early to mid twentieth centuries, the state had been able to borrow at home and overseas at reasonable rates of interest. This would suggest a degree of market confidence in monetary and fiscal institutions of the period. Over the second half of the twentieth century, this proved to be no longer the case. Della Paolera, Irigoin and Bózzoli (2003) confirm that from the 1850s to the 1930s the fiscal accounts often registered a primary surplus (that is, net of interest payments). From the 1940s onwards, this was not so (2003, p. 71; see also Ministerio de Economía y Producción, 2006, slides 22 and 23). Real interest charges rose, and it proved virtually impossible for the state to borrow in the national currency. Given the softening exchange rate, which further raised the cost of borrowing as debt was largely denominated in US dollars, commissions, amortisation payments and interest charges came to account for a significant proportion of state expenditure, and consequently the public sector deficit (Beckerman 1990; Vitelli, 1999).

In the post-World War II period, the fragility of Argentinian fiscal institutions became all too clear. As reflected in Figure 2.5, the country diverged from regional standards of fiscal competence, and lagged further and further behind global standards of state credibility suggested by the tax/GDP ratio presented above. For much of the twentieth century, Argentine fiscal institutions struggled to maintain the level of extractive power achieved in the late nineteenth century, when the standard for state economic involvement was much lower. This stylised survey also indicates that public sector deficits were a pronounced feature of Argentinian fiscal history long before the hyperinflation that marked the transition from the Alfonsín to the Menem presidencies in 1989–90. Such was the magnitude of the budgetary problem, and the background to the Convertibility Plan.

Convertibility and the Budget in the 1990s: Government Revenue and Expenditure

The Convertibility Plan was introduced by Menem's fourth Minister for the Economy, Domingo Cavallo, on 1 April 1991. It was based on a new monetary system, further opening of the economy, and a promised thorough reform of the state — including a retooling of fiscal institutions. The new monetary order was, in effect, a bimonetary arrangement based on the local currency and the dollar. Following a substantial devaluation, the domestic currency was to be completely backed by dollar and foreign reserves held by the Central Bank, which would function as a Currency Board. The Central Bank was freed from political control and prohibited from monetising the fiscal deficit. Apart from a small fiduciary limit, domestic currency would only be issued against dollar reserves and the Bank would exchange currency for dollars at the official rate on demand. The new parity was sanctioned by Act of Congress rather than a Central Bank directive. This was designed to give the arrangement greater credibility by, apparently, committing the political class as a whole to the project — or at least those voting for it in Congress. The peso lost legal tender status: creditors could require debt repayment in dollars. The government, however, would only accept pesos in payment of taxes and settlement of accounts with official agencies.

Opening the economy, along with the liberalisation of exchange transactions and abolition of price controls, was intended to discipline the private sector. A hard currency would deliver hard prices and compel economic agents to take hard, rational decisions. Reform of the state meant removing the principal pressure points on the budget. These were the public corporations, the social security funds and the provinces. The federal budget was to be brought into balance by tax reform — modernising the fiscal structure and increasing the efficiency of tax collection. The disposal of state enterprises had a dramatic impact. Capital inflows strengthened the external accounts, helped reduce overseas indebtedness, and brought windfall budgetary gains. Loss-making enterprises that could not be sold were closed: some were transferred to the provinces, supposedly in line with the devolution of responsibility for service provision to the provinces and municipalities. The 'problem' of social security was also solved by privatisation — a switch from state agencies to private pension funds.

Despite flaws, the Convertibility Plan appeared to work, mostly because there was a large measure of popular support and some distribution (though not an equitable distribution) of pain. During the early years, there was growth with low inflation. From 1991 to 1994 inclusive, output grew at an annual rate of a shade under 8 per cent: inflation averaged a fraction over 28 per cent a year, but the consumer price index fell sharply from 84.0 per cent in 1991 to 3.9 per cent in 1994. Unemployment rose, but remained below double digits until 1994 despite the accelerating pace of privatisation, while investment increased. The project also survived major shocks, including several currencies crises in other emerging markets — the Tequila Crisis of December 1994, the

1997–98 Asian currency crises, the Rouble Crisis of August 1998, and the Cachaça Crisis of late 1999. The Plan also survived political shocks such as the resignation of Cavallo in July 1996, and the change of government in 1999.

After negative growth in 1995, following the Tequila Crisis, the economy recovered and growth rates remained positive until 1998, when growth stalled. From this point onwards, the economy began to contract — slowly at first, and precipitately after the end of 2001. Year-on-year inflows of foreign capital increased from 1993 to 1997 in real terms, and remained substantial until early 2000, though the rate of new inflows declined sharply after 1998. Increasing capital inflows helped to cover the trade deficit (most pronounced in 1992–94 and 1997–98) as privatisation receipts dried up after 1995. Foreign direct investment, particularly in the productive sectors, had a dramatic effect on competition, first in agriculture and later in manufacturing. Export growth testifies to efficiency gains in the productive sectors, not least during the early phase of Convertibility when the peso was over-valued. Similarly, a positive export performance around the turn of the decade was not simply a function of the post-1998 recession-cum-depression. Between 1991 and 2001, average annual total factor productivity gains were positive, unlike the experience of previous decades. Government indebtedness, however, remained high through the decade, and rose dramatically towards the end.

What did the 1990s deliver in terms of budgetary reform and fiscal discipline? Discipline was key. Closely modelled on the pre-World War I Gold Standard, the arrangement was a straitjacket that implied 'locking in' monetary policy and fiscal responsibility (López Murphy, 1995, pp. 123–24; della Paolera

Figure 2.6: The Argentine Consumer Price Index (CPI) and Federal Primary Surplus (FPS)

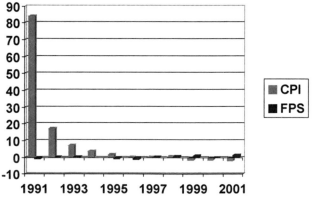

Source: INDEC

and Taylor, 2001, pp. 15, 17–18; della Paolera, Irigoin and Bózzoli, 2003). Theoretically, monetary discipline was built into the Plan, and rule compliance implied balancing the budget.

The sharp decline in the rate of consumer price inflation after the beginning of the decade suggests monetary discipline. The high bar for 1991 (84 per cent) shown in Figure 2.6 is residual inflation from 1990–91. Further declines in 1992 and 1993 indicate that the shock of the new currency arrangement was beginning to take effect. For most of the remainder of the period, annual average price increases were below 1 per cent, with negative price movements after 1999. Budgetary data also appear positive. Yet the picture is not quite so rosy. While a primary surplus was obtained on several occasions, official data show an annual average public sector deficit of around 2 per cent for the 1991–2001 period. This is partly explained by interest payments. Federal data also excluded the provinces, many of which continued to run deficits. In addition, a number of items of expenditure, financed through agreements with the World Bank and the Inter-American Development Bank, were kept off the books. This has led Teijeiro (2001) to argue that the average real deficit stood above 4 per cent, with a steep rise being recorded immediately before the collapse (2001, pp. 1–3).[4] Deficits of this order hardly indicate fiscal rectitude. On the contrary, they point to a loss of control — one that undermined the credibility of budgetary institutions and of the state itself (Damill, Frenkel and Rapetti, 2005, p. 5).

The principal explanations for a loss of control include transitional fiscal measures applied early in the Convertibility Plan period, aspects of the privatisation process and the structure of the budget. In effect, there was a lack of political will to affect a fundamental overhaul of budget institutions and mechanisms. Such palliatives as increasing the efficiency of revenue collection were no substitute for structural reform that would have shifted the public accounts from an over-dependence on pro-cyclical forms of taxation. Another factor was a reflection of provincial budgetary indiscipline. By the end of Convertibility, as much as 20 per cent of the money stock may have been made up of 'inconvertible' provincial notes issues. In effect, the provinces monetised deficits by printing promissory notes, which circulated as currency. Several small interior provinces had resorted to this mechanism during the early years of Convertibility. Although the Constitution prohibited the provinces from printing money, little was done about the issue of provincial quasi-currency. Initially, the provinces involved had little economic weight, and the political costs of bringing errant governors and provincial finance ministers to book in the early 1990s may have been considered not worth the effort. However, by the end of the decade, when the province of Buenos Aires began printing *patacones*, it was another matter. But by then the precedent had been set and the straitjacket was beginning to slip as the economy shrank. Yet as Mussa (2002) asserts: 'Enumerating the many things that contributed to Argentina's tragedy [the 2001 crisis], however, should not obscure the critical failure of Argentine economic policy that was the fundamental cause of disaster — namely, the chronic inability of the Argentine authorities to run a reasonable fiscal policy.' (2002, p. 4)

Notwithstanding his efforts to install and sustain the Plan, Cavallo made two early decisions that were to generate long-term budgetary difficulties. First, he preferred to reduce expenditure rather than increase revenue in order to restore budgetary equilibrium. Second, he implemented tax waivers and rebates to compensate local producers for residual inflation, the initial over-valuation of the peso and the 'shock' opening of the economy. Tariff reform meant that raw materials were admitted free of duty; intermediate goods paid 11 per cent; finished goods paid 22 per cent; and export tariffs were abandoned. The abrupt opening of the economy, coupled with decapitalisation during the 1980s, meant many local firms were uncompetitive. In order to restore business confidence, and to foster new investment, the government sought to reduce operating costs by granting tax breaks. Reductions in social insurance contributions were also devised as mechanisms to reduce labour costs, increase business confidence, and stimulate consumption. Consistent with the declared objective of easing labour taxes and promoting labour market flexibility, the government declared that reducing and redistributing the burden of social insurance payments was intended to increase profits and consumption (Rapoport, 2000, pp. 981–82; Gerschunoff and Llach, 2003, p. 440). The strategy worked. During the first years of Convertibility, growth was driven basically by domestic consumption. Around the middle of the decade, exports surged largely due to substantial investment in the rural sector and, to a lesser extent, in manufacturing — again assisted by the removal of export tariffs and duty changes which reduced the cost of importing capital goods and intermediate products.

Removal of export taxes and the paring of production and labour taxes, however, came at a cost. Value-added tax (VAT) became the principal mechanism in the fiscal arsenal. Over the decade, rates were raised in response to revenue crunches, first from 15 to 18 per cent and then to 21 per cent — a level substantially above that applied in most other countries. During the same period, the rate of corporation tax increased by only two percentage points, from 33 to 35 per cent. Hikes in VAT rates accounted for the lion's share of the growth in tax receipts during the 1990s. Income tax yielded more modest gains, as did social insurance contributions, until rates were reduced and the system was partly privatised (Tanzi, 2000, pp. 14–28; Rapoport, 2000, pp. 981–82; Teijeiro, 2001, pp. 6–7).

At various points before his resignation in 1996, Cavallo alluded to the need to reform the tax structure in order to modernise the budget. He also acknowledged that while Convertibility was essential for stability, the peso–dollar connection should be regarded as a transitional mechanism, one that could be replaced by an arrangement based on a trade-weighted basket of currencies. (This is a topic to which he would return in 2001 when reappointed to the Economics Ministry.) Unfortunately, apart from modernising the administration of the Tax Office, and enhancing the efficiency of tax collection, little was achieved by way of budget reform. In part, the problem was one of timing. Time was necessary to embed the Plan, and this ruled out a sudden change in the exchange anchor. Fiscal and budgetary restructuring also depended on the economic conjuncture. Reform and a redistribution of the tax burden are politically easier to effect during periods of growth, though growth itself can undermine the imperative for reform. While some budgetary pressures — for example, the re-election campaign of Menem in 1994–95 — are relatively easy to predict, others are not. However it is the case that, in small, open economies like the Argentine, exogenous shocks must be expected. Even if the timing of crises is difficult to forecast, they are an inevitable hazard. Perhaps Cavallo was unlucky. Occurring a few months before the 1995 elections, the Tequila effect meant both an exogenous crisis and the electoral cycle derailed any serious stab at fiscal reform. A year later, Cavallo was no longer in office. Nevertheless, his obvious frustration with the slow pace of reform, and increasingly frequent references to 'criminal mafias' and 'corruption', suggest there were profound institutional constraints on fiscal reform (Cavallo, 2001). The return of growth could have provided another window of opportunity for budgetary restructuring, but by this stage the odds were increasingly stacked against root-and-branch change.

The short-term fiscal consequences of privatisation were broadly positive (Manzetti, 1999, pp. 119–33). Virtually at a stroke, a large budget pressure point was removed. As detailed above, state-owned enterprises generated losses, not surpluses. Many were heavily indebted, both domestically and overseas, having issued dollar-denominated bonds they were unable to service. Most offered execrable services. State firms were regarded as bastions of corruption and privilege, milked by union bosses and politicians. This explains the overwhelming public support for privatisation, and indeed Convertibility itself. It was assumed that private operators could not be worse, and might even be considerably better at managing productive industries and public services. The public had lost patience with the post-World War II model (Manzetti, 1999, pp. 77–89; della Paolera and Taylor, 2001, p. 231). Privatisation reduced public spending (and excised future expenditure commitments). There was also a modest reduction in debt. And successful privatised firms paid taxes —

they made a positive, rather than negative, contribution to the budget. But there were downsides. First, cash proceeds from sales were treated as income, temporarily making the budget position appear far healthier than it really was. Second, in the rush to privatise, little account was given to creating the necessary regulatory environment. In many sectors, state monopolies were transformed into private monopolies. Even when regulatory agencies were formed after privatisation, they were weak — in part because they had no input in framing operating criteria laid down in privatisation decrees. Third, particularly in the first phase of privatisation, there was a lack of transparency. Although, once appointed to the Economics Ministry, Cavallo promised to make tendering and disposal practices more accountable, a path-dependent pattern of privatisation had already been established. As a result, real efficiency gains from the disposal of state firms were initially minimal. Fourth, the process may have entrenched powerful business lobbies capable of subverting future reform — not least a redistribution of the fiscal burden or reductions in operating subsidies promised to private operators of public utility companies. While, as a sector, business may have been institutionally weak, several *grupos* enjoyed access to power and had a substantial influence on the pattern and pace of privatisation, including conditions of sale and operation (Palermo and Novaro 1995; Llanos, 2002; Schneider, 2004, pp. 185, 193). There was another downside: before the privatisation of some state enterprises many workers were encouraged to take early retirement, a move that shifted the fiscal burden from public companies about to be sold to state pension funds that would remain in government hands.

If the fiscal consequences of privatisation were broadly positive, the partial privatisation of social insurance (and the hybrid pensions system that resulted) was largely negative. As observed above, Argentinian administrations had historically treated social insurance contributions as income. By the 1980s, like state corporations, pension funds had become a major pressure point in the budget. Privatisation was again the preferred solution. There was, however, a critical difference. While the sale of enterprises transferred from the public to the private sector current and future 'profits and losses', hybrid pension privatisation did not. Although those in employment were encouraged to go private, the residual state system continued to be responsible for the payment of existing pensions. While state funds were in deficit, until privatisation they still enjoyed substantial income flows from working members. As those in work moved to private pension schemes, official funds suffered a haemorrhage of receipts without a corresponding reduction in liabilities. Before transfers began to bite, social insurance receipts had accounted for around a third of total tax receipts (Rapoport, 2000, p. 982). According to Szlezak (2006), it was the fiscal implications of social security reform in the 1990s that finally

Figure 2.7: The Argentine Open Unemployment as a Percentage of the Economically Active Population

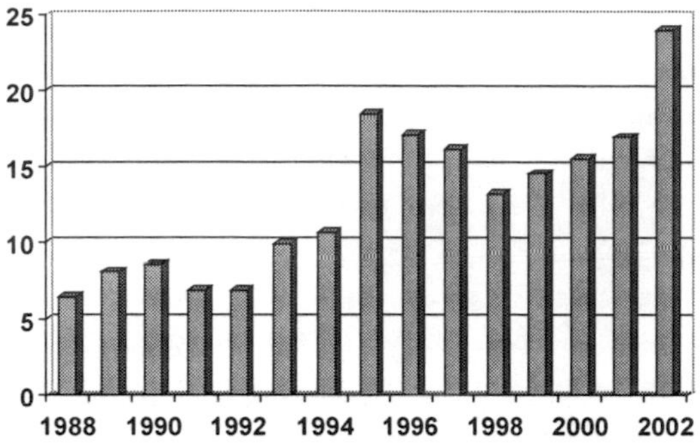

Source: INDEC

brought down Convertibility. Pension privatisation transformed an income flow into a debt flow. In short, payments into the private funds, resources that governments had previously received as income, now reached the public treasury in the form of new debt — pension funds were required to invest a large proportion of contribution income in public bonds. After 1997, the flow of private pension fund credit to the Treasury would be constrained by rising unemployment and contribution evasion.

During the 1990s, there was an intense debate about the cause and nature of unemployment. Did observed trends signal transitional, frictional or structural adjustments in the labour market? Apologists for government strategy pointed to job growth (or the creation of sustainable employment); critics of the regime emphasised rising unemployment and under-employment. As the data in Figure 2.7 show, unemployment was a persistent problem, and there was a considerable step-up in unemployment in the middle of the decade.

Unemployment was a profound social and economic problem. Given the bias of the fiscal system, it was also a budgetary problem, not because the state was responsible for the payment of unemployment benefits (there were none), but because revenue streams were overly dependent on consumption taxes. Employment levels influenced the yields of VAT and income tax. In addition, as unemployment rose, there was a parallel growth of the informal economy which lay largely beyond the fiscal horizon, even outside the reach of many consumption taxes. For example, while the salaried tended to make purchases in supermarkets and 'shoppings' — entities that could avoid the surveillance of the fiscal authorities only with great difficulty — those who found irregular work in the informal economy tended to spend in small corner shops, where informal credit may have been available and fiscal supervision nonexistent, and/or they may have engaged in barter. These were the only survival strategies available to those on or below the poverty line. Unemployment and poverty undermined the viability of a pro-cyclical fiscal system.

How was the growing fiscal deficit financed? Privatisation receipts, treated as income, covered a significant proportion of the deficit before 1995, when disposals tended to tail off. There was nothing left to sell. Already in 1994, as part of the Brady Plan, the government began to issue new debt. The Tequila Crisis temporarily diluted the appetite of foreign markets for new Argentinian debt, so the government turned to the local capital market, only to return to overseas centres with a vengeance in 1996. However, from 1998 currency crises in Asia, Russia and Brazil reduced international liquidity and increased the cost of foreign borrowing. By this stage, analysts were also beginning to question the durability of Convertibility, placing additional constraints on new overseas bond issues. Once again, the government turned to the domestic market. Local institutions absorbed an increasing amount of paper, at lucrative rates and commissions. Finally, in 2001 the government compelled Pension Funds to swallow huge amounts of official paper. By 1998, before new overseas borrowing proved difficult, the total (public and private) foreign debt to foreign exchange earnings ratio stood at 500 per cent. At the same time, the public debt/GDP ratio stood at 40 per cent. These ratios signalled irresponsible borrowing, a shift from credible to non-credible fiscal institutions as illustrated in Figure 2.1. While the sources of indebtedness changed over time, there was a constant and steady reliance on floating new debt to close the fiscal gap (Rapoport, 2000, pp. 981–82; Teijeiro, 2001, pp. 4–5; Mussa, 2002, pp. 4–8; Damill, Frenkel and Rapetti, 2005).

Between 1991 and 1999, primary public expenditure grew by 85 per cent, but total expenditure increased by 101 per cent (Machinea, 2002, pp. 15–16, 36). Moreover, while the rate of increase in primary expenditure tended to level off after 1994 (having risen steeply between 1990 and 1994), total expenditure proved much more difficult to control. Relatively modest between 1994 and 1997, the gap between primary and total expenditure widened every year thereafter. This reflected the faster growth in debt service, a rising charge that would place ever-greater pressure on other items of expenditure, hence the desperate efforts to reduce government payroll costs in 2000 and 2001, and Cavallo's last-ditch 'zero deficit' strategy in 2001.

During the decade, the fiscal base became narrower and heavier, focused on a limited range of indirect taxes that bore heavily on a circumscribed spectrum of society. Rising unemployment (and the increasing weight of the informal economy) led to a decline in the tax take. The burden of taxation, a function of the limited spread of the revenue base, coupled with the structure of the system to encourage evasion. This undermined both the credibility of the fiscal regime and 'social solidarity'. Commenting approximately one year before the crisis, Tanzi argued that the only way to increase tax revenue was to reduce tax rates. He also predicted that unless the system was modified to make it more equitable and efficient, fiscal institutions would implode (*Clarin*, 31 December 2000).

The inability of the political class to grasp the nettle of radical fiscal and budgetary modernisation is neatly captured by the departure of Cavallo from office in 1996, amidst claims of the influence of 'corrupt mafias' on government, and the rotation of Ministers of the Economy in 2001. A full explanation for the resignation/sacking of Cavallo in 1996 may never be given, yet it is probable that the imbalance in the fiscal accounts, the structure of the budget, and the distribution of taxing and spending powers between the federal government and the provinces were important considerations. During his two week tenure at the Palacio de Hacienda in 2001, super-orthodox Minister López Murphy proposed both expenditure cuts and a redistributive tax hike. The political class and other influential interests might have stomached either one of these fiscal and budgetary adjustments; they could not countenance both. Hence Minister López Murphy had a short shelf life. Yet it is unlikely that even such radical surgery could have saved Convertibility at this late stage. As Tanzi had predicted, given the pro-cyclical character of the tax system the country was already ensnared in a Keynesian trap. With the economy contracting, fiscal revenue dipped. Attempts to increase revenue flows by raising tax rates simply pushed the country deeper into recession, necessitating a further round of tax hikes which reduced private consumption even more, and forced the government to borrow irresponsibly, shifting institutional arrangements from the upper to the lower circuit outlined in Figure 2.1.

Credibility and Fiscal Political Economy

What was the structure of the budget? Returning to the discussion of credibility, fiscal solidarity and control over expenditure outlined in the opening section, who paid taxes and who benefited from government expenditure, and how did the fiscal burden change over time?

As has been implied, for much of the latter part of the twentieth century, everyone paid the inflation tax, though some were better able than others to minimise the cost of monetary disorder — or indeed maximise opportunities for distributive gain. From the 1940s until the decade of Convertibility (and once again today), the export sector shouldered a disproportionate share of the tax burden, as did those who were unable to avoid paying income tax and social insurance contributions. Who benefited? Largely the so-called urban alliance of business and organised labour, as well as the state apparatus itself, notably the military who administered a large segment of government firms that included iron and steel production, motor vehicle manufacture, the merchant marine and air transport.

Reforms associated with Cavallo in 1991 meant that the structure of taxation — and the distribution of the fiscal burden — changed dramatically. At the outset of the Menem presidency in 1989, VAT accounted for around 12 per cent of total federal government revenue, income tax for 12.5 per cent, and social insurance contributions for 17 per cent. By the end of the decade, the proportions were, respectively, 40, 19 and 21 per cent (INDEC, FIDE and MECON respectively; Tanzi, 2000, pp. 21–28; Rapoport, 2000, p. 982). (In strong fiscal states, the proportion of revenue raised through VAT and income tax is approximately equal.) This meant that consumers and salaried workers increasingly financed the fiscal costs of sustaining Convertibility. The unemployed also bore a disproportionate share of transitional and structural adjustment costs, as did those who had previously depended on the 'inclusive populist state'. Who received? All benefited from monetary stability. Yet some sectors enjoyed more direct gains from state largesse than others.

As suggested above, until the default of 2002, domestic and foreign bondholders absorbed a rising share of government expenditure in the form of high interest rates. Indeed, efforts in 2001 to effect voluntary funding operations with domestic and foreign creditors were a stark reminder, if one was needed, that bondholders were receiving a generous return and an unsustainable share of government spending. Spiralling interest charges rang alarm bells about irresponsible borrowing in international financial centres during the last years of Convertibility, and were ultimately instrumental in the decision of the IMF to pull the plug. While Cavallo claims that the Fund was never fully committed to the Plan, relations with Buenos Aires deteriorated rapidly when Washington took the position that 'emergency' aid was being used to finance payments to private creditors and capital flight (Cavallo and Cottani, 1997, pp, 17–22; Damill, Frenkel and Rapetti, 2005, pp. 25–26, 38). Businesses, particularly local firms, also benefited from state largesse. First, they benefited from the disposal of government enterprises on generous terms. Second, they benefited from deficit-fuelled government contracts and subsidies. Privatisation strengthened the ascendancy of large domestic conglomerates, which came to enjoy near monopolistic positions in such sectors as transport, energy, the media, and iron and steel. Some of these groups neatly fit Cavallo's depiction of 'business mafias'. They enjoyed immunity from taxation while experiencing the benefits of fiscal generosity, and monetary stability (Manzetti, 1999, pp. 99– 119, 133–41; Romero, 2001, pp. 288–89). And the political class also gained — individually and collectively — as the scandal of discretionary pensions and mushrooming provincial expenditure confirmed. Although the federal budget was brought back broadly into *primary* balance, uncontrolled provincial expenditure destabilised the national accounts. One of the intractable defects of the tax system is that the federal government was largely responsible for raising revenue while the provinces functioned as spending machines controlled by local political 'mafias'. The structure of the budget during Convertibility simply made distributional conflict more transparent.

As already argued, taxation is largely a matter of consent. Even in the case of strong, efficient states, the effectiveness of the fiscal system depends on the willingness of the taxed to pay. There is a contract between state and society to deliver public goods in exchange for fiscal extractions: willingness to pay also depends on perceptions of equity and fiscal solidarity. This means that the state delivers and is able to discipline free-riders, and that public expenditure is under democratic control. The initial achievements of the Convertibility Plan seemed to indicate that an important public good was being delivered. Over time, corruption, evasion and the narrowness of the tax base — increasingly dependent on regressive consumption taxes borne by a shrinking spectrum of groups engaged in the formal sector — suggested that solidarity was being undermined, and that free-riders were escaping discipline. Tax evasion was peculiar neither to the Argentine nor to the period. Prebisch observed in 1956 that Argentinian fiscal institutions were becoming more regressive, in stark contrast to other developed countries and earlier periods of Argentinian fiscal experience (Prebisch, 1956, pp. 19, 51). According to official estimates, fully half of income tax payments were being evaded during the 1960s (República Argentina, 1967). By the 1990s, Argentinian tax rates were considerably higher than in Latin American countries like Mexico and Chile. And compared with Chile, where VAT approximated to levels prevailing in countries of the European Union, evasion (or avoidance) was significantly greater (*Clarín*, 31 December 2000; Tanzi 2000, p. 23). Once again, a decrease in fiscal justice found collective expression in widespread tax evasion.

Concluding Remarks

Characterising the state as the agent of its citizens, specifically the agent to which politically enfranchised citizens assign the task of effecting collective choices about resource allocation and income distribution, Grossman assumes that taxation is the means by which the state prevents free-riding on the provision of public goods (Grossman, 2001, p. 453). But what happens if the state is unable (or unwilling) to apply a credible fiscal regime? That is, what happens if free-riders consume such public goods as monetary stability yet gradually avoid the fiscal burden necessary to sustain the supply of public goods? Inevitably, fiscal solidarity, budgetary control and the supply of goods are jeopardised. So too is state credibility. This seems to be confirmed by the story of the political economy of taxation in the Argentine during the late twentieth century.

References

C. Arza (2004) Distributional Impact of Social Policy: Pensions Regimes in Argentina Since c.1944, unpublished doctoral dissertation, University of London.

M. Beckerman (1990) 'El impacto fiscal del pago de la deuda externa: la experiencia argentina, 1980–86' *Desarrollo Económico*, no. 116.

F. Capie (2001) 'The Origins and Development of Stable Fiscal and Monetary Institutions in England', in Michael D. Bordo and Roberto Cortés Conde (eds.), *Transferring Wealth and Power from the Old to the New World: Monetary and Fiscal Institutions in the Seventeenth Through the Nineteenth Century* (Cambridge: Cambridge University Press).

D. Cavallo (2001) *El peso de la verdad* (Buenos Aires: Planeta 1997).

D. Cavallo and J.A. Cottani (1997) 'Argentina's Convertibility Plan and the IMF', *American Economic Association Papers & Proceedings*, vol. LXXXVII, no. 2, pp. 17–22.

D. Cavallo and J.C. de Pablo (2001) *Pasión por crear* (Buenos Aires: Planeta).

F. Comín and D. Díaz Fuentes (2006) 'La evolución de la hacienda pública en Argentina, España y México, 1820–1940' mimeo, paper presented at the XIV International Economic History Congress, Helsinki, August.

M. Damill, R. Frenkel and M. Rapetti (2005) 'La deuda argentina: historia, default y reestructuración' (Buenos Aires: CEDES Doc. de Trabajo).

M.J. Daunton (2001) *Trusting Leviathan: The Politics of Taxation in Britain, 1799–1914* (Cambridge: Cambridge University Press).

G. della Paolera and A.M. Taylor (2001) *Straining at the Anchor: The Argentine Currency Board and the Search for Macroeconomic Stability, 1880–1935* (Chicago: University of Chicago Press).

G. della Paolera, G.M. Alejandra Irigoin and C.G. Bózzoli (2003) 'Passing the Buck: Monetary and Fiscal Policies', in G. della Paolera and A.M. Taylor (eds.), *A New Economic History of Argentina* (Cambridge: Cambridge University Press), pp. 46–86.

P. Gerschunoff and L. Llach (2003) *El ciclo de la ilusión y el desencanto: un siglo de políticas económicas argentinas* (Buenos Aires: Ariel).

H.I. Grossman (2001) 'The State in Economic History', in M.D. Bordo and R. Cortés Conde (eds.), *Transferring Wealth and Power from the Old to the*

New World: Monetary and Fiscal Institutions in the Seventeenth Through the Nineteenth Century (Cambridge: Cambridge University Press).

S. Haber, D.C. North and B. Weingast (2002) 'The Poverty Trap', *Hover Digest*, no. 4.

F.J. Herschel and S. Itzcovich (1957) 'Fiscal Policy in Argentina', *Public Finance*, vol. XII, nos. 2 & 3.

J.M. Hobson (1997) *The Wealth of States: A Comparative Sociology of International Economic and Political Change* (Cambridge: Cambridge University Press).

R. Hora (2001) *The Landowners of the Argentine Pampas: A Social and Political History 1860–1945* (Oxford: Oxford Historical Monographs).

C.M. Lewis (1993) 'Social Insurance: Ideology and Policy in the Argentine, c. 1920–1966', in C. Abel and C.M. Lewis (eds.), *Welfare, Poverty and Development in Latin America* (London: Macmillan), pp. 175–200.

C.M. Lewis and P. Lloyd-Sherlock (2002) *Social Insurance Regimes: Crises and 'Reform' in the Argentine and Brazil Since* c. *1900*. LSE Working Paper.

M. Llanos (2002) *Privatization and Democracy in Argentina: An Analysis of President–Congress Relations* (London: Palgrave).

R. López Murphy (1995) 'Los planes de estabilización en el MERCOSUR', *Ciclos*, no. VIII, pp. 123–24.

J. L. Machinea (2002) 'Currency Crises: A Practitioner's View', mimeo, Brookings Trade Forum, May.

L. Manzetti (1999) *Privatization South American Style* (Oxford: Oxford University Press).

Ministerio de Economía y Producción, Subsecretaria de Programación Económica (2006) XXIII Reunión Plenaria del Foro Permanente de Direcciones de Presupuesto y Finanzas de la República Argentina 'Evolución macro y proyecciones', slides 22 and 23.

M. Mussa (2002) *Argentina and the Fund: From Triumph to Tragedy* (Washington DC: Institute for International Economics).

C. North Douglass (1994) 'Institutions and Credible Commitment', mimeo.

C. North Douglass and R.P. Thomas (1973) *The Rise of the Western World: A New Economic History* (Cambridge: Cambridge University Press).

P. K. O'Brien (1988) 'The Political Economy of British Taxation, 1660–1815' *Economic History Review*, vol. XXXXI, no. 1, pp. 1–32.

P. K. O'Brien and P.A. Hunt (1999) 'England, 1485–1815', in R. Bonnet (ed.), *The Rise of the Fiscal State in Europe, c. 1200–1815* (New York: Oxford University Press), pp. 53–100.

M. Obstfeld, J.C. Shambaugh and A.M. Taylor (2004) *The Trilemma in History: Trade-offs Among Exchange Rates, Monetary Policy and Capital Mobility* (Cambridge, MA: NBER).

M. Olson Mancur (1993) 'Dictatorship, Democracy, and Development', *The American Political Science Review,* vol. LXXXVII, no. 3, pp. 567–76.

O. Oszlak (1982) *La formación del estado argentino* (Buenos Aires: Editorial de Belgrano).

Palermo Vicente and Marcos Novaro *Política y poder en el gobierno de Menem* (Buenos Aires 1995)

R. Prebisch (1956) 'Mesa Redonda en la Universidad de Córdoba, Buenos Aires, Secretaría de Prensa de la Presidencia de la Nación', *Desarrollo Económico y Política Social* (Buenos Aires).

M. Rapoport (2000) *Historia económica, política y social de la Argentina, 1880–2000* (Buenos Aires).

República Argentina, Presidencia de la Nación, Secretaria del Consejo Nacional de Desarrollo, S. P. E. N (1967) *Estudios de Política Fiscal en la Argentina (Versión Preliminar)* no. V, p. 19.

República Argentine, Presidencia de la Nación, Secretaría de la Prensa (1956) *Moneda sana o inflación incontenible (the so-called* Plan Prebisch*)*, (Buenos Aires).

D. Rock (1975) *Politics in Argentina, 1890–1930: The Rise and Fall of Radicalism* (Cambridge: Cambridge University Press).

L.A. Romero (2001) *Breve historia contemporánea de la Argentina* (Buenos Aires: Fondo de Cultura Económica).

B.R. Schneider (2004) *Business Politics and the State in Twentieth-century Latin America* (Cambridge: Cambridge University Press).

L.M. Snider (1987) 'Identifying the Elements of State Power: where do we begin?', *Comparative Political Studies,* vol. XX, no. 3, pp. 314–56.

K.L. Sokoloff and E.M. Zolt (2006) 'Inequality and the Evolution of Institutions of Taxation: Evidence from the Economic History of the Americas', mimeo.

P. Szlezak Phillip (2006) The Political Economy of Pension Privatisation in Argentina, 1990–2005, unpublished DPhil thesis, Oxford University.

V. Tanzi (1987)'Qualitative Characteristics of the Tax Systems in Developing Countries', in D. Newbury and N. Stern (eds.), *The Theory of Taxation for Developing Countries* (New York: Oxford University Press).

V. Tanzi (2000)'Taxation in Latin America in the Last Decade', paper presented at the Fiscal Reforms in Latin America Conference, November.

V. Tanzi and H. Zee (2000) *Tax Policy for Emerging Markets: Developing Countries* (Washington DC: IMF).

M. Teijeiro (2001) 'Una vez mas: la política fiscal …' available from www.cep.irg.ar.

M.A. Veganzones and C. Winograd (1997) *Argentina in the 20th Century: An Account of Long-awaited Growth* (Paris: OECD).

G. Vitelli (1990) 'Las lógicas de la economía argentina: inflación y crecimiento', mimeo.

G. Vitelli (1999) *Los dos siglos de la Argentina: historia económica comparada* (Buenos Aires: Prendergast).

L. Weiss and J.M. Hobson (1995) *States and Economic Development: A Comparative Historical Analysis* (Cambridge, MA: Polity Press).

Notes

[1] For a counter view, see O'Brien (1988 pp. 1–32), and O'Brien and Hunt (1999, pp. 53–100). O'Brien estimates that the British state captured about 15% of national income in 1700, rising to around 30% by 1810, at the height of the Napoleonic Wars, a proportion substantially above that for continental Europe. It was this proportion that demonstrated the strength — 'fiscality' — of the British state.

[2] For comments on the history of taxation, see Comín and Díaz Fuentes (2006); Sokoloff and Zolt (2006, pp. 15–28, 33–39).

[3] The OxLAD data is broadly comparable with that provided by Tanzi (2000, p. 9) and Sokoloff and Zolt (2006, pp. 34–35 and Table 18).

[4] For calculations based on official data, see Mussa (2002, pp. 5–6).

3

FISCAL SUSTAINABILITY AND DEFICIT POLITICS IN THE UNITED STATES

Dennis S. Ippolito

The key to the short-term fiscal outlook in the United States is tax policy. Tax cuts enacted in 2001 and 2003 have contributed significantly to the large federal deficits of the past several years, but many of these cuts are scheduled to expire after 2010. Unless they are extended, revenue-GDP levels are expected to rise and bring the budget close into balance by 2012. The politics of tax policy, then, will largely determine whether structural deficits in the United States are eliminated over the next decade.

The long-term fiscal outlook presents a more complicated challenge. In 10 to 15 years, demographic pressures will begin to escalate the costs of federal retirement and healthcare entitlements. Absent changes in existing policy, it will be difficult to finance these entitlements, while funding defence and other national needs at required levels and maintaining revenue-GDP levels that are politically acceptable and economically viable. Concerns about fiscal sustainability in the United States, then, involve the projected costs and budgetary impact of three major retirement and healthcare entitlements: Social Security, Medicare, and Medicaid.[1]

There is a direct, albeit modest, linkage between the current and future outlooks. To the extent that debt-GDP levels remain high because of immediate deficits, the fiscal sustainability time horizons for controlling entitlement cost pressures become much shorter. Another, less obvious, linkage relates to spending policy. Mandatory programmatic spending-GDP levels have doubled over the past several decades, and the United States now devotes well over half its budget to entitlement programmes. This entitlement expansion has been accommodated by corresponding cutbacks in discretionary programmes, primarily defence, keeping the overall spending-GDP levels relatively stable. But with the projected trajectory for long-term mandatory spending moving sharply higher, these tradeoffs will no longer suffice, and policy-makers in the United States will finally have to confront the fiscal limits of the entitlement state.

The Short-Term Outlook

When the Bush administration took office in 2001, the Congressional Budget Office (CBO) described the federal budget outlook as 'bright' (Congressional Budget Office, 2001a, p. xiv). The CBO's baseline projections showed surpluses totalling $5.6 trillion for FY2002–11, with annual surplus-GDP levels climbing above 5 per cent over this period. Since 2001, this outlook has been transformed by economic shocks and policy changes. Deficits — actual and projected — for FY2002–11 are likely to be well above $2.0 trillion.

While a weak economy early in George W. Bush's first term sharply depressed revenues, a series of tax cuts have kept revenue levels low during the subsequent economic recovery. In addition, defence spending has increased substantially since the 11 September 2001 terrorist attacks in the United States. Defence-GDP levels, which had fallen to 3 per cent in 2001, are now running at approximately 4 per cent. The gap between revenues and spending has been further widened by large domestic spending increases. Indeed, since 2001 the spending-GDP ratio for mandatory and discretionary domestic programmes has risen by about as much as has defence.

The fiscal consolidation success that the United States enjoyed during the 1990s was not unique. A number of advanced democracies matched or exceeded the deficit-reduction record in the United States, and many have since experienced cyclical reversals in their fiscal outlooks. The reversal in the United States, however, largely reflects structural or policy changes, in particular the Bush administration's efforts to cancel the defence cutbacks and especially tax increases that made fiscal consolidation possible.

Table 3.1: Outlays, revenues and deficits as a percentage of GDP, fiscal years 1950–89

		Average annual level		
Fiscal Years		*Outlays (%)*	*Revenues (%)*	*Deficits(%)**
1950–59	(7)	17.6	17.2	0.4
1960–69	(8)	18.7	17.9	0.8
1970–79	(10)	20.0	18.0	2.1
1980–89	(10)	22.2	18.3	3.9

*   For each decade, these are average net deficits (i.e., deficits minus surpluses). The numbers in parentheses are the annual deficits for each period.

Source: US Government (2006, p. 25).

The Road to Balanced Budgets

The deficit problem the United States faced during the early 1990s was rooted in long-term spending policy changes. From the 1950s through the 1980s, outlay-GDP levels rose steadily, while revenue levels changed very little (see Table 3.1). As outlays continued to climb, the frequency and magnitude of deficits increased. During the 1980s, deficit-GDP levels averaged nearly 4 per cent, and debt-GDP levels soared.

This upward shift in spending was driven by domestic programmes. In particular, spending policy priorities were shifting from defence to social welfare programmes. During the 1950s, for example, defence spending accounted for well over half the budget; defence-GDP levels remained above 10 per cent through the latter part of that decade. By the late 1970s, the defence budget share had been cut in half, and defence-GDP levels were under 5 per cent. Over this same period, mandatory spending for entitlement programmes was moving in the opposite direction and offsetting the decline in defence. Between 1960 and 1980, the mandatory spending-GDP level went from less than 5 per cent to almost 10 per cent. This 'welfare shift' transformed spending policy, making it more difficult to control spending growth and deficits.

Within this mandatory spending category, retirement and healthcare entitlements accounted for a disproportionate share of the overall growth. Social Security, which was established in 1935, grew fairly slowly until 1965, when Medicare and Medicaid were enacted. The Johnson administration coupled these new healthcare entitlements to greatly increased Social Security cash benefits (Ippolito, 2003, pp. 190–97). Social Security benefits were then raised by an additional 50 per cent between 1967 and 1972, with automatic cost-of-living adjustments (COLAs) supplied in 1972. As a result, real spending for Social Security doubled during the 1970s, while inflation-adjusted spending for Medicare and Medicaid went up by 250 per cent. By 1980, the spending-GDP level for these three programmes was 6 per cent, while total mandatory spending was climbing towards 10 per cent (Congressional Budget Office, 2007, p. 149).

The Reagan Deficits

While the Reagan defence build-up and tax cuts dominate most analyses of budget policy during the 1980s, the battles over spending policy and deficits were much broader. The budget programme that Ronald Reagan presented to Congress in 1981 called for sharp reductions in domestic discretionary spending and in entitlement programmes. Reagan was advocating, in effect, a return to pre-Great Society spending policy — high defence budget shares, scaled-back domestic programmes, narrowly defined 'social safety net' entitlement policies.[2] These spending retrenchments were controversial from the outset, and Reagan's actual accomplishments fell well short of his goals. He was able to erase the discretionary domestic expansions of the 1970s, but efforts to modify the 'universalisation of social benefit programmes' were largely frustrated. Congress rejected any major cutbacks in Social Security and Medicare, and other non-means-tested entitlements were preserved largely intact.

As shown in Table 3.2, spending policy changes during the Reagan presidency affected the balance between defence and non-defence discretionary spending and, to a lesser extent, social welfare entitlements for the poor. Mandatory spending-GDP levels were stabilised but not substantially reduced. High rates of growth in Social Security and, especially, Medicare persisted, and overall spending remained at very high levels.

Table 3.2: Spending-GDP Levels, Fiscal Years 1981–89 (%)

Fiscal Year	Discretionary Spending		Mandatory Spending		
	Defence	Nondefence	Entitlements*	Interest	Total
1981	5.2	4.9	9.9	2.2	22.2
1982	5.8	4.3	10.4	2.6	23.1
1983	6.1	4.2	10.6	2.6	23.5
1984	5.9	3.9	9.4	2.9	22.1
1985	6.1	3.9	9.7	3.1	22.8
1986	6.2	3.7	9.4	3.1	22.5
1987	6.1	3.4	9.1	3.0	21.6
1988	5.8	3.4	8.9	3.0	21.2
1989	5.6	3.4	9.0	3.1	21.2

*   Includes offsetting receipts.
Source: Congressional Budget Office (2007, pp. 145–49).

On the tax side, the two defining measures of the Reagan presidency were the Economic Recovery Tax Act of 1981 and the Tax Reform Act of 1986. The former was an enormous package of individual and corporate tax cuts, estimated at $750 billion for FY1981–86 (Ippolito 2003, p. 233). Larger than expected deficits led Congress to repeal some corporate tax preferences in 1982 and 1984, but the Reagan administration blocked efforts to raise individual tax rates.

The 1986 Tax Reform Act, enacted in the midst of high deficits, marked an important shift in structural tax policy. For both individuals and corporations, tax rates were greatly reduced, while tax preferences were curtailed or eliminated.

The overall revenue changes over time were expected to be deficit neutral, but the tradeoffs between rates and preferences worked differently for individuals and corporations. For corporations, reductions in preferences outweighed the effects of lower rates, resulting in net tax increases. For individuals, the tradeoffs were reversed, and all income tax liabilities for an estimated six million low-income taxpayers were eliminated as well. Even more important from the standpoint of Republican tax philosophy, marginal rates were sharply reduced. For high-income taxpayers, the 1986 *Tax Reform Act* essentially provided a flat tax of 28 per cent on all taxable income.

The basic elements of the Reagan tax programme — lower tax burdens for individuals and other structural tax reforms to promote economic growth, along with reduced revenue-GDP levels — were maintained in the face of heavy deficits. Revenue-GDP levels fell from 19.6 per cent in 1981 to approximately 17.5 per cent from 1983–86. Revenues rebounded modestly over the next three years, but peak levels were only slightly above 18 per cent of GDP, some three percentage points below spending. The budget policy impasse of the Reagan years, then, was rooted in Congress's refusal to cut the largest component of federal spending — retirement and healthcare entitlements — and Reagan's refusal to increase the largest revenue source — individual income taxes. The resulting deficits averaged almost 4 per cent of GDP from 1981–89, and publicly held debt as a percentage of GDP rose from 25 per cent to 40 per cent over this period.[3]

Deficit Reduction in the 1990s

In response to these deficits, Congress passed legislation requiring the budget to be balanced over a six-year period.[4] The 1985 deficit control act did not change existing policy but instead provided for automatic spending cuts, primarily in discretionary programmes, if Congress and the president subsequently failed to enact tax and spending laws that would keep budgets within prescribed deficit ceilings. These deficit-reduction controls had no serious impact on Reagan, but they forced his successor, George H. Bush, to negotiate a massive deficit-reduction agreement with the Democratic-controlled Congress in 1990. Three years later, Bill Clinton used the Bush precedent to expand tax increases and to extend spending controls. In FY1998, the federal budget registered its first surplus since 1969. In FY2000, the surplus exceeded $236 billion.

This dramatic change in fiscal policy began with an unexpected and rapid deterioration in the deficit outlook in 1990. When the Bush administration's FY1991 budget was submitted to Congress in January 1990, it stated that the statutory deficit ceiling for 1991 ($64 billion) would be met without major tax increases or spending cuts. It also forecast a balanced budget by 1993 (US Government, 1990, pp. 9–10). Over the next few months, however, deficit estimates turned sharply negative. By June, the projected deficit for FY1991 was $230 billion and climbing (Ippolito, 2003, p. 247). Since discretionary programmes could not possibly absorb the spending cuts needed to comply with the statutory deficit ceilings, Bush called on Congress to negotiate a multiyear deficit-reduction programme.

The Omnibus Budget Reconciliation Act of 1990 that finally emerged from these negotiations had a decidedly Democratic tilt. Of its estimated $480 billion in deficit reduction for FY1991–95, nearly one-third involved revenue increases. The top marginal rate for individuals was raised (to 31 per cent); high-income taxpayers were also targeted for higher Medicare taxes along with reduced deductions and personal exemptions. Spending cuts were aimed almost exclusively at defence; entitlement benefits were largely exempted.

OBRA 1990 did, however, implement new budget controls that the Bush administration had proposed. These included multi-year discretionary spending caps, so-called PAYGO restrictions on tax cuts and entitlement benefit increases, and enforcement procedures to prevent violations of the spending caps or PAYGO controls.[5] Nevertheless, George Bush paid a heavy political price among Republicans for abandoning his 'no new taxes' pledge, and this price was electorally amplified by an apparent lack of progress in the deficit outlook. Despite the tax increases, revenue levels were being dragged down by a weak economy, and deficits were worsening. When Reagan left office, the deficit was $150 billion. Three years later, with the largest deficit-reduction bill in history having been signed into law, the deficit was over $290 billion.

Under Clinton, a similar scenario seemed to be unfolding. The Omnibus Budget Reconciliation Act of 1993 was a $430 billion package of tax increases and spending cuts that promised a one third reduction in baseline deficits over FY1994–98. The tax increases in OBRA 1993 were much larger than those enacted in 1990 — an estimated $240 billion over five years, with most of these additional revenues coming from upper-income taxpayers. The top marginal rate for individuals was raised from 31 per cent to 39.6 per cent; higher Medicare payroll taxes and Social Security benefit taxes were also imposed on high-income taxpayers.

In large part because of these tax increases, OBRA 1993 barely passed the House and Senate. Republican opposition was unanimous, and a number of Democrats deserted Clinton as well. Moreover, the deficit situation remained gloomy in the run-up to the 1994 mid-term elections, contributing to a surprising Republican victory. Since the New Deal, Democratic control of Congress had seemed close to permanent — Republicans had captured the House and Senate for two years after World War II, and another two years after Korea. Republicans had also held the Senate for six years under Reagan. Otherwise, Democratic majorities had been nearly continuous and typically quite large.

With their 1994 breakthrough, Republican congressional leaders, particularly the new House Speaker, Newt Gingrich, revived and expanded the Reagan effort to reduce the size of government. Their first initiative was a constitutional balanced-budget amendment, which easily passed the two thirds majority threshold in the House but failed by one vote in the Senate. The Republicans then launched a multi-year balanced budget programme, combining a massive package of spending cuts — nearly $900 billion over seven years when compared to baselines — with a $245 billion cut in taxes (Ippolito, 2003, pp. 265–72).

These Republican spending cuts were aimed exclusively at domestic programmes, particularly entitlements. Medicare was targeted for a $270 billion reduction; Medicaid was to be cut, capped, and turned over to the states as a block grant; and welfare entitlements for the poor were sharply reduced as well. A Reconciliation Bill containing the entitlement spending reductions and tax cuts was approved by Congress in November. A parallel effort to slash discretionary domestic programmes focused on the FY1996 appropriations Bills Congress was considering.

The 1995 Reconciliation Bill was vetoed by President Clinton in early December. By that time, Clinton also had vetoed a series of domestic appropriations Bills that Republicans had cut well below his recommendations. The latter confrontation proved to be pivotal. Budget negotiations between the White House and congressional leaders collapsed in acrimony, partial government shutdowns occurred in November and December of 1995, and the public response to the shutdowns and related battles over budget policy forced a Republican retreat. Clinton subsequently exploited this advantage during the final round of FY1996 appropriations decisions, and he continued to keep Republicans on the defensive when FY1997 bills were negotiated prior to the 1996 election. After the election, a new round of budget policy talks began, but the balanced-budget agreement that the White House and Congress finally reached in early 1997 left in place the individual tax increases enacted in 1993.

The 1997 agreement included two Reconciliation Bills. The Tax Reconciliation Bill provided for a net reduction of $80 billion over five years — lower capital gains taxes and child tax credits on the Republican side, and expanded low-income and education tax credits sponsored by Clinton. The spending savings in the companion 1997 reconciliation were estimated at $260 billion over five years. About half of this amount came from extending discretionary spending caps through 2002. There were also substantial entitlement savings, particularly in Medicare, but these did not involve benefits. Instead, sharp reductions were made in the scheduled payment formulas for hospitals, physicians and healthcare providers, and Medicare Part B premiums were increased.

According to Clinton and congressional Republicans, the 1997 budget agreement represented a real breakthrough. For at least several years, deficits would remain in the $50–70 billion range, but the budget would be balanced — if only barely — in 2002 (*Congressional Quarterly Almanac*, 1998, pp. 2-18). In fact, deficits were disappearing much faster — revenue-GDP levels were surging well above official projections and spending-GDP levels were moving in the opposite direction (Ippolito, 2003, p. 285). In FY1998, the budget registered an unexpected surplus of nearly $70 billion. Two years later, the surplus had tripled.

The policy components of deficit reduction during the 1990s are shown in Table 3.3. Well over two-thirds of the shift from large deficits to large surpluses was provided by defence cuts and individual income tax increases. Domestic spending, mandatory and discretionary, was essentially flat for the period. Defence-GDP levels, by comparison, were the lowest in 50 years, but any serious partisan debate over defence spending was muted by the post-Cold War environment and the Republican focus on tax cuts. Republican differences with the Clinton administration over defence budgets involved marginal increases,

Table 3.3: Policy components of deficit reduction, 1990–2000 ($ billions and % of GDP)

FY 1990	= –$221	FY 2000	= +$236
Revenues	= 18.0% GDP	Revenues	=20.9% GDP
Outlays	= 21.8%	Outlays	= 18.4%
Deficit	= -3.9%	Surplus	= +2.4%

	FY 1990	FY 2000	Change
Revenues	18.0% GDP	20.9% GDP	+2.6% GDP
Individual	8.1	10.3	(+2.2)
Corporation	1.6	2.1	(+0.5)
Payroll	6.6	6.7	(+0.1)
Other	1.6	1.6	(+0.0)
Outlays	21.8%	18.4%	-3.4%
Discretionary defence	5.2	3.0	(-2.2)
Discretionary non-defence	3.5	3.3	(-0.2)
Mandatory programmatic	9.9	9.8	(-0.1)
Net interest	3.2	2.3	(-0.9)
	21.8	18.4	-3.4

Source: Congressional Budget Office (2007, pp. 143–47).

not substantial buildups. On the tax side, by comparison, partisan differences were magnified as revenue-GDP levels soared to World War II peaks. In 1944 and 1945, revenues had climbed to 20 per cent of GDP. From 1998–2000, revenues again moved above the 20 per cent mark. In 2000, revenues were 20.9 per cent of GDP, the same as in 1944 (US Government, 2007, pp. 25–26).

Even worse from the Republican standpoint was the upward shift in individual income tax levels. From the end of World War II through the mid 1990s, individual income tax-GDP levels averaged about 8 per cent (US Government, 2007, pp. 33–34). For FY1997–99, the average was almost 9.5 per cent. In FY2000, the income tax-GDP share reached 10.3 per cent, the highest level ever recorded.

The key budget policy battle over fiscal consolidation — whether to balance the budget at high or low revenue levels — had been won by Clinton and congressional Democrats. Despite their takeover of Congress in 1995, Republicans never came close to restoring the revenue levels or income tax policies of the Reagan era. Moreover, Republicans failed to force substantial cutbacks in domestic spending. Indeed, once budget surpluses were in place and surplus projections became increasingly optimistic, Republican antipathy towards domestic programmes began to wane. In 1999 and 2000, Republicans joined Clinton in circumventing the budget enforcement controls on spending, boosting discretionary domestic spending and expanding healthcare and veterans' entitlements.[6]

Surplus projections by 2000 were so large and seemingly permanent — Clinton's budget that year trumpeted 'decades of surpluses to come' (US Government, 1999, p. 3) — that competing plans for surplus budgeting were a central feature of the presidential election campaign. George W. Bush highlighted the Republican commitment to large, permanent tax cuts that would lower revenue levels and, not coincidentally, eliminate future surpluses that would otherwise be available for new domestic spending. For Al Gore and the Democratic Party, smaller and targeted tax cuts represented a contrasting fiscal approach to preserve high revenue levels and finance an ambitious domestic agenda. In addition, Democrats emphasised 'saving' the Social Security surpluses — that is, balancing on-budget taxes and spending — as a way to postpone serious problems with entitlement financing indefinitely.[7] Thus, the pivotal issue in surplus budgeting — as it had been in deficit budgeting — was whether to balance budgets, and to accommodate domestic spending pressures, at high- or low-revenue levels.

Deficit Budgeting Returns

With George W. Bush's victory in 2000, the predictable first priority for the 107th Congress was a massive tax cut. The Economic Growth and Tax Relief

Reconciliation Act of 2001 (EGTRRA) was the largest tax cut in two decades, with an estimated revenue cost of $1.35 trillion over 10 years (Congressional Budget Office, 2001b, p. 8). But as this legislation was moving through Congress, the economy was slowing and the September 11 attacks turned this slowdown into a recession. The attacks also triggered emergency domestic spending and additional defence spending for the emerging war on terrorism.

The economic downturn, spending increases and tax cuts during 2001 erased some $4 trillion of the $5.6 trillion in surpluses projected in January (Congressional Budget Office, 2002, p. xiii). The remainder soon evaporated as well, as revenue-GDP levels fell more quickly and sharply than anticipated, discretionary spending levels continued to climb, and mandatory spending moved steadily upward. As Table 3.4 indicates, the budget policy shift from 2000–05 was essentially the reverse of what had occurred during the 1990s. Individual income tax-GDP levels dropped by 2.8 percentage points, and defence-GDP levels rose by one percentage point. Taken together, individual income taxes and defence accounted for about three-quarters of this surplus-deficit shift.

Table 3.4: Policy components of the surplus–deficit reversal, 2000–05 ($ billions and % of GDP)

FY 2000	= + $236	FY 2005	= - $318
Revenues	= 20.9% GDP	Revenues	= 17.6% GDP
Outlays	= 18.4%	Outlays	= 20.2%
Surplus	= +2.4%	Deficit	= -2.6%

	FY 2000	FY 2005	Change
Revenues	20.9% GDP	17.6% GDP	-3.3% GDP
Individual	10.3	7.6	(-2.7)
Corporation	2.1	2.3	(+0.2)
Payroll	6.7	6.5	(-0.2)
Other	1.6	1.3	(-0.3)
Outlays	18.4%	20.1%	+1.7%
Discretionary defence	3.0	4.0	(+1.0)
Discretionary non-defence	3.3	3.9	(+0.6)
Mandatory programmatic	9.8	10.8	(+1.0)
Net interest	2.3	1.5	(-0.8)
	18.4	20.2	+1.7%

Source: Congressional Budget Office (2007, pp. 143–47).

Figure 3.1: Total Revenues and Outlays as a Percentage of GDP, 1966–2017

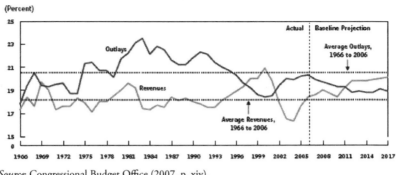

Source: Congressional Budget Office (2007, p. xiv).

Since 2005, outlays have remained at approximately 20 per cent of GDP. Revenue-GDP levels have rebounded to almost 18.5 per cent — close to the historical average for the last 50 years but well below the levels during Bill Clinton's second term (see Figure 3.1). If the economy performs reasonably well during the remainder of Bush's presidency, and wartime defence requirements diminish, deficits should continue to fall but not disappear.

The immediate post-Bush outlook, in turn, will be shaped by tax policy outcomes over the next few years. Numerous tax cut provisions enacted during the Bush presidency — including the entire 2001 EGTRRA — are scheduled to expire. Unless Bush persuades a Democratic-controlled Congress to make some or all of these cuts permanent, revenue-GDP levels will rise abruptly after 2010. A further uncertainty is the fate of the alternative minimum tax, a several decades-old supplemental income tax aimed at high-income taxpayers that limits the extent to which they can use tax preferences to reduce income tax liabilities. Because this tax has not been adjusted in terms of income thresholds, it is now affecting millions of middle-income taxpayers and significantly increasing their tax burdens. The Bush administration and Congress have thus far provided temporary AMT relief, but the revenue costs from extended or permanent coverage adjustments will be extremely high (Congressional Budget Office, 2007, pp. 88–89).

Finally, the deficit record of the Bush administration has translated into rising publicly held debt-GDP levels, but this ratio is likely to remain below 40 per cent for the next five to 10 years. In terms of historical comparisons, debt-GDP ratios in this range are not particularly striking (see Figure 3.2). But there are features of the current debt situation that raise legitimate concerns about long-term impact. First, the percentage of debt held outside the United States has roughly tripled — to almost 45 per cent — over the past few decades (Congressional Budget Office, 2007, p. 19). In addition to the potential political complications that heavy Chinese and other foreign holdings of US debt might

Figure 3.2: Debt Held by the Public as a Percentage of GDP, 1940–2017

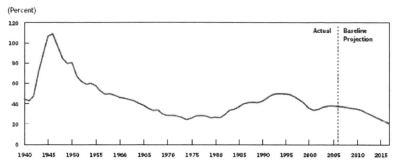

Source: Congressional Budget Office (2007, p. 10).

introduce, there are uncertainties about interest rate and financing pressures. Second, the deficit and debt problems associated with future spending policy will make it much more difficult to maintain a stable fiscal path. The long-term fiscal outlook, then, extends and potentially magnifies current concerns regarding federal debt.

The Long-Term Outlook

Partisan conflicts over spending policy and revenue levels will likely sharpen as the costs of entitlement programmes begin to mount. There are some two dozen entitlements that the federal government finances in whole or in part, with the major beneficiary populations being the elderly, the poor, federal civilian and military retirees and veterans. Current costs for most of these programmes are substantial — income security entitlements for the poor, for example, are approximately $200 billion, while federal civilian and military retirement along with veterans' pensions and insurance are an additional $150 billion (Congressional Budget Office, 2007, p. 55). Under current policy, almost all of these programmes will continue to grow in coverage and costs over time.

The long-term fiscal sustainability of entitlement policy, however, chiefly depends on three major retirement and healthcare entitlements: Social Security, Medicare, and Medicaid. In 2006, these three programmes accounted for more than 75 per cent of total mandatory spending; over the next decade, that percentage is expected to climb to almost 90 per cent (Congressional Budget Office, 2007, p. 50). In addition, spending-GDP levels for these programmes will continue to rise.

The Sources of Current Growth

At present, the growth in retirement and healthcare entitlements is being driven largely by programmatic rather than demographic factors (Congressional

Budget Office, 2007, p. 61). Cost of living and other automatic adjustments in Social Security and Medicare, for example, will increase spending by an estimated $256 billion in 2017; other statutory benefit increases will raise Social Security, Medicare and Medicaid outlays by nearly $500 billion. By comparison, increases in caseloads — that is, the beneficiary populations for these programmes — will have comparatively modest effects, adding an estimated $340 billion to programme costs in 2017.

The impact of demographic pressures on retirement and healthcare entitlements, then, will remain limited over the next 10–15 years. Nevertheless, cost increases under current law are expected to raise outlay-GDP levels by more than two percentage points between 2006 and 2017, with most of this increase being accounted for by the Medicare programme (Congressional Budget Office, 2007, p. 50). Cost growth in other entitlements is expected to lag well behind, which will moderate the increase in total mandatory spending-GDP levels. Eventually, however, demographic pressures will begin to push mandatory spending levels much higher, particularly if healthcare costs are not controlled. The long-term fiscal problem for the United States, then, is much more serious for Medicare and Medicaid than for Social Security.

Dependency Ratios

Whatever the general uncertainties of long-term demographic projections, several demographic shifts appear to be reasonably predictable. First, the number of future retirees in the United States will grow rapidly as the large baby boomer generation reaches retirement age. Second, life spans for these retirees are expected to increase, bringing the share of the population aged 65 and older to approximately 20 per cent by 2050 (Congressional Budget Office, 2005a, p. 9). Third, low fertility rates will likely result in an abrupt slowdown in the growth rate for the labour force in the United States, even with allowances for future immigration.

Population aging, then, will have a significant impact on dependency ratios — that is, the ratio between workers and retirees. In the United States, favourable dependency ratios — about 5:1 over the past few decades — have helped make it possible to finance entitlement expansions without great difficulty. These ratios, however, are now expected to fall to fiscally undesirable levels over the next half century — an estimated 3:1 by 2030 and approximately 2.5:1 by 2050 (Congressional Budget Office, 2005b, p. 21). As ratios decline in this fashion, future worker cohorts will face greatly increased tax burdens to finance retirement and healthcare benefits if current policy commitments remain largely in place. It is also possible that a contracting labour force would result in lower economic growth, making the financing problems even more serious.

An obvious response to these demographic shifts would be public policies that encourage people to remain in the workforce longer — discouraging early retirement, raising the normal retirement age, and extending the transition to full retirement by providing partial benefits to supplement part-time work. In fact, a number of these adjustments have already been made in the Social Security programme (Ippolito, 2003, p. 310). Benefit reductions for early retirement (age 62) will increase for future retirees under current law. The normal retirement age is now being raised to 66 and will be moved up to 67 during the 2020s. And the financial penalties for post-retirement work have been eased. In 2000, for example, the Social Security 'earnings test' that penalised high-income retirees who continued to work from ages 65–69 was repealed.

Long-term cost projections for retirement and healthcare entitlements, however, already take these adjustments into account. While additional changes to encourage longer working careers could certainly be implemented, the impact on dependency ratios would probably be modest. These types of policy adjustments would also have a much smaller impact on healthcare entitlement costs than on Social Security costs, but it is the Medicare and Medicaid cost scenarios that present the more daunting fiscal challenge. Indeed, reasonably straightforward policy reforms could reduce or even eliminate the projected upward shift in Social Security spending-GDP levels over the next several decades.

Social Security

The fiscal concerns over Social Security are often confused with the technical solvency of trust funds that finance the programme.[v8] The critical issue, however, is the budgetary impact of the programme — how Social Security affects the government's overall spending and revenue needs. If its spending-GDP level moves significantly upward, Social Security will require adjustments in aggregate budget policy — increased revenues through payroll taxes, cutbacks in other spending programmes or borrowing. The magnitude of projected Social Security cost increases, then, is the appropriate focus for reform proposals.

With the benefit formulas and retirement age criteria now in place, Social Security will grow fairly slowly over the next decade. The outlay-GDP level for FY2017, for example, is 4.8 per cent, compared with 4.2 per cent for 2006 (Congressional Budget Office, 2007, p. 50). By 2030, however, the Social Security share of GDP will have risen to about 6 per cent (Congressional Budget Office, 2005b, p. 10). The spending path from 2030–50 is then relatively flat, peaking at around 6.5 per cent.

Social Security's financing 'problem' is not minuscule. A 2+ percentage point increase in GDP, for example, would necessitate very substantial payroll

Figure 3.3: Federal Spending Under Current Law and Under Three Illustrative Options for Slowing the Growth of Social Security

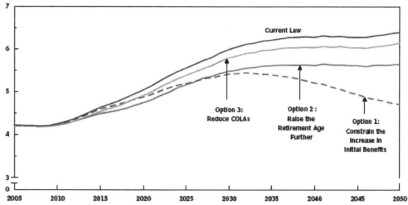

(Percentage of gross domestic product)

Note: COLAS=cost-of-living adjustments.

Source: Congressional Budget Office (2005b, p. 23).

tax increases if the programme were to remain entirely self-financing. But the Social Security spending path can also be lowered significantly, and fairly predictably, by structural changes that lower per beneficiary costs (see Figure 3.3). A reduction in the cost-of-living adjustments that are applied annually to retirees' Social Security benefits, for example, would significantly reduce the long-term growth in spending. (The specific consumer price index (CPI) currently used for this purpose possibly overstates the effect of inflation on retirees, and the illustration in Figure 3.3 represents a 'CPI minus 0.3 percentage point' modification to correct for this possible overstatement.) A less generous inflation adjustment would lower Social Security-GDP levels over the short term and slow their rise thereafter. A lesser CPI reduction would obviously erase some of these savings, as would efforts to restrict the CPI changes to high-income retirees.

The retirement age option combines an increase in the normal retirement age with future adjustments that would correspond to increases in life expectancy. Under current law, the normal retirement age is being raised to 66 (between 2003 and 2009), and it will then rise to 67 (between 2021 and 2027). By moving up the latter transition and then making future adjustments based on increased life expectancy, Social Security-GDP levels would peak at about 5 per cent over the next few decades and decline slightly thereafter (Congressional Budget Office, 2005b, p. 23).

The most significant change in future spending, however, would result from a less generous initial benefit formula. Under current law, a retiree's initial benefit incorporates a wage index adjustment — that is, the retiree's lifetime earnings are adjusted for changes in the average annual earnings for the entire labour force. By substituting price indexing for wage indexing in determining the initial benefits for future retirees, Social Security-GDP levels would increase slightly until about 2030, at which point they would begin to fall gradually. By 2050, Social Security would account for roughly the same share of GDP that it does today (Congressional Budget Office, 2005b, p. 22).

Of course, this change would significantly lower lifetime benefits that future retirees receive. Workers whose eligibility begins in 2030, for example, would face a reduction of more than 20 per cent when compared with current law benefits (Congressional Budget Office, 2005b, p. 22). For those retiring in 2050, the corresponding reduction would be almost 40 per cent. 'Progressive indexation,' which would retain wage indexing for low-income retirees but apply price indexing to upper-income retirees, would produce lesser, but still significant, savings.

Any structural reform that appreciably lowers long-term Social Security growth necessarily means that future retirees will receive lower benefits over their lifetimes than current law would provide. This 'benefit gap' has given rise to a debate over private retirement accounts that would supplement Social Security benefits for future retirees. The Bush administration unsuccessfully proposed a 'partial privatisation' initiative in 2005; its plan called for a portion of future payroll taxes to be diverted to individual investment-based retirement accounts. The administration argued that long-term growth in these accounts would more than compensate future retirees for necessary reductions in their Social Security benefits.

While partial privatisation schemes would not affect current or near-term retirees, the diversion of some portion of payroll taxes to fund private accounts would mean substantial transition costs (i.e., borrowing) to fund current and near-term benefits. In addition to these financing difficulties, privatisation options would affect the income replacement and income redistribution components of the traditional Social Security programme. A major concern is that the redistributive effects of the benefit structure now in place would be weakened by the introduction of supplemental private accounts. Finally, there is disagreement over whether private accounts could, in fact, eliminate the benefit gap under a retrenched Social Security programme.

Nevertheless, the Social Security financing problem is not particularly complex. The fiscal dimensions of the problem are predictable and relatively limited. The various policy reform options are also reasonably well understood in terms of their fiscal effects, although their potential programmatic effects are hotly disputed. With healthcare entitlements, by comparison, the potential fiscal sustainability issues are enormous, and the policy options uncertain.

Medicare and Medicaid

Over the past several decades, healthcare spending in the United States has grown much faster than the economy, and costs for the Medicare programme have risen faster than healthcare spending generally. When the Medicare programme began, spending levels were quite low — 0.2 per cent of GDP and 4 per cent of total healthcare expenditures in 1967 (Congressional Budget Office, 2003, p. 4). In 2007, the Medicare spending-GDP level is expected to climb above 3 per cent, which represents about one-fifth of total healthcare spending (Congressional Budget Office, 2007, p. 50). The growth in Medicaid spending has been less steep, with federal programme outlays currently accounting for approximately 1.5 per cent of GDP.

Past spending growth in both programmes reflects expanded beneficiary populations, but the primary factor in Medicare and Medicaid spending has been per beneficiary costs. The number of Medicare beneficiaries has doubled over the past 30 years. In real terms, however, Medicare outlays have increased by a factor of 10 (Congressional Budget Office, 2005b, p. 29). Over the same period, real spending for Medicaid has risen at an even higher rate. For both programmes, costs per beneficiary have risen much faster than per capita GDP — 'excess cost growth' for Medicare averaged 2.9 per cent from 1970–2004, while Medicaid's average was slightly lower (Congressional Budget Office, 2005b, p. 7).

This excess cost growth phenomenon appears to have resulted primarily from changing patterns of medical practice, notably the increased use of new and costly medical technologies. Curbing such growth in the future, however, is absolutely critical in terms of sustainable Medicare and Medicaid spending. For example, if excess cost growth remains close to past levels — 2.5 percentage points per year — Medicare and Medicaid spending would exceed 8 per cent of GDP by 2020 and then climb to nearly 22 per cent in 2050 (see Figure 3.4). In their long-range forecasts, Medicare programme trustees assume that excess cost growth can be lowered to 1 per cent. Even under this more optimistic assumption, Medicare spending-GDP levels would still nearly triple by 2050, and total federal costs for Medicare and Medicaid in 2050 would rise to approximately 12.5 per cent of GDP. If excess cost growth were entirely eliminated in these long-term projections, Medicare and Medicaid spending-GDP levels would track those for Social Security — from 4+ per cent today to 6+ per cent in 2050. Even the most positive scenario, in other words, does not entirely eliminate the fiscal sustainability problem for healthcare entitlements.

The need for effective healthcare cost controls is unambiguous, but the policy options for Medicare and Medicaid lack the simplicity and predictability of Social Security reforms. An increase in the eligibility age for Medicare, for example, would likely have a limited impact on long-term costs (Congressional

Figure 3.4: Total Federal Spending for Medicare and Medicaid Under Different Assumptions About Excess Cost Growth

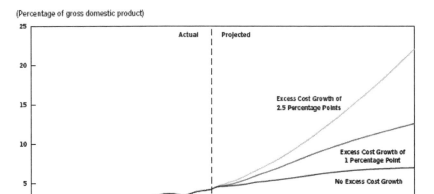

(Percentage of gross domestic product)

Source: Congressional Budget Office (2005b, p. 32).

Budget Office, 2005b, p. 33). Lowering the federal government's share of healthcare costs by transferring a greater share to beneficiaries and to the states might yield significant savings but could also unduly limit access to healthcare.

Targeting the healthcare cost transfers on high-income Medicare beneficiaries resolves the access problem but creates other difficulties. The 2003 Medicare prescription drug legislation, for example, contains income-based surcharges on enrollee premiums for Supplementary Medical Insurance (Medicare Part B covering physicians' and outpatient services). The new premium surcharge is being phased in from 2007–09 and is expected to affect 2–5 per cent of the 40 million Part B enrollees; premiums for these enrollees could quadruple over this period. While these additional premiums are intended to stabilise the federal government's share of Part B costs, they could also discourage participation in the programme and thereby increase federal costs over the long term. A similar concern applies to the Part D prescription drug benefits. The premium structure now in place is expected to offset a portion of the federal government's subsidy costs and to make possible additional subsidies for low-income beneficiaries. Whether participation rates and projected premium offsets will effectively control federal costs is unclear, since the Part D programme has only recently been implemented.

Another approach to controlling costs focuses on comprehensive efficiencies in healthcare services. A greater emphasis on lower-cost services and more effective care management might provide adequate care at reduced per beneficiary costs. It is also possible that increased competition from private health plans could help control Medicare costs. These and other strategies for making healthcare more efficient, however, are largely untested, and there is no consensus on whether such reforms would yield the very substantial savings needed to stabilise the growth in Medicare and Medicaid.

The federal government's role in funding healthcare services for a greatly expanding beneficiary population presents an enormous political and policy challenge. If excess cost growth in Medicare and Medicaid continues to remain high, the budgetary resources to sustain these programmes will require levels of taxation (or borrowing) that are as unlikely as they are unprecedented. As the gap between promised benefits and available resources inevitably widens, the political challenge for policy-makers will be enormous.

Conclusion: Entitlements and Taxes

Over the past half-century, spending-GDP levels in the United States have averaged just over 20 per cent of GDP; the average revenue level has been approximately 18.5 per cent. With the exception of a brief period at the end of the 1990s, deficits have been chronic and debt-GDP levels have increased by more than 50 per cent since the mid-1970s. Thus, even as defence cutbacks were used to finance most of the 'welfare shift', the federal government was usually unable to balance its budget with the relatively modest tax increases needed to cover the remainder.

The short-term fiscal outlook in the United States illustrates the continuing relevance of this de facto revenue ceiling. Under the Bush administration's fiscal program, large tax cuts have been kept in place during wartime and in the face of continued deficits. The administration is committed as well to making these tax cuts permanent, which would in all likelihood guarantee that structural deficits will continue indefinitely.

This structural deficit problem is not especially severe in terms of magnitude and, as noted previously, deficits will shrink or even disappear if the 2001 and 2003 tax cuts are not extended past 2010. What is remarkable about the current deficit situation is that it reflects relatively modest pressures on the spending side of the budget. Outlay-GDP levels are now slightly below long-term averages and well below those of the 1980s. Nevertheless, the revenue levels to finance this lower spending have been resisted.

In this context, the fiscal sustainability of retirement and healthcare entitlements becomes much more challenging. Under 'mid-range' assumptions, spending for Social Security, Medicare and Medicaid would be nearly 20 per cent of GDP by 2050 — about the same size as the entire federal budget today. The federal budget today, however, also includes defence, discretionary domestic programmes and other entitlements that account for about 10 per cent of GDP. Defence and homeland security needs are unlikely to disappear, and federal domestic commitments will certainly persist as well. To accommodate these federal responsibilities at realistic levels while maintaining Social Security, Medicare and Medicaid in their current form, spending-GDP levels would have to be substantially higher than those of the past 50 years.

Financing these higher spending levels would mean a major departure from historical revenue trends in the United States. Revenues have been kept below the fairly stable spending levels of the past several decades; raising taxes to cover much higher spending levels projected in the future will necessitate a dramatic change in the politics of taxation. The problem of fiscal sustainability in the United States is therefore defined, in large part, by the tax levels that are politically and economically viable. It is further shaped by federal policy responsibilities that extend beyond social welfare commitments to the elderly.

In the years ahead, policy-makers in the United States will be forced to revisit some basic issues about the size and role of the federal government. Maintaining the welfare state in its current form almost certainly means that the budget flexibility to support other national needs will shrink, and the tension between taxes and deficit financing will mount. At the same time, retrenching the welfare state to take into account demographic realities and fiscal constraints will be complicated and politically difficult. Nevertheless, a sustainable fiscal path cannot be achieved without significantly rebalancing the government's commitments to the elderly against its other responsibilities and its resources.

References

Congressional Budget Office (2001a) *The Budget and Economic Outlook: Fiscal Years 2002–2011* (Washington, DC: CBO).

Congressional Budget Office (2001b) *The Budget and Economic Outlook: An Update* (Washington, DC: CBO).

Congressional Budget Office (2002) *The Budget and Economic Outlook: Fiscal Years 2003–2012* (Washington, DC: CBO).

Congressional Budget Office (2003) *The Long-Term Budget Outlook* (Washington, DC: CBO).

Congressional Budget Office (2005a) *CBO Testimony: Implications of Demographic Changes for the Budget and the Economy* (Washington, DC: CBO).

Congressional Budget Office (2005b) *The Long-Term Budget Outlook* (Washington, DC: CBO).

Congressional Budget Office (2007) *The Budget and Economic Outlook: Fiscal Years 2008–2017* (Washington, DC: CBO).

Congressional Quarterly Almanac 1997 (1998) (Washington, DC: *Congressional Quarterly*).

Ippolito, Dennis S. (2003). *Why Budgets Matter: Budget Policy and American Politics* (University Park, PA: Pennsylvania State University Press).

US Government (1981) *Fiscal Year 1982 Budget Revisions* (Washington, DC: Government Printing Office).

US Government (1990) *Budget of the United States Government, Fiscal Year 1991* (Washington, DC: Government Printing Office).

US Government (1999) *Budget of the United States Government, Fiscal Year 2000* (Washington, DC: Government Printing Office).

US Government (2006) *Historical Tables, Budget of the United States Government, Fiscal Year 2007* (Washington, DC: Government Printing Office).

US Government (2007) *Historical Tables, Budget of the United States Government, Fiscal Year 2008* (Washington, DC: Government Printing Office).

Notes

[1]   Social Security provides cash benefits to retired and disabled workers (along with eligible spouses, children, and survivors). In 2006, Social Security programme outlays totalled $544 billion. Medicare is the federal programme that provides subsidised medical insurance for the elderly and for eligible disabled persons. Part A (Hospital Insurance) is financed by Medicare payroll taxes. Part B (Supplementary Medical Insurance) is a voluntary programme covering physicians' and outpatient services and is financed by beneficiaries' premiums and general federal funds. Part D is the new component that covers prescription drugs and is financed by premiums and federal funds. Total Medicare outlays in 2006, excluding offsetting receipts, totalled $374 billion. Medicaid is a joint federal programme that funds medical care services for the poor — expenditures for Medicaid are heavily concentrated on the elderly and disabled. In 2006, Medicaid outlays by the federal government were $181 billion (about 57 per cent of total programme spending). Because such a large portion of Medicaid spending goes for long-term and other care of the elderly, it is usually included in the fiscal scenarios that focus on demographic trends and retirement and healthcare entitlements.

2   The Reagan programme was set out in the FY1982 Budget Revisions. The short-term goal was to balance the budget in 1984 at just over 19% of GNP, with more than one-third of the budget directed toward defence.

3   After World War II, publicly held debt in the United States was nearly 110 per cent of GDP. Three decades later, the level had dropped below 25%. There was a slight rise in the late 1970s, followed by the sharp climb in the 1980s.

4   The Balanced Budget and Emergency Deficit Control Act of 1985 mandated a $172 billion deficit ceiling in 1986, with successively lower ceilings until the budget was balanced in 1991. The Supreme Court invalidated a key enforcement provision in this legislation in 1986, and a revised version was passed the following year that extended the deficit-reduction schedule through 1993.

5   The discretionary spending caps placed annual limits on appropriations for defence and non-defence programmes. For each fiscal year covered by the agreement, combined tax policy and entitlement benefit changes — that is, the net effect of legislated tax cuts and benefit increases — could not increase baseline deficits.

6   As a result of these bipartisan increases, discretionary outlays were $130 billion above statutory limits in FY2000 and 2001.

7   The on-budget/off-budget distinction is artificial. Revenues and outlays of the two Social Security trust funds (OASI and DI), as well as transactions of the Post Office, are excluded from the totals and other accounts in the budget. 'Saving' the social security surpluses, then, meant balancing the budget without taking into account the surpluses of revenue over-spending in the Social Security program. With the current deficit situation, Social Security surpluses help to finance, in effect, on-budget deficit.

8   The Social Security trust funds include revenues from payroll taxes and reserves in the form of government securities. It is assumed that benefit payments will begin to exceed payroll tax revenues in 10–12 years and that the reserves in the trust funds will be exhausted around 2040. Under current law, the Treasury is authorised to continue paying benefits as long as there are positive balances in the trust funds. If that balance fell to zero at some future point, spending authority would be limited to incoming payroll taxes and therefore could not cover all of the benefits defined by existing law. Payroll taxes, however, could be raised to cover the shortfall, or the law could be changed to reduce benefits. The technical solvency of the trust funds, then, is an artificial issue. The real problem with Social Security is how the programme as currently defined affects the government's overall revenue and spending needs, and these overall needs, in turn, have to be considered in terms of their economic, political and social impact.

4

THE PUBLIC BUDGET AND THE US CURRENT ACCOUNT DEFICIT

Iwan Morgan

Introduction

The United States is the lone superpower of the post-Cold War era, but it is also the world's most indebted nation. In something of an understatement, former Clinton Treasury Secretary Larry Summers observed (2004a, p. 48): 'There is something odd about the world's greatest power also being its greatest debtor.' This has never happened before. At the peak of its global power in 1914, Britain ran a current account surplus equivalent to some 9 per cent of its GDP. In 2006 the United States operated a current account deficit amounting to $856.7 billion, equivalent to 6.5 per cent of its own GDP and 1.7 per cent of global GDP (BEA, 2007, 2006b). In effect, the United States ran a loss of some $2.3 billion a day in its dealings with the rest of the world. To finance this, it needed to pull in some 70 per cent of all the rest of the world's global capital flows (Rajan, 2005b). In 2006, America's trade deficit made up 95 per cent of its current account deficit, and the remainder came from interest payment to foreign holders of US assets and net unilateral transfers abroad on programmes like foreign aid. The US budget deficit is not directly a component in the current account deficit, but the two are intimately connected. Many analysts regard them as 'twin deficits' on the grounds that the growth of the current account deficit since 2001 has reflected the collapse in US public saving brought about by the return of huge budget deficits (Dudley and McKelvey, 2004; Frankel, 2005; Godley et al., 2005).

In theory, a nation's current account balance measures the surplus or deficit of its spending over its income or, equivalently, of its investment over saving (public and private) (Congressional Budget Office, 2007). A current account deficit results from a nation spending more than it earns. In this circumstance, the only way it can increase investment spending is by attracting foreign capital to fill the gap between domestic saving and domestic investment. In the case of the United States, foreign investors (both public and private) financed its current account deficit by buying domestic US assets, such as government securities, bonds, stocks and real estate. This enabled American government, businesses and citizens to live beyond their means, whether as consumers of foreign capital or of goods.

In the 1990s, countries like Finland, Sweden and South Korea that ran large current account deficits typically saw these decline — whether due to lower exchange rates or economic slowdown — when they reached 4.0–4.5 per cent of GDP (Mann, 1999; Weller, 2004). The United States has evidently bucked this norm. In 2007, however, there was a decline in the current account deficit for the first time in six years. It fell sharply to $738 billion, equal to 5.3 per cent of GDP. Opinion remained divided as to whether the external imbalance had been brought under control or whether it still posed a potential threat to America's economic wellbeing. What was not in dispute was that the United States still needed to borrow more than $2 billion a day in 2007 to cover its shortfall in saving. Consequently, there was broad agreement that a conversion of the US federal budget position from deficit to surplus was fundamental to America's achievement of a 'soft landing' from its situation of international indebtedness.

This chapter reviews the recent development of the US current account deficit, assesses the risk it poses to the wellbeing of the American economy, and examines the link between America's internal budget deficit and external imbalances. In so doing, it underscores two themes of particular relevance to this book. It illustrates how the United States was able to sustain large internal public budget deficits without negative response from external financial markets, and also maintain its 'small fiscal state' tax base in spite of growing demands on its public purse.

Development of the US External Imbalance Since 1981

The Reagan era was the turning point in the development of large imbalances in America's economic dealings with the rest of the world. The national current account was almost continuously in surplus from 1960 to 1982 (excepting 1971, 1972, 1977 and 1978), but thereafter has consistently been in deficit (excepting 1991). The United States, the world's largest creditor with net foreign assets of $141 billion in 1981, metamorphosed into the world's largest creditor with net liabilities of $111 billion by 1985. The huge budget deficits (averaging 5 per cent of GDP in FY1982–86) generated by the Reagan administration's 1981 tax cuts and defence expansion underlay this transformation. These fiscal imbalances soaked up nearly three-quarters of US private savings in Ronald Reagan's first term. Over the course of the 1980s, the net national savings rate (private savings minus government borrowing) declined precipitously from an annual average of 6.9 per cent GDP in the previous decade to 2.8 per cent. As a result, the United States grew dependent on inflows of foreign savings to maintain investment growth (Sloan, 1999).

The large external imbalances presented Reagan-era policy-makers with difficult tradeoffs that had some parallels with those facing their early twenty-first century counterparts. The Federal Reserve initially kept interest rates 2 per cent higher on average than those of Western Europe and Japan to attract overseas capital. However, the resultant strong dollar produced a growing trade deficit. To correct this, Treasury officials negotiated the Plaza Accord of 1985 with America's then G-5 partners to allow the dollar to decline against their currencies. This devaluation eventually sparked fears of a dollar-strike by foreigners seeking to offload declining dollar assets — a concern which helped to precipitate the Wall Street stock market crash of 1987. Only heavy purchase of Treasury securities by the Japanese and West German central banks and interest rate hikes by the Federal Reserve calmed market fears and led to a new dollar rally (Frankel, 1995). The experience of the late 1980s therefore points to the problems of a 'soft dollar' solution to external imbalances, but also indicates that foreign governments have a crucial interest in maintaining the wellbeing of the American economy as the engine of global growth.

Nevertheless, parallels between the initial and second phase expansion of America's external imbalances should not be overdrawn. They were entirely different in scale. The current account deficit peaked in the Reagan era at only 3.5 per cent GDP in 1987, barely half its level in 2006. In 1985, the US Net International Investment Position (NIIP) deficit — the imbalance in its capital account between external financial assets and liabilities — equalled only 2.7 per cent GDP. However, it deteriorated precipitously from 5 per cent GDP in 1997 to 21.6 per cent GDP at the end of 2005. By then, foreign-owned US assets totalled $12.7 trillion, some $2.7 trillion more than the value of assets that the United States held abroad (BEA, 2006a; EPI, 2006a). According to one estimate, the United States needed to attract $7–8 billion in foreign direct investment and financial capital every working day in 2006 to make up the net shortfall (which also covers its own annual capital exports). Without this inflow of capital to sustain economic growth, the shock to its financial markets, and consequently its economy, would have been very significant. The likely consequences would have been a sharp decline in the exchange rate of the dollar, higher interest rates, a fall in equity prices and a weakening of the housing market (Bergsten and Truman, 2007).

Moreover, the second-phase expansion of the current account deficit was more complex than the earlier one. The chronic budget deficits operated during the presidencies of Ronald Reagan and George H.W. Bush were steadily reduced to produce a new cycle of balanced budgets in Bill Clinton's second term. In contrast to the 1980s, however, fiscal surpluses coincided with renewed expansion of the current account deficit. Even though balanced budgets sucked out purchasing power, the economy boomed in the 1990s thanks to a huge rise in private expenditure relative to income. With inflows of foreign capital making up this gap, the US current account deficit grew from under 2 per cent GDP in 1996 to 4 per cent GDP in 2000. In this period, however, the growth of the current account deficit was benign because it financed an investment boom that helped drive the economy to new heights of productivity (Cline, 2005).

Although a mild recession and associated reduction of private spending interrupted this upward trend briefly in 2001, imbalances became increasingly large and intractable from 2002 onward as projected budget surpluses turned into the actuality of large budget deficits. In 2001, the Congressional Budget Office had forecast cumulative fiscal surpluses in excess of $5.6 trillion in the next 10 years, but the Bush tax cuts and economic slowdown transformed its fiscal scenario. Within two years, its projections had changed dramatically to forecast deficits totalling $1.4 trillion (Ippolito, 2003). The United States underwent a fiscal deterioration of 6 per cent GDP from FY2000 to FY2004 (2.4 per cent surplus to 3.6 per cent deficit), almost comparable to that experienced in the Great Depression downturn from FY1930 to FY1934. The positive flow of public saving had partially counterbalanced the growth of external imbalances in the late 1990s, but the reversion to negative flow significantly enhanced America's need to borrow from abroad in the first years of the twenty-first century. Now, however, the inflow of foreign capital financed government dis-saving and high private consumption based on credit because it allowed the United States to maintain low interest rates. In other words, it did not have comparable benefits in contributing to a long-term growth in productivity, as had been the case in the 1990s (Cline, 2005).

Viewed in proportional terms to the economy, the US NIIP in the early twenty-first century is not particularly large. Brazil had an investment deficit in excess of 60 per cent when it encountered financial crisis in 1998, and Argentina operated one of 80 per cent at the time of its 2000 crisis. Assuming that the US current account deficit does not worsen dramatically and economic growth continues along the 10-year trajectory forecast by the Congressional Budget Office in 2004, the US NIIP deficit will not hit 60 per cent GDP until 2014 (Bivens, 2004). Moreover, it was only in the last quarter of 2005 that the balance of income on foreign assets turned negative. In other words, the net flow of investment *income* was hitherto positive in America's favour in spite of the *asset* deficit. Two factors explain this apparent paradox: one is the declining dollar, which boosted the value of US foreign assets; the other is the fact that only 45 per cent of US assets abroad are in fixed interest holdings compared with 65 per cent of foreign assets in the United States. With the balance on foreign asset income remaining negative in 2006-07, however, it appeared likely that the NIIP deficit would continue to deteriorate steadily (Godley et al, 2005; Labonte, 2005; EPI, 2006b; Mann, 2005; BEA, 2007, 2008).

Global Saving Glut Theory and its Critics

To the US Federal Reserve, and by extension the Bush administration, the world's appetite for US assets was a sign of America's economic strength rather than weakness. This view reflected confidence that global capital flows to those countries that can turn it to most productive use. US labour productivity increased by an annual average of 2.7 per cent from 1996 to 2006 thanks to improvements in information technology, business processes, inventory management and retailing. Some analysts contend that this acceleration, which is unmatched by other G-7 nations, inevitably raises the investment rate because investors — both domestic and foreign — want to take advantage of the higher rate of return to domestic capital (Levey and Brown, 2005; Tamny, 2006; Valderrama, 2007).

The most cogent expression of the view that the current account deficit was benign was Federal Reserve Chair Ben S. Bernanke's 'global saving glut' theory. This argued that: (1) a high level of worldwide savings relative to investment opportunities put downward pressure on world interest rates and diminished the 'home bias' of investors; (2) this advantaged countries which could provide the best combination of investment return and security; and (3) in this regard, the profitability, security and efficiency of US capital markets drew foreign investors like bees to the honey-pot (Bernanke, 2005).

This assessment discounted the danger that foreigners might disrupt the American economy through rapid liquidation of their dollar assets. Its adherents assumed that foreign official institutions, which had significantly increased their holdings of US Treasury securities since 2001, had an interest in preserving America's economic wellbeing because their aim was to maintain favourable exchange rates that gave their own countries' exports competitive advantage in the US domestic market. Moreover, the 50 per cent share of treasuries held by foreigners in 2006 amounted to no more than 20 per cent of total long-term US securities. It was therefore evident that America's capital markets were sufficiently large and flexible to accommodate any compositional diversification in foreign dollar holdings (Bergsten and Truman, 2007).

The *Economic Report of the President* for 2006 epitomised the upbeat assessment of cause and effect in the American current and capital accounts (*Economic Report*, 2006, Ch. 6). According to this rosy scenario, foreign investors were rational actors with an interest in sustaining America's economic growth rather than damaging it. Since their concern was to allocate their capital in the most efficient manner, it was deemed unlikely that capital flows would change rapidly because the fundamental economic determinants that attracted them in the first place were long-term and likely to endure. This obviated the danger of a massive and painful current account adjustment brought about by market flight from the dollar (Poole, 2005; Labonte, 2005).

Some critics of the Bernanke theory argued that it underestimated the significance of the sharp increase in foreign purchases of treasuries and other government securities. Foreigners increased their share of US Treasuries held by the public from 30 per cent in 2000 to 55 per cent in 2004. By far the largest share of these purchases — just over 70 per cent — was made by central banks, particularly those based in Asian countries that sought to manipulate the exchange value of their currency against the dollar to the benefit of their export trade (McKinnon, 2005; EPI, 2006b). In the opinion of former Council of Foreign Relations Chair Peter G. Peterson, America's growing dependency on central bank purchase of government securities constituted a level of risk in both economic and national security 'that no great power should be taking'. Drawing an analogy with the reserve crisis that compelled Britain into a humiliating withdrawal from the Suez intervention of 1956, he warned that the United States could be vulnerable to a dollar-strike by the People's Republic of China (PRC) in the event of an East Asian regional confrontation between the two powers (Peterson, 2005, p. 12). Like-minded analysts pointed out that central banks were not motivated by the same long-term profit calculations as private direct investors, so their reserve purchases were likely to be more volatile and less governed by concerns about the impact of their actions on America's economic wellbeing (Roubini and Sester, 2005).

On balance, the volatility argument appeared a remote contingency when measured against the reality of the rest of the world's seemingly insatiable appetite for American assets. Moreover, the symbiotic relationship between the United States and its foreign government creditors represented something of a balance of financial terror. In a new version of mutually assured destruction, other governments were unlikely to implement a dollar-strike because the resultant diminution of the dollar's exchange value would do significant damage to their own export-driven economies (Summers, 2004). Arguably, a more pertinent critique of the rosy scenario of America's indebtedness concerned foreign capacity to supply it with the growing volume of capital necessary to sustain economic growth.

A question mark hung over the capacity of Asian central banks to expand their dollar purchases to keep pace with the growth in America's borrowing needs as projected at the time of writing. According to one estimate, Asian central banks held some 60 per cent of global foreign-exchange reserves by late 2004, a portion well in excess of Asia's shares of global trade and global gross domestic product. In 2005, one country — the PRC — was responsible for 80 per cent of the increase in Asian reserves, while a number of countries — India, Malaysia, Taiwan and Korea — significantly slowed their accumulation (Roubini and Sester, 2004, 2005; BIS, 2006, p. 93). As a result of these interventions, China overtook Japan as the world's largest holder of foreign exchange reserves in early 2006. Some $700 billion of its estimated $1 trillion total reserves were in US dollars (Peters, 2007; Council of Foreign Relations, 2007). However, the growing reliance of the United States on this one country to fund its indebtedness carried obvious risks. If an internal banking crisis or an upward adjustment in its presently under-valued currency caused China merely to slow down its purchase of dollar assets, the consequences for the American economy could be severe.

The longer that the PRC, or indeed any country's central bank, goes on stockpiling dollar reserves, the greater the losses incurred from dollar devaluation will be. The rational-actor response to such a danger is to diversify reserve holdings. There is evidence that this is already taking place, since the dollar share of global foreign exchange purchases by central banks dropped from its peak rate of 76 per cent in 2004 to 53 per cent in 2005 (BIS, 2006). The short-term nature of so many Treasury securities also means that buyers now have flexibility and sellers become increasingly dependent on new issues being taken up. By early 2007, many central banks — such as those of Russia, Switzerland and Saudi Arabia — had signalled their intention to diversify reserve holdings in a manner that would not provoke instability in the financial markets (Peters, 2007). Whether this outcome can be guaranteed is another matter, however, because many private investors take their cue from the decisions of central banks, which can easily roil their herd instinct. Exemplifying this danger, South Korea's announcement in February 2005 that it intended to diminish the overwhelming preponderance of US dollars within its $200 billion foreign reserve portfolio spooked a sharp one-day fall on the Dow index. To reassure the markets, Seoul had to issue a clarification that it would only slow down dollar purchases, not sell off existing assets (*The Economist*, 2005).

The capacity of foreign private investors to take up any slack in foreign official investment should not be taken for granted. The scale of private inflows has grown so vast that its long-term sustainability is very much open to doubt. Foreigners accounted for virtually the entire increase in the total holdings of all long-term US securities, including equities and corporate bonds, from 2000 to 2005. It requires considerable optimism — some would say blind faith — to believe that the volume of inflow can continue into the foreseeable future. Optimists may ask where else foreign money can go, but the answer to this question is no longer clear cut. The creation of the euro as the common currency of a Euroland economy almost as large as America's has provided a true international financial alternative to the dollar for the first time since 1945. International investment in eurobonds exceeded that in dollar bonds in 2005–6. The US financial market ($48 billion) was still considerably larger than that of the Eurozone ($27 billion) by the end of 2006, but the Eurozone was growing twice as fast (Bergsten and Truman, 2007). If (or more likely, when) the French and German economies emerge from their relative stagnation, international investment in the euro and the Eurozone will also gather pace to the probable detriment of the volume flowing into the United States.

Even if the inflow were sustained, problems of financing it would sooner or later arise. The huge injections of foreign capital permitted US interest rates to be kept at historically low levels from 2001 through 2004. This eased the cost of massive borrowing from abroad and obviated the 'crowding out' effect of public deficits on private investment and growth. However, easy money led to real estate inflation that had to be doused through incremental interest rate hikes in 2005–6. This helped to provoke the crisis in the sub-prime mortgage market that led in turn to financial crisis and a credit crunch when the problems of holding bad mortgage debts began to hit financial institutions from mid 2007 onwards. To avert financial catastrophe and restore liquidity to the banking system, the Federal Reserve responded by again slashing interest rates. Nevertheless, the crisis signified that monetary conditions in the early years of the twenty-first century were exceptional, and that a return to normality would bring with it an increasingly onerous burden of debt service. If rates on short-term Treasuries rose even modestly, the US government itself would likely face an increase of between $30 billion and $50 billion in its annual interest repayments.

The 'Soft Dollar' Strategy

If the Bush administration appeared relatively unconcerned by the investment deficit, the same could not be said about its attitude towards the trade gap component of America's current account deficit. It aimed to resolve America's trade imbalance by a dollar devaluation strategy intended to boost exports and choke off the flow of cheap imports (Bergsten, 2004). This is not a solution available to debtor countries with foreign borrowings denominated in foreign currency, because devaluation increases the cost of debt servicing and frightens off foreign creditors. The United States, however, has the unique advantage that fully 95 per cent of its debt is denominated in its own currency because of the dollar's effective position as the world's reserve currency (Persaud, 2004; Bonner and Wiggin, 2006). According to William Poole of the Federal Reserve Bank of St Louis, this means that a decline in the foreign exchange value of the dollar works not as an accelerator of financial crisis but as part of a self-correcting mechanism. Dollar-denominated US liabilities remain unchanged in domestic value but the US holdings abroad, two-thirds of which are in foreign currencies, correspondingly appreciate and contribute with the diminishing effect of dollar decline on imports to orderly reduction of the current-account deficit (Poole, 2005).

The main problem with this scenario is that the dollar has been unable to float freely on the world currency markets. It declined from its early 2002 peak through 2004 by some 30 per cent against the euro and sterling, and by some 20 per cent against the Japanese yen and the Canadian dollar before rebounding somewhat under the impact of higher US interest rates in 2005–6. However, the Asian countries with which the United States continued to have large trade deficits formally pegged their currencies to the dollar to maintain export advantage (Labonte and Makinen, 2004; McKinnon, 2005). According to some estimates, the Chinese renminbi will need to undergo a 25 per cent appreciation against the dollar to achieve an appropriate degree of adjustment (Rajan, 2005b). In mid 2005, Beijing did initiate a 2.1 per cent revaluation of its currency as part of a new framework of flexibility, but change since then has been anything but rapid. In the first 18 months of the new flexibility, the renminbi appreciated only 6.5 per cent against the dollar (Council of Foreign Relations, 2007). Although it would rise somewhat more quickly thereafter, the increase was only 10 per cent compared with the 17 per cent fall in the dollar's value in relation to the euro in the period from April 2007 to April 2008.

If China were to allow a 25 per cent renminbi appreciation, this would not serve to reduce automatically its trade surplus with the United States. Some 65 per cent of China's exports to the United States are based upon PRC imports from other Asian countries of components and raw materials. If the latter did not allow their currencies to rise, the cost of China's imports from its neighbours would decline and the increase in its export prices to the United States would be modest. It is difficult to estimate the benefits of this to the United States–China trade balance. Chinese exports to the United States actually grew over the 18-month period in 2005–6 during which the renminbi rose by 6.5 per cent against the dollar. American manufacturing simply could not meet domestic consumer demand in the short term because so many plants had been shut down in the previous decade in the face of cheap imports. One result of renminbi appreciation, therefore, could well be the enlargement of the trade deficit in the short term because US consumers would end up buying costlier Chinese or other Asian goods. In the medium term, some estimates put the potential trade gap reduction between $20 and $40 billion from its 2006 level of $232 billion. Only if there were a coordinated upward revaluation of other Asian currencies in line with the renminbi would the benefits be significantly greater than this (Chinn and Steil, 2006; Council of Foreign Relations, 2007).

The dip in China's exports in late 2007 prompted some analysts to declare that the corner had been turned insofar as reducing the massive imbalance in its trade with the United States was concerned. Nevertheless, this did not produce a significant reduction in America's overall trade deficit, which only declined from $838 billion in 2006 to $815 billion in 2007. Despite the added advantage of a cheaper dollar for US exports, the converse effect of rising oil prices ensured that the dollar volume of imports remained high. More worryingly for analysts who anticipated that rising exports would prop up the ailing economy against the effects of the housing slump and credit crunch, the trade gap widened again in early 2008. In February, when oil price decline resulted in a 1.6 per cent drop in foreign petroleum sales, total imports jumped in value by 3.1 per cent, the biggest monthly gain for a year. Clearly American consumers had not lost their appetite for foreign products, even after six months of bad economic news at home (Bureau of Economic Analysis, 2008; Grynbaum, 2008).

On the other hand, the United States should be careful what it wishes for in relationship to its trade with China because a major revaluation of the renminbi could have adverse consequences for both the PRC and itself. A 25 per cent increase in the value of the renminbi against the dollar, were it to come about, would reduce the value of China's 2006 dollar reserves by $175 billion, equivalent to 7 per cent of GDP. This prospect would increase the likelihood of a sell-off of US Treasuries long before the devaluation had run its full course in order to forestall instability in China's banking sector. Moreover, the slowdown in the PRC's economy resulting from renminbi appreciation would have a corresponding impact on its East Asian trading partners, which in turn would have damaging effects for the entire global economy. Alternatively, a stronger currency might encourage the Chinese to go on a shopping expedition for US assets that were now going relatively cheaply. If the world's fourth-largest economy started buying up the likes of General Motors, Boeing, Exxon-Mobil or even Microsoft, ordinary Americans would find it difficult to retain belief in their nation's economic sovereignty (Setser and Roubini, 2005; Pesek, 2005, 2006; Bonner and Wiggin, 2006).

At present, China's own savings are primarily focused on the development of its own economy. Capital investment accounted for a remarkable 45 per cent of its GDP in the early years of the twenty-first century, compared with 15 to 20 per cent in the United States and Western Europe. More than two-thirds of the foreign capital buying in the United States in 2006 came from Europe. By 2007, more than five million Americans worked for domestic affiliates of foreign companies. This trend would accelerate if the Chinese joined the buying spree. In line with the iron rules of economics, the rest of the world is not going to cover the low levels of US saving without getting something in return.

As economist Matthew Slaughter observes: 'We have to sell them something. There's no metaphorical free lunch for the United States' (McGregor, 2007; Emmott, 2008; Goodman, 2008).

The Public Deficit Reduction Solution

The soft-dollar strategy arguably does not provide the United States with a means to reduce its dependence on foreign capital that is either economically sensible or under its direct control. Currency value issues are really a symptom of the broader causes underlying the United States–China trade deficit. The United States consumes too much, and China saves too much. The trade deficit can only be substantially addressed if both countries modify their economic behaviour through appropriate macroeconomic policies. In the case of China, this means increasing government non-investment expenditures on health care, education, welfare and pensions in order to free up for consumption the income that Chinese citizens presently save to pay for these. In America's case, it means expanding the level of public saving through reduction of the federal deficit.

A comparison of key fiscal indicators from the Clinton and Bush presidencies casts light on the factors associated with the deficits operated by the latter. Buoyant tax revenues averaging 20 per cent of GDP — a level unmatched since World War II — produced four consecutive balanced budgets in Clinton's second term. These were primarily generated by economic growth, but presidential success in preventing a Republican-led Congress from cutting taxes was also significant. A secondary factor in the restoration of fiscal responsibility was the retrenchment of defence spending from a real annual average of $339.5 billion in FY1990–95 to $287.7 billion in FY1996–2000. The change in the fiscal situation under Bush was dramatic. The tax cuts of 2001 and 2003 were significantly more instrumental than a mild recession in reducing average annual receipts to 17.1 per cent of GDP in FY2002–05, the lowest level since the second half of the 1950s. Meanwhile, prosecution of the 'War on Terror' and the Iraq war/occupation resulted in defence spending increasing in real terms (FY2000 dollars) from $297.5 billion (3 per cent GDP) in Clinton's last budget to $417.2 billion (4 per cent GDP) in FY2005. The president's FY2008 budget plan indicated that defence spending would peak at $461 billion (4.2 per cent GDP) and then decline steadily to $384.2 billion (3.1. per cent GDP) by FY2012. Such projections cannot be taken at face value, however, because of the Bush administration's tendency to fund military operations in Afghanistan and Iraq through emergency supplemental requests rather than through the regular budget planning process. In all likelihood, defence spending will continue to rise in real terms so long as the United States is engaged in these conflicts. Moreover, in contrast to Ronald Reagan's social programme retrenchment, the conservative Bush surprised many by also presiding over a growth in discretionary domestic spending from 3.1 per cent GDP in FY2001 to 3.8 per cent GDP in FY2005.

Bush promised a change of course during his second term to bring the fiscal imbalances under control. In 2004 he set himself the goal of reducing the deficit, estimated then at the artificially high level of $531 billion, by 50 per cent by the time he left office. In October 2006 he declared game over two years early with the release of official data showing that the FY2006 deficit was down to $248 billion. On current projections, the White House estimates that the budget will eventually record a small surplus in FY2012. Nevertheless, it required a leap of faith to believe that the federal government was back on the path of fiscal righteousness from which it strayed in 2001. However good the current figures looked on the surface, it did not require much digging to find worrying portents about the future. In the opinion of former Congressional Budget Office Director Robert Reischauer, among others, the FY2006 data represented no more than the calm before the storm (Abramowitz and Baker, 2006).

As the Bush budgets began their downward spiral into the red, Vice President Cheney reportedly commented that Ronald Reagan had proved that deficits didn't matter (Suskind, 2004, p. 291). Some four years later, the White House's celebrations at having reduced the FY2006 deficit to $260 billions indicated how far the Republicans had travelled from their one-time identification as the party of fiscal orthodoxy. Shifting attention from the dollar amount, the administration contended that a deficit of only 1.9 per cent GDP was in line with historical standards. This is very much open to question. The FY2006 deficit occurred in the fifth year of a strong economic recovery. It only looked good in comparison with the 4.3 per cent GDP average of the Reagan–Bush Sr. deficits of FY1982–93 and the 3.6 per cent GDP average of FY2003–05. The annual deficit average was a mere 0.9 per cent GDP from FY1947 to FY1982. It rose only to 2.1 per cent GDP in the economically troubled 1970s. The debt-GDP ratio also rose by 4.4 per cent from 2001–06, compared with a 16.4 per cent decline in the Clinton era and a 70.4 per cent decline from 1947 through 1981. The Bush era expansion may be less than the 23.4 per cent debt-GDP growth in the Reagan–Bush Sr. years, but the fact that interest payments constituted the fastest rising component of inflation-adjusted budget expenditure from FY2003 ($143 billion) through FY2008 ($214 billion projected) attested to its significance.

The president's claims on behalf of his FY2001 and FY2003 tax cuts, the jewels in his economic policy crown, were also questionable. In July 2006, he declared that the economic growth fuelled by tax relief was responsible for pumping up revenues to record levels in FY2005–6. In the president's eyes, this was ample justification to extend his tax cuts beyond their scheduled expiry in 2008 and 2010 (Bush, 2006). Such rhetoric was reminiscent of Ronald Reagan's advocacy of the 'Laffer curve' rationale for tax reduction in the 1980s, and just as spurious. The message that tax reduction was the best way to generate deficit-reducing economic growth ignored the evidence of the recent past. In the five years following the tax increases enacted as part of Clinton's deficit reduction plan of 1993, annual real economic growth and annual revenue growth respectively averaged 3.8 per cent and 8.3 per cent in contrast to 3.1 per cent and 4 per cent in the five years since Bush first cut taxes in 2001. Moreover, the Bush deficits would have been even smaller and may well have disappeared altogether had the 2001 and 2003 tax cuts not been enacted in the first place. According to analysis of US Treasury data by the independent Congressional Research Service, the Bush tax cuts only generated additional revenue worth about 7 per cent of their $1.1 trillion five-year cost (Horney, 2006; Montgomery, 2006).

The economic growth of 2005–6 was not unusually strong in comparison to comparable stages of earlier business cycles. To attribute it to structural fiscal factors was wishful thinking. There was certainly no evidence that the tax cuts paid for themselves. More plausibly, the revenue surge to 18.4 per cent GDP in FY2006 was a cyclical rebound from the historically low levels of the Bush first term. This buoyancy also served to counterbalance the abnormally high costs of military operations in Iraq and Afghanistan and the post-Hurricane Katrina reconstruction. However, this masking effect would vanish if the economy slumped into a deep recession as a result of the credit crunch and real estate slump. The Bush administration's forecast that a slowdown in the economy will cause the deficit to balloon once more from $162 billion (1.2 per cent GDP) in FY2007 to $410 billion (2.9 per cent GDP) in FY2008 suggests that its anticipation of a balanced budget in FY2012 is fiscal fantasy (Office of Management and Budget, 2008).

There is another worry regarding the budgetary consequences of a new economic slowdown. Some analysts expressed concern that the post-2001 recovery only generated a 0.9 per cent average annual increase in jobs over five years, which was much lower than the 2.5 per cent average for comparable periods of recovery following previous recessions since 1945. Accordingly, a new recession would likely have significant effect on the relatively anaemic rate of employment growth, with serious consequences for the continuation of deficit-reducing revenue enhancement (Aron-Dine and Shapiro, 2006).

Even were the revenue flow delivered by the current tax regime to remain strong, it could not compensate for the significant increase in spending on pension and medical entitlements after the baby boom generation begins to retire from 2012 onwards. According to official estimates, aggregate outlays on

Social Security, Medicare and Medicaid will increase about 7 per cent in real terms every year and expand from 8.4 per cent to 10.4 per cent of GDP from FY2006 through FY2015. Owing to an ageing population, rising medical costs and the prescription drug benefits enacted in 2003, Medicare will be the fastest growing of these programmes. Its outlays are forecast to rise from 2.6 per cent to 3.9 per cent of GDP over this 10-year period (Congressional Budget Office, 2005; Kogan and Horney, 2006; Concord Coalition 2006; Government Accountability Office, 2008).

Action to correct the fiscal deficit would be a case of accepting some degree of pain in the present to lay the foundations for a better future. It is far easier to sell this message politically when the economy is in trouble than when it is undergoing a prolonged cycle of expansion. The last time the United States engaged in a major fiscal correction was in the Clinton era, but this itself was an effort to mitigate the economic effects of a correction in the external imbalance. While the current account deficit declined from 3.5 per cent to about 1 per cent GDP between 1987 and 1990, GDP per capita grew at only half the rate and consumption grew at only one third the rate in the previous four years of economic expansion from 1983 through 1986. Viewed in this light, Bill Clinton's famous 1992 mantra — 'It's the economy, stupid' — tapped into popular concern not only about job losses, but also about stagnation in standards of living (Truman, 2004).

There is some diversity of opinion regarding the extent of current account adjustment required the second time round, but an imbalance of between 2.5 per cent and 3.5 per cent GDP is broadly considered sustainable in view of America's unique appeal to foreign investors (Mann, 2003; O'Neill and Hatzius, 2004). There is correspondingly greater agreement that the goal for the fiscal deficit should be to reduce it steadily to zero or a small positive figure in order to: (1) provide some scope for manoeuvre for fiscal policy when needed; (2) increase the overall rate of saving in the economy; and (3) prepare for the demographic future. The most expeditious means of achieving this adjustment in the short term would be to allow the Bush tax cuts to expire on schedule rather than renew them. However, the prospective expansion of entitlement spending as the baby boomers retire suggests that benefit reductions and/or payroll tax hikes may be necessary in hitherto sacrosanct programmes like social security and Medicare (Gale and Orszag, 2004; Rubin et al., 2004; Bergsten, 2007).

In the short run, this adjustment will certainly slow down the economic growth rates achieved in 2005–6, but the long-run effect should be beneficial if the experience of the 1990s is any indication. Reducing the budget deficit should also contribute to lower interest rates and may be associated with a weaker currency, which would tend to narrow the current account deficit and offset some of the short-term drag of fiscal policy. Though there is considerable variation in the estimates, the economic literature suggests that every $100 of budget deficit reduction yields from $20 to $50 in trade deficit reduction (Truman, 2004; Chinn and Steil, 2006).

Conclusions

The second-term Bush administration sought to reduce America's external deficit through a combination of dollar devaluation and growth-related closure of the domestic budget gap in the belief that the current account adjustment could be managed in an orderly and relatively painless manner. Critics of this approach argued that it was an ineffective short-term fix for a long-term problem. In their view, it did nothing to address the structural global imbalances that underlay the development of the intractable US external deficit since 2002 — namely China's tendency to save too much and America's tendency to save too little. In the opinion of Larry Summers (2004b), among others, low national saving was the most serious economic problem that the United States had faced since the Great Depression because it resulted in unsustainable dependence on foreign capital and public borrowing, both of which had far-reaching implications not only for America but also for the rest of the global economy.

The United States may have limited capacity to change the economic habits of the PRC, but it can do something about its own incapacity to save. Getting the US government to save more should prove easier than getting individuals to set income aside for the future. Social security presently offers too strong a safety net for middle-income Americans to worry about their economic security in old age, and low-income Americans are simply too hard pressed with getting by in the present. Reduction of the public deficit would go some way in the first instance to address the problems of being a low-saving nation. It could also strengthen America's hand in negotiating a broader adjustment in the global economy that has become dangerously over-dependent on US borrowing and consumption to sustain its growth.

The divided government circumstances of George Bush's final years as president were not conducive to significant action to address the structural elements of the public deficit. A Republican president sought to defend his tax programme and congressional Democrats did not want their party's 2008 electoral prospects blighted by charges that they were tax-and-spend liberals. Nevertheless, budget deficit reduction should rank high on the agenda of the next administration, Democrat or Republican, if America's external imbalances remain high.

In an age of pre-emptive geopolitical strategy, the Bush administration showed a curious reluctance to engage in geo-economic pre-emption because of its optimism that the global imbalances did not pose a serious threat. This constituted a substantial gamble that the eventual adjustment process would produce a soft landing for the economy instead of a hard one. It is impossible to predict at what juncture a slowing down of foreign investment might occur, but American policy-makers would do well to remember the commonsense adage that things that can't go on forever tend not to. There was no better summary of the risk that the United States was taking with its burgeoning current account deficit than IMF chief economist Raguram Rajan's observation that the optimists had to be right every day, whereas the pessimists needed to be right only once (Elliott, 2006).

At the time of writing in early 2008, some analysts believed that the recent reduction in the US current account deficit signified a diminished risk of disorderly adjustment. Others worried that the dollar decline that underlay this could spiral out of control because it was taking place against a background of doubt over, first, America's economic fundamentals amidst the worst crisis to hit its financial system since the 1930s, and, second, the capacity and will of other nations to meets its still vast need for foreign capital. One of these, Jeffrey Frankel of Harvard University, doubted that foreigners would continue to act like 'chumps, over and over again' by accepting low or negative returns net of dollar depreciation (Guha, 2007).

Even a soft landing is unlikely to be relatively painless for the United States, and could be higher in some regards than those from a hard one. It is conceivable that future living standards could grow more slowly after the former than after the latter. The dollar could decline for a longer period and eventually by a greater extent, with a resultant reduction in its purchasing power for foreign goods and services. Furthermore, the expectation of its continued fall would make dollar assets less useful as a medium of exchange and instrument of investment. This could have serious consequences for the dollar's reserve-currency status that endows the United States with unique advantages as a debtor nation (Eichengreen, 2005; Congressional Budget Office, 2007).

Time may well be running out on the United States' small fiscal state if its capacity for low-cost borrowing from foreigners diminishes. The demographic time bomb represented by the retirement of the baby boom generation is certain to put upward pressure on entitlement spending as currently constituted. A nation whose population growth is increasingly fuelled by immigration from Latin America and Third World countries in other parts of the world will also need to invest heavily in education to maintain its economic competitiveness in the future. Meanwhile, as demonstrated by the Iraq war, the costs of being the world's only military superpower are likely to grow. If it can no longer borrow so easily from abroad, the United States could soon be faced with the alternatives of paying for all this through tax increases or reducing the scope of its social provision and national security undertakings.

References

M. Abramowitz and P. Baker (2006) 'Painting a Rosy Budget Picture', *Washington Post,* 11 October, p. A6.

A. Aron-Dine and I. Shapiro (2006) 'Job Growth Has Slowed Significantly in 2006', Center of Budget and Policy Priorities, 13 October.

C.F. Bergsten (2004) 'Foreign Economic Policy for the Next President', *Foreign Affairs*, vol. 83, no. 2, pp. 88–101.

C.F. Bergsten (2007) 'The Current Account Deficit and the US Economy: Testimony Before the Budget Committee of the United States Senate', 1 February, available from www.iie.com/publications/papers/print. cfm?doc=pub&ResearchID=705.

C.F. Bergsten and E.M. Truman (2007) 'Why Deficits Matter: The International Dimension', testimony before the House Budget Committee, 23 January, available from www.iie.com/publications/print. cfm?doc=pub&ResearchID=704.

B.S. Bernanke (2005) 'The Global Saving Glut and the US Current Account Deficit', The Sandridge Lecture, Virginia Association of Economics, 10 March, available from www.federalreserve.gov.

Bank of International Settlements (BIS) (2006) *Seventy-sixth Annual Report* (Washington DC: BIS).

L.J. Bivens (2004) 'Debt and the Dollar: The United States Damages Future Living Standards by Borrowing Itself into a Deceptively Deep Hole', *EPI Issue Brief,* no. 203 (14 December).

B. Bonner and A. Wiggin (2006) *Empire of Debt: The Rise of an Epic Financial Crisis* (Hoboken, NJ: John Wiley and Sons).

Bureau of Economic Analysis (2006a) 'Value of Foreign Investments in the US Rises More Than Value of US Investments Abroad in 2005', 29 June, available from www.bea.gov.

Bureau of Economic Analysis (2006b) 'US Current Account Deficit Increases in Second Quarter 2006', 18 September, available from www.bea.gov.

Bureau of Economic Analysis (2007) 'US International Transactions: Fourth Quarter and Year 2006', 14 March, available from www.bea.gov.

Bureau of Economic Analysis (2008) 'US International Transactions: Fourth Quarter and Year 2007 Current Account', 17 March, available from www. bea.gov.

G.W. Bush (2006) Remarks by the President on the Mid-Session Review, 11 July, https://wwww.whitehousegov/news/releases/2006/07/20060711-1.html.

M. Chinn and B. Steil (2006) 'Why Deficits Matter', *The International Economy* (Summer), pp. 18–23.

W. Cline (2005) *The US as a Debtor Nation* (Washington, DC: Institute of International Economics, 2005).

Concord Coalition (2006) 'Concord Coalition Warns that Sustained Deficit Reduction Will Require More than Revenue Surprises', 17 August.

Congressional Budget Office (2005) *The Budgetary and Economic Outlook: Fiscal Years 2006 to 2015* (Washington, DC: Congressional Budget Office).

Congressional Budget Office (2007) 'Will the US Current Account Have a Hard or Soft Landing?' (Washington, DC: Congressional Budget Office).

Council of Foreign Relations (2007) *US–China Relations: An Affirmative Agenda, A Responsible Course*, Task Force Report, April.

J. Cranford (2005) 'The Deficit's Hard Truths', *CQ Weekly*, 26 September, pp. 2554–61.

W.C. Dudley and E. McKelvey (2004) 'The US Budget Outlook: A Surplus of Deficits', *Global Economic Paper*, no. 106 (31 March) (New York: Goldman Sachs).

Economic Report of the President (2006) (Washington, DC: Government Printing Office).

Economist (2005a) 'Collywobbles', 26 February, pp. 82–83.

B. Eichengreen (2005) *Sterling's Past, Dollar's Future: Historical Perspectives on Reserve Currency Competition*, Working Paper No. 11336 (Cambridge, MA: National Bureau of Economic Analysis).

L. Elliott (2006) 'Leaders Risk Taking Us Back to 1930s, Says IMF', *The Guardian*, 20 April, p. 25.

B. Emmott (2008) 'Asia is Not Immune to the Financial Malady of the West', *The Guardian*, 11 April.

Economic Policy Institute (EPI) (2006a) 'Increases in Foreign Liabilities Financed Through Sale of Government Securities', 30 June.

Economic Policy Institute (EPI) (2006b) 'US Current Account: Costs of Foreign Borrowing Pile Up', 18 September 18.

J. Frankel (1995) 'The Making of Exchange Rate Policy in the 1980s', in M. Feldstein (ed.), *American Economic Policy in the 1980s* (Chicago: University of Chicago Press), pp. 293–341.

J. Frankel (2005) 'The Twin Deficits', Bellagio Group Paper, Amsterdam, 20 January.

W. Gale and P. Orszag (2004) 'The US Budget Deficit: On An Unsustainable Path', *New Economy*, vol. 11, no. 4, pp. 236–42.

W. Godley, D. Papadimitriou, C. Dos Santos and G. Zezza (2005) *The United States and Her Creditors: Can the Symbiosis Last?* The Levy Economics Institute of Bard College (September), available from www. levy.org.

P. Goodman (2008) 'Two Outcomes When Foreigners Buy Factories', *New York Times*, 7 April.

Government Accountability Office (2008) *The Nation's Long Term Fiscal Outlook: January 2008 Update* (Washington DC: GAO).

M.R. Grynbaum (2008) 'US Trade Deficit Grows Unexpectedly', *New York Times*, 10 April.

K. Guha (2007) 'Risk Remains of a "Disorderly Adjustment"', *Financial Times*, 17 October.

J. Horney (2006) 'A Smoking Gun: President's Claim that Tax Cuts Pay for Themselves Refuted by New Treasury Analysis', Center for Budget Policy and Priorities, 27 July.

D.S. Ippolito (2003) *Why Budgets Matter: Budget Policy and American Politics* (University Park, PA: Pennsylvania State University Press).

R. Kogan and J. Horney (2006) 'Deficit Announcement Masks Bigger Story: Long-Term Outlook Remains Bleak', Center for Budget and Policy Priorities, 11 October.

M. Labonte (2005) 'Is the Current Account Deficit Sustainable?' Congressional Research Service, 13 December.

M. Labonte and G. Makinen (2004) 'Changing Causes of the US Trade Deficit', Congressional Research Service, 12 October.

D.H. Levey and S.S. Brown (2005) 'The Overstretch Myth', *Foreign Affairs*, vol. 84, no. 1, pp. 2–7.

C.L. Mann (1999) *Is the US Trade Deficit Sustainable?* (Washington: Institute for International Economics).

C.L. Mann (2003) 'How Long the Strong Dollar?' in F. Bergsten and J. Williamson (eds.), *Dollar Overvaluation and the World Economy* (Washington, DC: Institute for International Economics).

C.L. Mann (2005) 'Breaking Up is Hard to Do: Global Co-dependency, Collective Action and the Challenges of Global Adjustment', *CESifo Forum*, January, pp. 16–23.

R. McGregor (2007) 'A Unique Animal in the World Economy', *Financial Times,* 17 October.

R.I. McKinnon (2005) 'Trapped by the International Dollar Standard', available from http://ideas.repec.org/a/eee/jpomo/v27y2005i4p477-485.html.

L. Montgomery (2006) 'Lower Deficit Sparks Debate Over Tax Cuts' Role', *Washington Post*, 17 October, p. D1.

W.M. Morrison (2005) *China–US Trade Issues*, CRS Issue Brief for Congress, 26 August.

Office of Management and Budget (OMB) (2008), *Budget of the United States Government FY2009: Historical Tables* (Washington DC: OMB).

J. O'Neill and J. Hatzius (2004) 'US Balance of Payments Unsustainable, But …' *Global Economics Paper 104* (New York: Goldman Sachs).

A. Persaud (2004) 'When Currency Empires Fall', October 12, available from www/321.gold.com/editorials/persuad/persuad101204.html.

W. Pesek Jr. (2005) 'If China Shuns Dollar, Look Out US Bonds', 28 January, available from www. bloomberg.com/apps/news?pid.

—— (2006) 'For US, China Isn't the Problem', *International Herald Tribune,* 14 December, p. 7.

J. Peters (2007) 'Appeal of Euro Strengthens Against US Dollar', *International Herald Tribune*, 1 January, p. 8.

P.G. Peterson (2005) 'Old Habits Must Change', *The Banker*, no. 1, pp. 12–13.

W. Poole (2005) 'How Dangerous is the US Current Account Deficit?', 9 November, available from www.stlouisfed.org/news/speeches/2005/11_o9_o5.htm.

R. Rajan (2005a) 'Global Current Account Imbalances: Hard Landing or Soft Landing', 15 March, available from www.imf.org/external/np/speeches/2005/031505.htm.

R. Rajan (2005b) 'Global Imbalances: An Assessment', 25 October, available from www.imf.org/external/np/speeches/2005/102505.htm.

K. Rogoff (2005) 'America's Current Account: A Deficit of Judgement', available from www.globalagendamagazine.com/2005/kennethrogoff.asp.

N. Roubini and B. Setser (2004) *The US as a Net Debtor: The Sustainability of External Imbalances*, November, available from www.stern.nyu.edu/globalmacro/Roubini-Setser-US-External-Imbalances.pdf.

N. Roubini and B. Setser (2005) *Will the Bretton Woods 2 Regime Unravel Soon? The Risk of a Hard Landing in 2005-2006*, February, available from www.stern.nyu.edu/globalmacro/.

R. Rubin, P.R. Orszag and A. Sinai (2004) 'Sustained Budget Deficits: Longer-Run US Economic Performance and the Risk of Financial and Fiscal Disarray', Allied Social Science Annual Meetings, The Andrew Brimmer Policy Forum 'National Economic and Financial Policies for Growth and Stability', 4 January.

B. Setser and N. Roubini (2005) 'Our Money, Our Debt, Our Problem', *Foreign Affairs*, vol. 84, no. 4, p. 198.

J.W. Sloan (1999) *The Reagan Effect: Economics and Presidential Leadership* (Lawrence, KA: University Press of Kansas).

L.H. Summers (2004a) 'America Overdrawn', *Foreign Policy*, July/August, pp. 47–49.

L.H. Summers (2004b) *The United States and the Global Adjustment Process*, Stavros S. Niarchos Lecture, Institute for International Economics, 23 March, available from www.iie.com/publications/papers/summers0304.htm.

R. Suskind (2004) *The Price of Loyalty: George W. Bush, the White House, and the Education of Paul O'Neill* (New York: Simon & Schuster).

J. Tamny (2006) 'The Current-Account Paradox', *National Review*, 20 January.

E.M. Truman (2004) 'Budget and External Deficits: Not Twins but the Same Family', Federal Reserve Bank of Boston Annual Research Conference, 14–16 January.

D. Valderrama (2007) 'The US Productivity Acceleration and the Current Account Deficit', *Federal Reserve Bank of San Francisco Newsletter*, 30 March, available from www.frsbf.org/publications/economics/letter/2007/el2007-08.html.

C. Weller (2004) 'The US Current Account Deficit: On An Unsustainable Path', *New Economy*, vol. 11, no. 4, pp. 243–48.

5

FOREIGN EXCHANGE AND THE DYNAMICS OF PUBLIC DEBT IN LATIN AMERICA[1]

Carlos E. Schonerwarld da Silva and Matías Vernengo

The notion that deficits and debt are not in themselves good or bad, but should be judged on the merits of the function that they play in the economy, is ultimately due to Abba Lerner (1943), who dubbed his views the 'functional finance' approach, in contrast to conventional wisdom based on 'sound finance'. In this view, deficits and debt should be judged by their effects on the economy. In other words, if deficits and debt promote economic growth and equitable income distribution, they should be seen as positive. It also implies that surpluses and falling debt are as good as the function they play in the economy.

This paper further develops the ideas presented in Vernengo (2006) to deal with the interaction of exchange rate and public debt dynamics. It is suggested that, under certain conditions, exchange rate appreciation may lead to a reduction of debt, in particular when primary surpluses are the rule. The preoccupation about this policy mix for Latin America is that the exchange rate reduces competitiveness and may have important effects on long-term growth. Also, permanent primary surpluses, in the presence of significant nominal deficits, imply that the interest rate bill is relatively large, and that transfers to the financial sector, which worsen income distribution, are large. It must be emphasised that, although we draw implications for Latin America as a whole, there are significant differences between countries and any conclusions must be reached with great caution.

The ideas developed in this paper are based on the seminal writings of Lerner (1943), Domar (1944) and Pasinetti (1997), extending the analyses to an open economy, where the exchange rate is vital to the dynamic of the public debt. In this sense, the paper can be seen as an extension of functional finance principles to the open economy. Furthermore, the paper discusses the recent dynamic of the public debt in Latin America based on the model developed. The next section presents the model; the following one discusses the relationship between the model and the Latin American experiences. The final section analyses the effects of the recent exchange rate policy over public debt. In particular, the paper focuses on heterodox alternatives that stabilise the public debt at a given level. The trade-off between inflation and unemployment is dealt with in the last section. Although inflationary pressures following exchange rate depreciation are relevant — in particular as a result of relatively high pass-through effects — the paper points out that unemployment problems are fundamental in the case of Latin America.

Functional Finance in the Open Economy

The relationship between the exchange rate and public debt is essentially mediated by two mechanisms. On the one hand, devaluation implies higher payments on local currency over debt denominated in foreign currency, and the reverse in the case of appreciation. On the other hand, the rise in public debt can increase the perception about the probability of a default and country risks, even if that perception is ultimately incorrect.[2] An increase in default and country risks may lead to a significant outflow of foreign currency, and as a result to a large devaluation of the exchange rate. It seems reasonable to assume that the recent trajectory of public debt in Latin America is to some extent affected by the dynamics of exchange rates.[3]

The dual relationship between the exchange rate and public debt has some peculiar effects on decisions regarding monetary policy. For example, an increase in the rate of interest affects directly the financial burden of the public debt, and, consequently, raises the nominal deficit and domestic debt. However, with higher interest rates the country will be a magnet for short-term capital, leading to an appreciation of the local currency, and as a result reducing the weight of the public debt denominated in foreign currency. The net effect on public debt will depend on the relative forces of the two effects. If the devaluation of the exchange rate leads to a reduction of the burden of the debt higher than the increase caused by the interest rate, the initial monetary policy will result in a positive net effect, so the public debt is going to be lower.[4]

Conventional wisdom about fiscal deficits is that they stimulate the economy in the short run, according to the Keynesian approach, but in the long run, given the macroeconomic identity (domestic saving equals to domestic investment plus net foreign investment), a reduction in domestic savings will diminish either the net formation of capital or foreign investment. In both cases, the growth rate will drop. In other words, deficits are good in the short run, but bad in the long run. Usually, in the long run, the negative effect on economic growth can be characterised by decreasing savings, followed by an interest rate increase, which in turn leads to a reduction of capital accumulation.[5]

It must be noted that the conventional result may be affected by market imperfections. Diamond (1965) shows that the failure of competitive markets to support optimal intertemporal allocations can stem from two sources: (1) the divergence between the planning horizon of individuals and the horizon of economic activity, evident in economies of overlapping generations; and (2) market imperfections, such as missing markets for the allocation of risks. Gale (1990) shows that, given financial market imperfections, public debt by introducing low risk securities may assist capital formation and economic growth. In that sense, even within the conventional neoclassical model there is some role for deficits and debt to affect growth positively.

If the monetary authority sets the interest rate exogenously, the causality between the interest rate and fiscal deficit might be reversed. Thus, a higher interest rate causes an increase on debt service payments leading to an increase in the nominal deficit. This sort of closure appears as the most relevant in the case of developing countries. Another important point, according to Abba Lerner (1943) and Evsey Domar (1944), is that deficits do not necessarily result in an expansion of public debt. Domar points out that the public debt-to-GDP ratio will raise if, and only if, the interest rate is higher than the growth rate. Pasinetti (1997) suggests that alternative monetary regimes have different effects on the sustainability of the public debt. In other words, the Bretton Woods era which was characterised by relatively low rates of interest was more prone to sustainable debt dynamics, and deficits were ultimately benign, whereas the post-Bretton Woods era is one where debt is more likely to be unsustainable and deficits more harmful.

However, the work of Lerner, Domar and the recent *aggiornamento* by Pasinetti (1997) emphasise cases in which public debt is completely denominated in local currency. Thus, to understand cases where a significant proportion of public debt is denominated in foreign currency, the explanation of how the dynamics of the exchange rate influences public debt turns out to be crucial. The extension of functional finance ideas to the open economy are based on two relationships depicted in Figures 5.1 and 5.2. First, the exchange rate is determined by interest rate differentials (a domestic rate higher than the foreign interest rate leads to appreciation), by the level of the current exchange rate vis-à-vis the desired exchange rate (if the current one is above the desired there will be pressures for appreciation), and by the level of public debt. In particular, it is assumed that higher levels of public debt may lead financial markets to suspect the sustainability of the fiscal stance and dump public bonds, leading to a depreciation of the domestic currency. This relationship is depicted by the e-dot curve in Figures 5.1 and 5.2.

The second relationship between public debt and the exchange rate results from the fact that, in developing countries, part of public debt is denominated

Figure 5.1: Stable Node

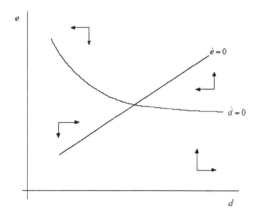

Figure 5.2: Saddle Path

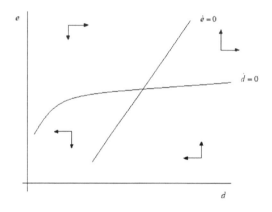

in foreign currency. Hence, a depreciation increases the value in domestic currency of public debt denominated in foreign currency, and vice versa in the case of an appreciation. The relationship between public debt and the exchange rate in this case is depicted by the d-dot curve. Figure 5.1 shows a stable case while Figure 5.2 depicts an unstable case. The stability conditions are broader than the one developed by Domar. In particular, the system would tend to be stable when the economy grows fast, the rate of interest is low, the exchange rate is not very sensitive to the level of public debt, and the amount of public debt denominated in foreign currency is small. In other words, now stability also depends on how much public debt affects the exchange rate, and how much the exchange rate affects public debt.

It is also crucial to note that an appreciation of the exchange rate is prejudicial to the growth of exports and to output growth. Export performance seems to be crucial for economic development, and exchange rate dynamics is central for exports. However, an appreciation still has the effect of reducing the burden of debt, but that does not necessarily mean that the economy is less prone to a currency and default crisis, since debts in foreign currencies must be paid with export proceeds. Hence, an appreciation may have an ambiguous effect, on the one hand leading to a lower level of debt, which may signal a more sustainable public debt, but by reducing external competitiveness may in fact be increasing the risk of default. In fact, a poor export performance may trigger a depreciation of the currency and lead to spiralling debt.[6]

Also, the risks associated with an appreciated currency may be compounded by fiscal austerity measures. The maintenance of primary surpluses at all times is sometimes seen as central for debt sustainability. However, if primary surpluses are maintained at the expense of public investment, which has positive effects on output growth, the effects may be counter-productive. Also, maintaining simultaneously primary surpluses and nominal deficits indicates that the government is paying the difference to the owners of public bonds.[7] Public bonds are usually held by banks, corporations, pension funds and wealthy individuals. Thus, the combination of primary surpluses and nominal deficits represents a significant transference of income from society as a whole to a few privileged groups. The redistributive process turns out to be important because in many cases primary surpluses result from reductions in public spending (Câmara Neto and Vernengo, 2004–05). Redistribution towards the wealthy may also be recessive, and by reducing growth make the sustainability of public debt more questionable.

In other words, a macroeconomic policy mix based on appreciated exchange rates and permanent primary surpluses might be compatible with decreasing debt-to-GDP ratios, but according to functional finance principles this is not necessarily good. If appreciation and surpluses make it more difficult for the economy to grow over time, the risks might be great, and debt dynamics may be unsustainable, even with falling public debt levels in the short run.

One may question why countries would maintain a policy mix that may hurt long-term growth prospects. An appreciated exchange rate which helps to stabilise the public debt-to-GDP ratio may also be central for anti-inflationary policies. In many developing countries, the pass-through effect of foreign prices on domestic inflation is relatively high, and exchange rate depreciation translates into significantly higher prices. Thus, central banks that are fundamentally concerned with price stability may use exchange rate appreciation as an important instrument in anti-inflationary policies.[8] Also, the notion that primary surpluses and lower debt are always good is a legacy of past debt crises, and has been firmly ingrained into IMF adjustment programmes, and the so-called Washington Consensus.

Functional finance ideas highlight some of the trade-offs associated with monetary, fiscal and exchange rate policies. Primary surpluses and appreciated exchange rates allow for lower debt-to-GDP ratios, and are central for maintaining price stability. However, this policy mix has negative impacts on income distribution and economic growth. Further, although the debt-to-GDP ratio is falling, it is not correct to assume that the risk of a currency crisis and default are falling. Low rates of growth and appreciated exchange rates indicate that small changes may lead to unsustainable debt dynamics. In particular, a small depreciation of the domestic currency may increase public debt denominated in domestic currency by a large amount.

The Latin American Case

The model developed in the previous section suggests that there may be significant problems with the current macroeconomic policy mix in several Latin American countries. In particular, we suggest that primary surpluses and decreasing debt are less benign than they might seem. They impose significant costs in terms of forgone growth and worsening income distribution, and may not lead to sustainable debt trajectories in the long run.

In Figure 5.3 we can see that the public debt of the central government, as well as that of the non-financial public sector, has shown a downward trend since 2003. At the level of the central government, the public debt-to-GDP ratio dropped from almost 60 per cent to 45 per cent. Regarding the non-financial public sector, the public debt-to-GDP ratio for 2005, calculated as a simple average, came to 48.6 per cent in 2005 in comparison to 55.9 per cent

Figure 5.3: Latin America (19 Countries): Public Debt (% of GDP)

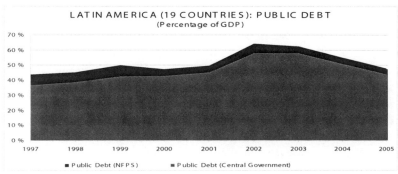

in 2004. There are three factors behind this downward trend: (1) the differential between growth and real interest rate; (2) the large primary surpluses and debt restructurings; and (3) the appreciation of many of the countries' currencies against the dollar (ECLAC, 2006).

The region's monetary policy-makers have had to cope with different sorts of challenges than they did in the past. The abundance of external resources stemming from higher exports and capital inflows has fuelled the appreciation of the countries' currencies. It is important to note that, for the most part, the expansion of exports has been associated with the expansion of the world economy, in particular the spectacular performance of China. In order to keep the appreciation under control, the countries' central banks intervened in the currency market, buying up foreign exchange in order to rein in their exchange rates. In turn, in an effort to ease the inflationary pressures generated by this strategy, the monetary authorities have had to sterilise the excess liquidity by engaging in open-market operations (ECLAC, 2005, p. 14).

The sterilisation process created pressure for an ever-increasing interest rate in order to capture the excess liquidity in the financial market via open-market operations, but it was not sufficient to neutralise the massive inflow of capital that arrived in the region after a certain degree of normality was regained in the aftermath of Argentina's crisis in 2001. The nominal interest rates, measured as the simple average of the interest rate in 19 countries, moved down since 2002 as shown in Figure 5.4. Also, inflation has been relatively volatile, but it has fallen after 2003 and been fundamentally subdued.

In Figure 5.5, the comparison of the nominal interest rate between the four biggest countries (in terms of GDP) in Latin America (Brazil, Argentina, Chile and Mexico) presents sizeable differences among them. Brazil presents an interesting and extreme case of the dangers of the current macroeconomic policy mix in Latin America because its nominal interest rate is the highest one, with the exception of Argentina during its crisis. The result of a very high nominal interest rate and a low and stable inflation rate is that the Brazilian real interest rate has been the highest in the world.[9] High rates of interest have significant effects on debt servicing, and on the exchange rate as we will see below.

The Latin American and Caribbean region grew by 4.5 per cent in 2005, thereby completing three consecutive years of positive growth. Figure 5.6 shows one of the most important determinants of the public debt-to-GDP ratio downward movement in Latin America. A combination of positive growth rate greater than the real interest rate pushed down the public debt-to-GDP ratio. Thus, it is one of the pillars necessary to understand why the public debt-to-GDP ratio went down very fast after 2003 in Latin America.

Figure 5.4: Latin America (19 Countries): Nominal Interest Rate and Inflation Rate

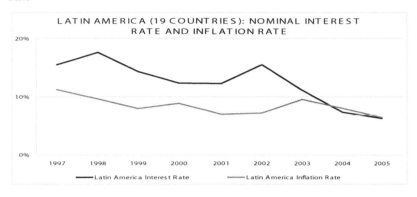

Figure 5.5: Latin America (19 Countries): Nominal Interest Rate

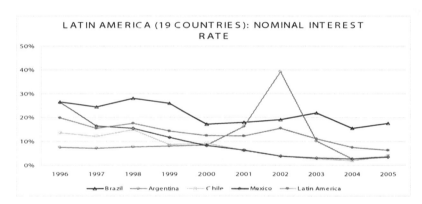

Figure 5.6: Latin America (19 Countries): Growth Rate and Real Interest Rate

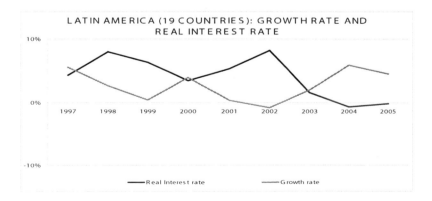

Between December 2004 and December 2005, the Latin American and Caribbean region's real effective exchange rate vis-à-vis the rest of the world appreciated by 8.3 per cent. Yet the extra-regional effective rate of exchange appreciated throughout 2005, hence a comparison of the average rates for 2004 and 2005 yielding a smaller figure (4.5 per cent). In 2005, the average appreciation of the real effective exchange rate relative to the rest of the world was almost twice as high for South America (10.1 per cent between December 2004 and December 2005) as the average for Central America, the Caribbean and Mexico (6 per cent). In contrast, the aggregate real effective exchange rate for the region vis-à-vis the rest of the world showed a slight depreciation (0.8 per cent) in the first four months of 2006 (ECLAC, 2006, p. 4).

The real exchange rate has been appreciating in Latin America since 2003. As already discussed, the pressure for appreciation was mainly caused by the large inflows of capital that re-entered Latin America after the Argentinean crisis in 2001 and were associated with the boom in the global economy since 2002 — in particular, the favourable shock to the terms of trade. Figure 5.7 displays the existence of a relationship between the real exchange rate and the public debt, so when the real exchange rate appreciated after 2003 the public debt-to-GDP ratio went down. Figure 5.8 seems to indicate that the exchange rate is an important element to understand public debt dynamics when the issue involves developing countries that do not have strong currencies and have debt partly denominated in foreign currency.

Note that the exchange rate appreciation that has taken place since 2003, at least for the region as a whole, is relatively small when compared with the depreciation of the previous years. Figure 5.8 shows the evolution of the real effective exchange rate for Latin America and also for the big four (Argentina, Brazil, Chile and Mexico). Since 2003, appreciation has been stronger than the average for Latin America in all countries except Argentina. It is interesting to note that Argentina has also had the most marked expansion since 2003, and the real exchange rate depreciation has certainly played a significant role.

The positive macroeconomic situation existing since 2002 provided a fertile ground for the countries of the region to make significant improvements in their fiscal accounts. At the end of 2004, the countries' central governments posted a weighted average primary surplus of 2.2 per cent of GDP, compared with 1.6 per cent in 2003. Meanwhile, the overall balance, which includes interest payments on the public debt, shows a decrease in the deficit from −1.8 per cent to −0.9 per cent of GDP (ECLAC, 2005). The primary surplus increased to 2.7 per cent of GDP in 2005, but the overall deficit remains negative owing to higher interest payments on the public debt (see Figure 5.9). Thus, the final variable with which we are concerned, primary budget surpluses, presented a consistent and significant result for a reduction of the public debt-to-GDP ratio.

Figure 5.7: Latin America (19 Countries): Public Debt and Exchange Rate

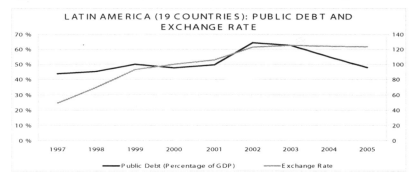

Figure 5.8: Latin America (19 Countries): Real Effective Exchange Rate

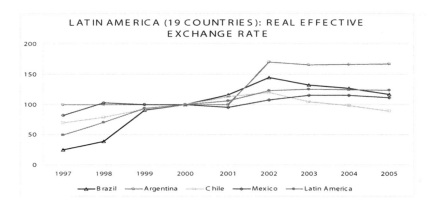

Figure 5.9: Latin America (19 Countries): Primary Budget Surplus/Deficit (% of GDP)

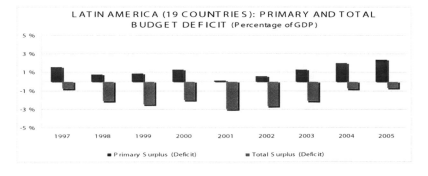

Figure 5.10: Latin America (19 Countries): Gross Fixed Capital Formation, Unemployment Rate and Growth Rate

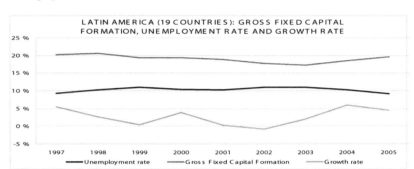

A noticeable impact on its labour markets has been caused by the region's relatively high rate of economic growth in recent years (ECLAC, 2006). In fact, 2005 was the third year in a row of marked increases in the employment rate. The 2005 rise of 0.5 percentage points takes the rate up to 53.6 per cent of the working-age population. The most relevant fact to bear in mind, however, is that these recent improvements are simply bringing the region's employment rate back to the levels of 1997 (Figure 5.10). Furthermore, unemployment remains high, with an estimated 18 million people out of work. Also, a sizeable percentage of new jobs are in low-paying positions, and the number of short-term employment arrangements in the formal sector is on the rise. Thus, the labour market's reactivation in 2005 has not yet led to any significant rise in real wages, which were up by just 0.5 per cent.

Since 2003, gross capital formation has expanded; however, it is slightly above 20 per cent of GDP and is still lower than before the series of financial crises that began in 1997. Arguably, the 'present investment coefficients are too low to sustain a fast enough growth rate to fuel job creation in the formal sector at the level needed to help alleviate the delicate social situation existing in Latin America and the Caribbean' (ECLAC, 2006, p. 14).

It is well known that there is a strong relationship across countries between rates of economic growth and the share of GDP devoted to investment. DeLong and Summers (1991) show that there is a positive correlation between GDP growth and equipment investment, and suggest that causality runs from the latter to the former. The correlation between investment and growth is also strong in Latin America, as can be seen in Figure 5.10. However, this empirical relationship falls short of demonstrating a causal link from investment to growth. The data demonstrate correlation more than causality, and a simple accelerator model suggests that causality is reversed. That is, firms invest if demand increases in order to maintain capacity utilisation at normal levels.[10]

Probably more important than investment per se is the constraint on public investment. Aschauer (1989a, 1989b) argues that, in the United States, public investment is much more productive than private investment, and that public investment in infrastructure crowds out private investment. In other words, even though private investment results from growth, public investment may very well promote economic growth. However, the permanent primary surpluses in Latin America imply a reduced fiscal space for governments to expand public investment. The lack of fiscal space for investment in infrastructure does not bode well for future economic performance in the region.

Increasingly, there is a consensus that infrastructure investment represents a serious constraint for long-term sustainable growth. For example, Brazil experienced a severe energy constraint in 2001 that affected industrial production significantly. Figure 5.11 shows that total infrastructure investment in Brazil had a decline of 2.8 per cent of GDP in a comparison between the 1980–85 and 1996–2001 periods. During the period 1980–85, Brazil invested around 5 per cent of its GDP in infrastructure, but had a sharp decline to 2.3 per cent of GDP during the period 1996–2001. The Brazilian story is not atypical. Chile was the only exception: it had an increase during the same period. The average performance for Latin America shows a reduction of infrastructure investment of around 1.8 per cent of GDP.

The relatively low levels of public investment in infrastructure, and the limited fiscal space to expand public investment, are not unique dark clouds over the current economic recovery in Latin America. As noted before, the economic recovery has been possible to a great extent due to spectacular Chinese economic growth and the less impressive, but significant, recovery in the United States after the 2001 recession. However, global imbalances may very well imply a reduced rate of growth of the global economy in the near future. According to a recent report by the Economic Commission for Latin

Figure 5.11: Latin America (19 Countries): Infrastructure Investment (% of GDP)

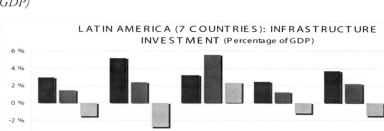

America and the Caribbean:

> While the world economy may succeed in dealing with the threat of
> inflation and in rectifying existing global imbalances without any steep
> downturn in its growth rate, these factors are still a source of uncertainty.
> Some indicators appear to be heralding a period of greater global volatility,
> and the possibility cannot be ruled out that this may dampen growth
> somewhat and trigger a reversal in the net direction of some capital flows
> back toward developed countries. (ECLAC, 2006, p. 3)

In that scenario, the lack of fiscal space for expansionary fiscal policies and the appreciated exchange rate, which reduces international competitiveness, suggest that the economic expansion in the region is more fragile than is usually assumed. Falling debt-to-GDP ratios were only possible because of the large primary surpluses and appreciated exchange rate. However, the primary surpluses constrained the ability of the public sector to increase infrastructure investment, imposing severe limits on growth. Also, the appreciation suggests that the economies in Latin America are vulnerable to a sudden slowdown of the world economy. If global imbalances actually lead to even a moderate global recession, and capital outflows, depreciation of Latin American currencies would lead to an increase of debt-to-GDP ratios even with large primary surpluses. Even worse, the contraction of foreign demand will take place in an environment in which domestic demand will not be able to compensate, and growth will most likely collapse.

In that situation, we would have the negative scenario of growing debt-to-GDP ratios, higher nominal deficits (even with primary surpluses) and a depreciating currency. The possibilities of defaults in such a case cannot be ruled out. It should be noted that there is a risk, as is always the case with generalisations, in emphasising the commonalities in the recent Latin American experience. The diversity of experiences in Latin America is great, and there are some important exceptions to our description of the limits to the foreign exchange rate and public debt dynamics we describe above. All in all, our analysis of the dynamics of the exchange rate and public debt is that the mix of appreciation and falling debt-to-GDP ratios should not be seen as sustainable in the long run, and that significant risks are still present.

Concluding Remarks

Our discussion of public debt dynamics in Latin America based on functional finance ideas suggests that falling debt-to-GDP ratios are not necessarily an indication that the risk of a currency crisis and default is decreasing. Low rates of growth and appreciated exchange rates indicate that small changes may lead to unsustainable debt dynamics, and in particular a small depreciation of the domestic currency may increase public debt denominated in domestic currency by a large amount and lead to a currency crisis and eventual default. Functional finance provides a cautionary tale for the recent Latin American experience.

Large primary surpluses, strong and appreciating exchange rates, and falling debt-to-GDP ratios do not, in our view, imply that Latin America has entered a new era of expansion, and that external crises are a thing of the past. A particular set of circumstances — for example, the global expansion, the positive shock to the terms of trade, and the incredible global liquidity provided by the large American current account deficits — appears to have put an end to the period of external crises that started with the Mexican Tequila Crisis in 1995 and culminated with the Argentinean debacle of 2001. However, the external conditions for the renewed period of international financial stability are flimsy at best. Lower debt-to-GDP ratios, permanent primary surpluses and appreciated exchange rates may, in fact, make things worse in the case of a reversal of external conditions.

In the same vein, our discussion suggests that growing debt, primary deficits and a depreciating currency should not be seen as signs of an impending crisis, particularly if public investment is creating the basis for the sustainable expansion of domestic demand, including a better distribution of income and promoting external competitiveness. More spending in infrastructure and social policies may be positive as an instrument to make domestic demand expansion the basis of sustainable economic growth. More depreciated exchange rates might reduce the external vulnerability in the long run. These measures may imply that, in the short run, primary deficits would be necessary and that debt-to-GDP ratios would increase. But this would be a small price to pay for a strategy of development that provided long-run sustainable and equitable growth in Latin America.

References

D. Aschauer (1989a) 'Is Public Expenditure Productive?' *Journal of Monetary Economics*, no. 23, pp. 177–200.

D. Aschauer (1989b) 'Does Public Capital Crowd Out Private Capital?' *Journal of Monetary Economics*, no. 24, pp. 171–88.

O. Blanchard (2005) 'Fiscal Dominance and Inflation Targeting: Lessons from Brazil', in F. Giavazzi, I. Goldfajn and S. Herrera (eds.), *Inflation Targeting, Debt, and the Brazilian Experience, 1999–2003* (Cambridge: MIT Press).

A. Câmara Neto and M. Vernengo (2004–05) 'Fiscal Policy and the Washington Consensus', *Journal of Post Keynesian Economics*, no. 27, pp. 333–43.

B. DeLong and L. Summers (1991) 'Equipment Investment and Economic Growth', *Quarterly Journal of Economics*, no. 106, pp. 445–502.

P. Diamond (1965) 'National Debt in a Neoclassical Growth Model', *American Economic Review*, no. 55, pp. 1126–50.

E. Domar (1944) 'The Burden of Debt and the National Income', *American Economic Review*, no. 34, pp. 798–827.

Economic Commission for Latin America and Caribbean (ECLAC) (2005) *Economic Survey of Latin America and Caribbean* (Santiago, Chile: ECLAC).

Economic Commission for Latin America and Caribbean (ECLAC) (2006) *Economic Survey of Latin America and Caribbean* (Santiago, Chile: ECLAC).

B. Eichengreen and R. Hausmann (2005) 'Original Sin: The Road to Redemption', in B. Eichengreen and R. Hausmann (eds.), *Other People's Money* (Chicago: Chicago University Press).

B. Eichengreen and A. Mody (2000) 'What Explains the Changing Spreads on Emerging Market Debt?' in Sebastian Edwards (ed.), *The Economics of International Capital Flows* (Chicago: University of Chicago Press).

R. Frenkel and L. Taylor (2006) 'Real Exchange Rate, Monetary Policy and Employment', DESA Working Paper no. 19.

Gale, D. (1990) 'The Efficient Design of Public Debt', in R. Dornbusch and M. Draghi (eds.), *Public Debt Management: Theory and History* (Cambridge: MIT Press).

W. Gale and P. Orszag (2003) 'The Economic Effects of Sustained Budget Deficits', *National Tax Journal*, no. 56, pp. 462–85.

M. Kalecki (1971) *Selected Essays in the Dynamics of a Capitalist Economy* (Cambridge: Cambridge University Press).

A. Lerner (1943) 'Functional Finance and the Federal Debt', *Social Research*, no. 10, pp. 38–51.

L. Pasinetti (1997) 'The Social Burden of High Interest Rates', in P. Arestis, G. Palma and M. Sawyer (eds.), *Capital Controversy, Post-Keynesian Economics and the History of Economics: Essays in Honour of Geoff Harcourt*. Volume I (London: Routledge).

L. Taylor (1998) 'Lax Public Sector, Destabilizing Private Sector: Origins of Capital Market Crises', CEPA Working Paper no. 11, Center for Economic Policy Analysis, October.

M. Vernengo (2006) 'Globalization and Endogenous Fiscal Crisis', in P. Berglund and M. Vernengo (eds.), *The Means to Prosperity: Fiscal Policy Reconsidered* (New York: Routledge).

Appendix: The Model

The dynamics of the exchange rate, defined as the domestic price (local currency) of foreign currency (US dollar), is determined by three factors presented in the following equation:

$$(1)\ \dot{e} = \sigma(i^* - i) + \theta(\overline{e} - e) + \mu d$$

Dots represent a change in the level — thus, *e-dot* is the change in the exchange rate (up is depreciation and down is appreciation). The primary factor is the traditional interest rate parity condition, according to which if the domestic interest rate, i, is higher than the foreign interest rate, i^*, the exchange rate will appreciate. On the other hand, if the domestic interest rate is below the foreign one, depreciation will follow. Equation (1) also assumes that if the actual exchange rate, e, is lower than the expected exchange rate, *e-bar*, there is a tendency to devaluation. The expected exchange rate is determined by perceptions of economic agents about the long-term rate of exchange rate that would be compatible with a sustainable current account. Finally, the international financial markets perception imply, particularly influenced by the risk agencies (e.g. Fitch, Moody's and Standard and Poors), a devaluation of the exchange rate when the public debt-to-GDP ratio, d, rises. We assume that a higher d implies higher risk of depreciation. The link may be weak, and also μ might catch other risk factors that are not affected by fundamentals. We assume that in a very open economy μ would be central for the dynamics of the exchange rate. In that sense, a depreciation may follow simply from a changing mood in international financial markets.

Further, we assume that deficits are financed by the issue of new bonds, and that prices are constant. In addition, we assume that public debt, in terms of local and foreign currencies, is indexed to the basic short term rate controlled by the central bank. The primary deficit $(G - T)$ is defined as the growth of the public debt (D-*dot*) minus the payment of interest on the outstanding debt. Thus, we have:

$$(2)\ (G - T) = \dot{D} - i(D_d + eD_f)$$

D_d is the public debt denominated in local currency and D_f is the share of public debt denominated in foreign currency. The dynamics of the public debt-to-GDP ratio is given by:

$$(3)\ \frac{\dot{d}}{d} = \frac{\dot{D}}{D} - g$$

In other words, the rate of growth of the debt-to-GDP ration is the difference between the rate of growth of public debt and the growth rate of GDP, g. Substituting (1) into (2), we obtain:

$$(4) \quad \frac{\dot{d}}{d} = \frac{(G-T) + i(D_d + eD_f)}{D} - g$$

Rearranging equation (4), we get:

$$(5) \quad \dot{d} = [i(\delta_d + e\delta_f) - g]d + \tau$$

Where δ_d and δ_f represent the shares of domestic and foreign debt in total public debt, and δ is the primary deficit as a share of GDP.

Equations (1) and (5) provide a system of equations that describe the exchange rate and public debt dynamics. The first equation expresses that an increase in public debt leads to a depreciation of the exchange rate. The relation is represented by the upward sloping *e-dot* curve in Figure 5.1. The more sensitive the exchange rate is to changes in the public debt-to-GDP ratio, the steeper the *e-dot* curve will be. It is expected that a more open economy, without capital controls, would have a steeper *e-dot* curve than an economy with capital controls and with a relatively closed capital account, since in the latter case the exchange rate would not be affected by international financial markets' perceptions about default and country risks.

The second equation suggests that a devaluation of the exchange rate increases public debt, depending on the value of the parameters. Figure 5.1 illustrates the equilibrium when there is a primary surplus, instead of a deficit. Certain conditions that can be expressed by using the Jacobian below (Equation 6) determine the local stability/instability of the system.

$$(6) \quad J = \begin{bmatrix} -\theta & \mu \\ i\delta_f d & i(\delta_d + e\delta_f) - g \end{bmatrix}$$

If the determinant of the Jacobian is positive and the trace is negative, then the system is a stable node as represented in Figure 5.1. Stability can also occur in the case of primary deficits, when the *d-dot* curve is positive sloped. On the other hand, if the determinant of the Jacobian is negative, then the system is an unstable saddle-path, as depicted in Figure 5.2.

The examination of the Jacobian shows that the system is more prone to instability if the rate of growth of the economy is low, the rate of interest is high, the sensitivity of the exchange rate to country and default risks is high and the share of foreign debt in total public debt is high. Instead of the conventional condition of stability according to which the system is stable if the rate of growth is bigger than the rate of interest, the system is unstable if:

$$(7) \quad g < \frac{i\theta(\delta_d + e\delta_f) + i\delta_f \mu d}{\theta}$$

This suggests that economies in which the public sector is heavily indebted in foreign currency and that have opened up the capital account of the balance of payments are more prone to currency crises. Also, it must be noted that crises are possible even in the absence of fiscal laxity, when primary surpluses are substantial (Taylor, 1998). The model also indicates that currency crises are likely to lead to default, as the exchange rate and the debt-to-GDP ratio move in the northeast direction in Figure 5.2.

Notes

[1]   Pontifícia Universidade Católica do Rio Grande do Sul and University of Utah. Preliminary versions of the paper were presented at the Institute of Latin American Studies (ILAS), London, Centro de Estudios de Estado y Sociedad (CEDES), Buenos Aires, and the Universidad Nacional Autónoma de México (UNAM). We would like to thank Manuel Agosin, Per Berglund, Roberto Frenkel, Irma Manrique, Diego Sanchez, Oscar Ugarteche and other conference participants for their comments. Responsibility for remaining errors is ours entirely.

[2]   The empirical evidence on the effects of public debt and other 'fundamentals' on default and country risks shows that the connection is weak. For example, Eichengreen and Mody (2000) argue that observed changes in fundamentals explain only a fraction of the emerging market debt spread over secure assets.

[3]   This paper develops a simple model (see Appendix) where the exchange rate is crucial to analyse the dynamic of public debt. For an earlier version that dealt with the Brazilian economy, see Vernengo (2006).

[4]   This adds a new twist to the conventional fiscal dominance argument, according to which an increase in the real interest rate makes domestic government debt more attractive and leads to a real appreciation, but if the increase in the real interest rate also increases the probability of default, then the effect may be to lead to a real depreciation. See Blanchard (2005).

[5]   The empirical evidence on the effects of fiscal deficits on the interest rate is that the effects are small. For a recent survey of the American case, see Gale and Orszag (2003), who argue that deficits equal to 3% of GDP would raise interest rates by between 60 and 180 basis points with a mean of 120. It must be noted that empirical studies seldom discuss causality. However, given that increases in interest rates — which might be influenced by monetary policy — affect debt servicing, it seems reasonable to consider whether causality runs from interest to deficits, rather than the other way round.

[6]   In that case, an external crisis leads to a fiscal crisis, something suggested in Vernengo (2006). For the advantages of relatively depreciated and competitive exchange rates, see Frenkel and Taylor (2006).

7   The nominal deficit is the difference between total spending and revenues, while the primary result excludes interest payments. Hence, the difference between the two is composed by interest payments on outstanding debt (Vernengo, 2006).

8   In that respect, target exchange rates that are low because of anti-inflationary policies may be central to explain exchange rate appreciation. In some cases, high domestic interest rates may also play a role.

9   For a discussion of the Brazilian case, see Vernengo (2006).

10 For a simple explanation of investment behavior using the accelerator, see Kalecki (1971).

6

FISCAL POLICY AND EQUITY: THE DILEMMAS FACING BRAZIL'S LABOUR GOVERNMENT[1]

Edmund Amann and Werner Baer

A recurrent theme in the development literature has been the question of whether increased efficiency can be achieved simultaneously with an increased degree of equity. Many have claimed that society has to choose one or the other.[2] For example, in the case of agriculture it has been suggested that a drastic redistribution of land ownership, though resulting in more equitable distribution of agricultural income, could also diminish productivity. Similar arguments have been presented with respect to the urban industrial sector. Many who have accepted the notion of a trade-off between equity and efficiency have suggested that both might be achieved sequentially. In other words, a period in which equity has been sacrificed for the sake of an efficient allocation of resources, resulting in high rates of economic growth, could lay the foundations for a period in which greater emphasis would be placed on a substantial redistribution of assets and income generated from them.

It is the purpose of this chapter to evaluate the latter proposition as it applies to the recent fiscal experience of Brazil, where in January 2003 Luiz Inácio Lula da Silva, the former trade union leader and head of Brazil's Workers' Party (PT)[3] took office. This was perceived by many Brazilian and foreign observers as portending a dramatic shift to the left in the governance of the country. In the run-up to Lula's victory, many harboured hopes that this new government would provide a real radical alternative to the policy profile pursued up until then. At the same time, the prospects of a Lula victory engendered fears among domestic and foreign investors that irresponsibility in fiscal and macro-economic policies and the erosion of established property rights would become the order of the day. It is ironic that these initial perceptions have been confounded by subsequent developments. Many of the early left-wing supporters were bitterly disappointed in the policies adopted by President Lula, while the domestic and foreign investment communities were not only pleasantly surprised by the actual policies adopted, but gradually became strong admirers of his government.

Examining the record to date of President Lula's administration, it becomes evident that his initial goal was to proceed in a cautious way by first establishing a reputation for fiscal prudence. This would lay the foundations upon which more radical structural reforms could be carried out. We shall argue that such a sequence, while not unfeasible, contains some contradictions, the nature of which may place in jeopardy the reformist social vision of Lula and his followers.

In this chapter, we shall first describe the socio-economic aims of the PT as it took over the reins of government. This will be followed by a brief description of the macroeconomic and fiscal policies adopted, their impact on the economy, and the institutional structural reforms launched. Next, bearing in mind the centrality of social reform to Lula and his followers, we shall present a preliminary assessment of the impact of these policies on some key social indicators. Finally, we plan to show how the adopted sequence of orthodox fiscal policies followed by drastic social reforms may not be entirely compatible, taking into account the path-dependency which inhibits radical departures from established norms in socio-economic policies.

The Socio-economic Vision of Lula and the PT in the Run-up to Power

Prior to the election of October 2002, the presidential candidate's party (the PT) issued a comprehensive manifesto which diagnosed Brazil's major socio-economic failings and outlined a number of policy initiatives designed to remedy them (Partido dos Trabalhadores, 2002). This policy document is distinguished by the fact that social development is considered a vital component, rather than a residual, of economic growth (Partido dos Trabalhadores, 2002, p. 30).

The document places a particular emphasis on the tackling of poverty and inequality, both long-term features of the Brazilian economy. For instance, it states that the grinding poverty of Brazil 'is not something transitory, but is the result of a historical legacy in which fundamental flaws were never tackled'. Recognising this, it is argued that there is no substitute for the implementation of thoroughgoing structural reforms. However, there is recognition that such reforms are likely to take a considerable period of time (in fact, many years) to accomplish (Partido dos Trabalhadores, 2002, p. 43).

The document states explicitly the need to promote rapid economic growth and international competitiveness as a backdrop to achieve social development. For that purpose, six key policy goals were specified: price stability; efficiency of the taxation system; provision of long-term finance; investment in research and development; education of the workforce; and selective investments in infrastructure. To promote simultaneous social development, the document advances a new strategic vision in which the tackling of poverty and inequality is to be performed in an integrated and coherent fashion.[4]

The social development programme proposed by PT contained two key components: a programme designed to tackle hunger (called *fome zero*)[5] (p. 43) and a minimum income guarantee (p. 41). Regarding the former, a number of measures were proposed, including direct support for family-based agriculture, the right of all family workers to social security benefits (whether in the formal or informal sector), and complementary income guarantees for all children from poor families, plus incentives for those children to obtain a basic education. In addition, the *fome zero* programme proposes yet more direct measures, including 'popular restaurants', food banks, modernisation of the food supply chain, the promotion of 'urban agriculture' and support for subsistence farmers (pp. 43–44). Perhaps the most publicised aspect of the *fome zero* programme was the introduction of a 'food card', a sort of cash card enabling the poorest families to obtain for free a certain quantity of food each month.

Closely allied to the *fome zero* programme was the second aspect of the PT's anti-poverty policy: the minimum income guarantee. The latter was supposed to operate in four ways: (1) to target children in poverty up to the age of 15, transferring payments to families whose income was equal to or less than the minimum wage;[6] (2) the launch of student grants for those between the ages of 16 and 25 coming from a low-income background; (3) a programme of minimum income guarantees and professional training for unemployed workers between the ages of 22 and 50; and (4) the 'New Opportunity' programme for unemployed workers between the ages of 51 and 66, offering retraining (pp. 42–43). Taken together, these initiatives were supposed to herald a new era in which growth and equity would be promoted simultaneously.

Macroeconomic and Fiscal Policy Under the Lula Administration

The domestic and international investment community's reaction to Lula's victory in October 2002 was one of nervous expectation. There was the fear that the new government would be tempted to default on part of the debt, that the foreign investor friendliness of the previous government would not be maintained, that there might be a reversal of the privatisation programme that had prevailed throughout the 1990s and that the fiscal responsibility established under President Fernando Henrique Cardoso would not be sustained. The growing concern of investors in the run-up to the election is well illustrated by the widening of the interest rate spread between Brazilian sovereign bonds and their US equivalents (Amann and Baer, 2006, p. 222). However, the interest spread declined right after the election of President Lula. This was the result

Table 6.1: Evolution of the Public Sector Primary Deficit By Component, 1985–2006*

	Primary Balance: States and Municipalities	Primary Balance: State–owned Enterprises	Primary Balance: Federal Government and Central Bank
1985	−0.10	−0.90	−1.61
1986	0.10	−1.29	−0.40
1987	0.59	−1.38	1.78
1988	−0.51	−1.42	1.01
1989	−0.31	−0.10	1.44
1990	−0.20	−1.73	−2.75
1991	−1.4	−0.33	−0.98
1992	−0.06	−0.41	−1.09
1993	−0.62	−0.76	−0.81
1994	−0.77	−1.19	−3.68
1995	0.18	0.07	−0.52
1996	0.54	−0.07	−0.37
1997	0.74	−0.05	0.27
1998	0.19	0.35	−0.55
1999	−0.21	−0.66	−2.36
2000	−0.54	−1.06	−1.85
2001	−0.8	−0.86	−1.68
2002	−0.72	−0.67	−2.16
2003	−0.81	−0.8	−2.28
2004	−0.9	−0.58	−2.7
2005	−0.99	−0.76	−2.59
2006	−0.84	−0.82	−2.21

* Negative figures indicate surpluses.

Source: Banco Central do Brasil.

of reassuring statements made by Lula and his incoming cabinet regarding the above-mentioned fears (2006, p. 222). Also, conscious of the sensitivities of international financial markets and the danger they held for currency stability, the newly elected government took rapid steps to assuage the anxieties of investors and multilateral institutions.

The centrepiece of the government's strategy in this regard was a reasserting of its predecessor's commitment to fiscal prudence. In concrete terms, this took the form of an elevating of the primary surplus from 3.49 per cent of GDP in 2002 to 3.89 per cent in 2003. By 2005, the primary surplus attained a peak of 4.34 per cent of GDP before falling back to 3.03 per cent in 2006 as pre-election political pressure mounted on the administration to raise spending. Table 6.1 indicates that, in the current decade, the pursuit of such impressive surpluses has been driven strongly by the activities of the federal government. However, one of the fundamental factors driving fiscal adjustment across the public sector over the longer term has been tough centrally mandated limits over patterns of spending in states and municipalities. Following the passage of the Law of Fiscal Responsibility in 2000, a spending ceiling for personnel costs was established across all levels of government while budgetary agreements were signed between the federal government and the majority of the states (Giambiagi, 2005 p. 184).

Such was the government's determination to pursue tight fiscal policy that it actually succeeded in surpassing the primary fiscal surplus it had pledged to the IMF. This was achieved through tight controls of growth in expenditures, combined with added vigour in generating revenues: in 2003, revenues increased by R$36 billion, while expenditures rose by only R$29 billion, while in 2004 revenues increased by R$64.6 billion while expenditures rose by R$54.3 billion.[7] In addition, the tax burden rose over the first two years of the government's term, reaching 36 per cent of GDP by 2004. By way of contrast, the tax burden of Chile, Mexico and Argentina in the same year stood at 17.3 per cent, 18.3 per cent and 17.4 per cent respectively.

The second plank of the Lula administration's orthodox approach to macroeconomic policy was the initial pursuit of relatively tight monetary policy. Throughout the first half of 2003, interest rates were kept at very high levels (by June 2003 the SELIC benchmark rate stood at 25.8 per cent) as the Lula government continued its policy of reassuring the international community. This policy was underpinned by the maintenance of the inflation-targeting framework established after the January 1999 maxi- devaluation.[8] It is important to emphasise that the average economic agent needing credit paid much higher interest rates than indicated by the SELIC, which is the country's prime rate. For instance, in 2003 interest rates charged to consumers reached such levels as 74.7 per cent in August, declining slightly to 69.4 per cent in October.[9]

The rates only began to be lowered slightly in the second half of the year, once the real began to appreciate in value against the US dollar, a development which stemmed from robust growth in commodity exports but also at least in part from a general weakness in the US currency. As the real strengthened (from an average of R$2.88 to the dollar in 2003 to R$2.13 in 2006), inflationary pressure lessened in tandem (see Table 6.2). This allowed Central Bank base rates to fall: by the end of 2006, the SELIC rate stood at 13.19 per cent, while by September 2007 it had fallen further to 11.18 per cent.

It should be remembered that the stabilisation which occurred with the introduction of the Real Plan was not based on inflation targeting, but rather

Table 6.2: Brazil: Price Changes and Real GDP Growth (yearly % change)

	Consumer Prices (IPCA)	General Prices (IGP–DI)	GDP Growth
1993	1,927.38	2851.33	4.92
1994	2,075.89	908.0	5.85
1995	66.01	15.02	4.22
1996	15.76	9.22	2.66
1997	6.93	7.11	3.27
1998	3.20	1.84	0.13
1999	4.86	19.91	0.79
2000	7.04	9.52	4.31
2001	6.84	10.23	1.31
2002	12.53	27.65	2.66
2003	9.30	6.94	1.15
2004	7.6	11.87	5.71
2005	5.69	1.42	2.94
2006	3.14	3.64	3.70

Sources: FGV, Conjuntura Economica; Banco Central.

on a combination of a more open economy, high interest rates, the covering of government deficits by non-Central Bank borrowing and the maintenance of an 'exchange rate anchor'.[10] Inflation targeting began with the devaluation of the real in January 1999, and the price stability maintained since that time has been attributed to this policy. The Lula administration has kept the inflation-targeting framework in place, a policy which has been justified in a lengthy article by Central Bank officials, strongly associated with the previous administration. They concluded that

> the inflation-targeting regime of Brazil is relatively new, but has shown
> to be important in achieving low levels of inflation, even in the context
> of large shocks. The presence of the Central Bank committed to pre-
> announced inflation targets has worked as an important coordinator of
> expectations and generated a more stable inflation scenario. (Minella et al.,
> 2003)

The retention of the inflation-targeting framework by the Lula administration places it in a dilemma, since such targeting implies that all other policy goals (including social objectives) would be subordinate to the primary goal of achieving a certain level of inflation. The primacy of inflation targeting has also raised concerns regarding its negative implications for growth and — through its impact on exchange rates — on competitiveness.

Social Impacts of Lula's Macroeconomic Policies

It should be stressed at the outset that structural policies aimed at improving social indicators operate with very long lags. Therefore, we would not expect to see dramatic improvements in these indicators over such a short time period (the first four or so years of Lula's government). Nevertheless, it cannot be denied that the tight fiscal and monetary policies that have been maintained have had short-term social impacts, not least through their effects on income levels.

The period between 1995 and the beginning of the Lula administration witnessed a protracted decline in real industrial wages (Amann and Baer, 2006). Against this background, given its social objectives, it was clearly of priority to the new administration to reverse this trend. However, the first two years of the Lula government proved to be a period in which real industrial wages failed to register a substantial increase (Amann and Baer, 2006). Data from DIEESE (which is the research arm of the trade unions) reveal that by 2006, average monthly real wages in Brazil's most populous and industrialised city, São Paulo, stood at R$1113. This represented only a modest increase over the R$1088 registered in 2003, the beginning of Lula's term. In 1998, by contrast, average monthly real wages in São Paulo were considerably higher, standing at R$1569. Similar trends are also evident for other large metropolitan areas in Brazil.

One of the most publicised trends associated with the Lula administration has been the improving trajectory of the Gini coefficient. Table 6.3 indicates a modest reduction in inequality between 2002 and 2005, with the Gini coefficient falling by 0.02 percentage points. What factors have driven this improvement and to what extent can it be attributed to the explicit anti-poverty programmes launched by the Lula administration?

In the first place, it should be noted that the fall in the Gini is modest compared with previous episodes, especially that of the early 1990s. During the latter period, the elaborate anti-poverty agenda of the Lula administration

Table 6.3: Gini Coefficient: Brazil, 1960–2005

1960	1970	1976	1977	1978	1979	1980	1981	1982	1983	1984
0.57	0.53	0.62	0.62	0.60	0.59	–	0.58	0.59	0.60	0.60

1985	1986	1987	1988	1989	1990	1991	1992	1993	1994	1995
0.60	0.59	0.60	0.62	0.64	0.61	–	0.58	0.60	–	0.60

1996	1997	1998	1999	2000	2001	2002	2003	2004	2005
0.60	0.60	0.60	0.59	–	0.60	0.59	0.58	0.57	0.57

Source: IPEA Date/IBGE.

was not, of course, in existence. The sharp improvements in the Gini then were largely the product of falls in the rate of inflation, which delivered sharp positive real income effects to the poorer in society (Thorp, 1998). When one examines the record of the Lula administration, to its credit inflation (see Table 6.2) has also fallen and this must form part of the explanation for narrowing in inequality. Another factor which needs to be taken into consideration is the sharp rises in the minimum salary that have occurred since 2002 (Pães de Barros, 2007). This has had an undeniably positive impact on the incomes of those in the bottom two deciles of the distribution. As will be seen, the rise in the minimum salary is rather a double-edged sword so far as tackling poverty is concerned, since its direct positive effects on the incomes of the poor need to be weighed against the reduced scope it creates for discretionary public sector spending on social investment. Pães de Barros (2007) argues that the explicit anti-poverty instruments of the Lula administration (notably the Bolsa Família) have also had a role in narrowing income inequality. However, as will be seen, the scale of these programmes has been strongly limited by fiscal constraints.

Lula's Explicit Social Policies

As mentioned above, President Lula began his mandate with *fome zero*, the aim of which was to directly tackle the problem of hunger. In subsequent months, the implementation of this programme fell into disarray. As one observer commented, 'it sowed bureaucratic confusion by creating extra ministries to tackle social problems (one for hunger and another for social assistance)'. In addition, according to the same source, the *fome zero* programme has been viewed by many observers as 'fuzzy and outmoded'.[11] A key difficulty faced by the *fome zero* programme has been that, in its multifaceted and loose-bound approach, the authorities have set themselves an enormous organisational challenge. On a practical level, these difficulties made themselves felt on the ground:

> Efforts to provide initial food relief to the 4 million poorest Brazilians ran into a logjam of problems, ranging from finding that many of them were illiterate and had no ID (and thus could not find out about or register for the aid) to local corruption and huge logistical snafus involved in delivering aid to people who live without roads, electricity, phones, or often fixed addresses. (Steffen, 2003)

Whatever the organisational imperfections of Lula's new social programmes, their effectiveness was always going to be limited by available resources. Unfortunately, the budget allocation for social programmes proved not to be as generous as the government had originally anticipated. This was a direct result of the fiscal pressures placed on Brazil by multilateral institutions (in particular the IMF), and the fact that the scope for discretionary spending was otherwise limited by debt servicing, transfers and personnel spending obligations (the latter driven strongly by rises in the minimum salary). It will be recalled that the IMF agreed to a new, more stringent, primary budget surplus target of 4.25 per cent of GDP (the old target having been 3.75 per cent). To achieve this, an extra cut of R$14 billion was required in the federal budget, of which R$5 billion had been destined for social expenditures. Of the latter sum, reductions in education spending contributed R$341 million, health R$1.6 billion, and social security R$247 million. Most surprising of all, given its profile, was the application of a R$34 million cut to the *fome zero* programme (Cruz, 2004).

It will be recalled that the second plank of the Lula administration's explicit anti-poverty agenda surrounded the notion of a family minimum income guarantee. In policy terms, this eventually saw the light of day in the form of the Bolsa Família programme. This programme provides cash transfers of between R$15 and R$95 per month, depending on the level of family income and the scale of previous benefits. Provision of these resources is conditional upon school attendance and the completion of regular medical checkups by children. The numbers covered by this programme have expanded rapidly in recent years, from 3.6 million families in 2003 to 11.1 million in 2006. The evidence regarding the effectiveness of the programme is mixed and somewhat contradictory. However, in Brazil's more disadvantaged regions — especially the north and north-east — the indications are that the programme has made real inroads into tackling extreme poverty (Pães de Barros, 2007). Still, it is important not to overstate the significance of the Bolsa Família since, because of fiscal constraints to be discussed below, its budget allocations have been surprisingly modest. Amann and Baer (2007) estimate that in 2006 the Bolsa amounted to just 2.5 per cent of government spending (or 0.5 per cent of GDP). By contrast, spending on debt servicing amounted to no less than 18 per cent of total government expenditure. This pattern of expenditure is likely to perpetuate income inequalities since the holders of government debt (and hence recipients of interest repayments) are clearly a more numerically concentrated and wealthier group than the beneficiaries of the Bolsa or the other explicit anti-poverty programmes designed by the Lula administration (Amann and Baer, 2007).

Lula's Structural and Fiscal Reforms

One major political and economic success of Lula in the first year of his mandate was the passage of a reform of the social security system. Such a reform was desperately needed. This becomes clear from the scale of social security spending in comparison with other social expenditures. According to Rands (2003, pp. 4–5), during 2002 the state had to allocate no less than R$39 billion to provide for the benefits of civil servants. This compares with total federal spending on

Table 6.4: Brazil: Distribution of Monetary and Non–Monetary Benefits by Income Groups (Deciles — %)

(a) Government Monetary Benefits

	1	2	3	4	5	6	7	8	9	10	Total
Total Benefits	2	3	3	3	5	7	7	9	15	46	100
Pensions	0	1	2	3	4	7	7	9	16	51	100
Unempl. insurance	6	6	8	12	12	9	13	11	14	9	100
Family support*	2	8	11	13	13	12	10	10	9	12	100
Old age support**	7	12	28	14	39	0	0	0	0	0	100
Children support***	35	38	19	7	1	0	0	0	0	0	100

*Abono salarial de salario–familia

** Amparo ao idoso

***Bolsas–escola, alimentação e criança cidadã

(b) Non–Monetary Benefits

	1	2	3	4	5	6	7	8	9	10	Total
Health	17	16	14	12	11	9	7	6	5	3	100
Education	6	6	6	6	5	5	10	12	17	27	100

Source: Rezende and Cunha (2002, p. 95).

health of R$30 billion. The important point to bear in mind is that these social security expenditures are targeted at a very restricted section of the population, that is, 3.5 million public servants and their dependants. In other words, although public expenditure on social security in Brazil may be extensive, its benefits are extremely concentrated. This may be seen in Tables 6.4(a) and (b), which show that the top decile of the income distribution received over half of the pension benefit in 2002. In contrast, the government-run social security system for private sector workers (the Instituto Nacional de Seguridade Social, or INSS) targets fewer resources (R$17 billion) at a much larger client group

(19 million people) (Rands, 2003). Thus, a reform was crucial if resources were to be conserved, but also more equitably distributed.

In December 2003, the Lula government succeeded in having its social security reform Bill passed by both Brazil's Senate and Chamber of Deputies. The reform increased the minimum retirement age for all civil servants; it required retired civil servants to contribute to the social security system if their monthly income exceeded R$1,440 per month; it limited the amount of pensions paid to widows and orphans of civil servants; it placed caps on civil servants' wages and retirement earnings; it placed a maximum cap for the whole civil service; and it set a cap on pensions paid to private sector retirees. In addition, numerous other measures were introduced to control spiralling social security costs.[12]

Over the longer term, these reforms are expected to deliver substantial savings, perhaps as much as R$50 billion in 20 years' time (Rands, 2003). In this sense, the reforms should have the ability to free up resources for alternative social expenditures while at the same time curbing the deficit-generating properties of the social security system. However, the reforms will take some time to have full effect and in this interregnum the government will find itself under continuing and stringent budgetary constraints. Unfortunately for the Lula government, its progress in limiting the growth of the social security deficit will be hampered — at least in the short term — by its raising of the minimum wage.[13] Under Brazilian law, increases in the minimum wage will automatically generate a rise in social security payments, since the latter are in effect indexed to the former. Thus we have a typical recurrence of the efficiency versus equity dilemma. Attempts to rationalise the social security system are constantly being confronted by the equity-based demand for higher minimum wages. A practical consequence of this dilemma is that the government — despite the reforms — is forecasting continued rises in the social security deficit, at least over the short term.[14]

Another major thrust in the government's attempt to achieve structural change consisted of a tax reform package introduced in the first half of 2003. Among the main items were: a unification of the ICMS tax across states (with a reduction in the number of rates from 44 to five), with a gradual shift from a production-based to a consumption-based tax;[15] the cessation of state tax breaks to inward investors; the transformation of the financial transactions tax (CPMF) from a temporary into a permanent tax; the federal compensation of states which issue tax credits to exporters;[16] the reform of the method of collecting the Cofins social security tax by switching the basis of its collection from wages to employers' value-added revenues;[17] and finally, the promotion of capital goods sales and exports by reductions in the incidence of the ICMS sales tax and the industrial products tax (IPI).[18]

While reform of the indirect taxation system was certainly needed in order to boost revenues and promote competitiveness (especially of exports), doubt remains as to whether the current measures are sufficiently extensive or thoroughgoing (Giambiagi, 2004). In addition, there remains the question of whether aspects of the reforms will actually function in practice, not least the provision granting state tax exemptions for exports.[19]

The Core Dilemma of the Lula Government

President Lula came to office with two major goals: the pursuit of a macroeconomic policy orthodox enough to win the approval of the international financial community; and the achievement of a greater degree of socio-economic equity. It seems that this was to be done in a sequential fashion, initially emphasising the former to be followed by the latter. The reason for adopting this sequence was, as mentioned above, that the domestic and international investor community looked on the victory of President Lula as a threat to their interests. Thus, in order to access foreign resources and ease negotiations over the external debt, the pursuit of orthodoxy assumed primacy over equity considerations. Unfortunately, the sequencing adopted may create difficulties. An initial period of economic orthodoxy, because of its effects on growth, might make it very difficult to allow for a subsequent large dose of policies aimed at greater socio-economic equity. That is to say, embarking initially on an orthodox policy path can determine subsequent sets of policies. At the same time, there are reasons to suspect that the pursuit of orthodoxy is not simultaneously compatible with rapid income redistribution. In other words, orthodoxy may not be compatible with rapid redistribution, either in the short term (while the orthodox policies are in place) or in the long term (because they do not give rise to the appropriate growth conditions).

Of course, the initial emphasis on orthodox macroeconomic policy may not necessarily be prejudicial to the realisation (either short or long term) of sharp improvements in equity. As the experience of Chile (and indeed Brazil in the mid 1990s) has shown, orthodox policies, partly because of their ability to rein in inflation, can benefit the real incomes of the poorest in society. At the same time, accompanied by institutional reform and shifts in the pattern of discretionary public spending, the maintenance of tight fiscal policy can be compatible with a redistribution of income favouring the poor. Also, it can be argued that orthodox policies, because they may result in inflation and exchange rate predictability, favour an acceleration in private sector investment. To the extent that this raises growth and creates a more amenable redistributive environment, once again the poor may benefit. However, in the case of contemporary Brazil, we argue that, for a number of reasons, the adoption of an initial emphasis on orthodoxy may not deliver a significantly more equitable outcome either in the short or long run.

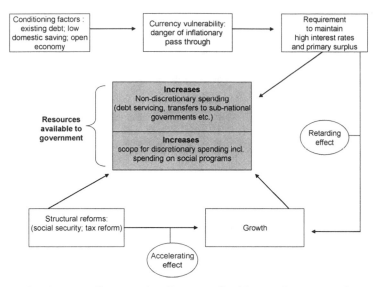

Figure 6.1: Factors influencing the allocation of public spending in Brazil

Is Orthodoxy Compatible with Redistribution? The Short Term

In the short term, the orthodox policies pursued in Brazil have not favoured rapid income redistribution. Still, it may have proved possible to achieve a greater measure of distribution had the government been able to operate in a proactive fashion. Unfortunately, aside from the lags in operation which would attach to any policy, this was not the case for two reasons. The first has to do with the limited scope for discretionary spending, while the second is connected with a failure (within existing spending constraints) for the public sector to intervene more effectively. Our argument regarding discretionary spending is illustrated in Figure 6.1.

In the centre of the figure, the shaded box indicates total resources available to the government, the allocation of which can be divided between discretionary and non-discretionary expenditures. The non-discretionary expenditures comprise contractually determined items over which the federal government has no control. The most important of these are debt servicing and the constitutionally determined transfers to sub-national governments. Discretionary spending would include social programmes aimed at improving equity. The key point to note is that the balance of discretionary versus non-discretionary expenditures will be determined by the macroeconomic policy stance adopted and the success encountered in implementing structural reforms.

Table 6.5: Brazil: Federal Government Expenditures (% distribution)

	1994	1995	1996	1997	1998	1999	2000	2001	2002	2003	2004
Current expenditures	50.0	55.2	53.0	43.8	40.2	38.4	40.6	48.8	50.2	44.1	48.4
Wages and benefits	12.9	16.2	14.2	11.5	9.6	8.8	9.4	10.8	11.1	9.1	9.8
Public debt service	7.1	7.1	6.6	5.4	6.2	7.5	6.3	8.8	8.2	7.6	8.2
Transfers to states and local govts	8.6	9.1	9.0	7.7	7.6	7.1	8.4	10.0	10.8	9.2	10.1
Social security	12.1	13.7	14.2	11.8	10.8	9.8	10.5	12.4	12.9	12.4	13.5
Other current expenditure	9.3	10.0	9.0	7.4	6.0	5.2	6.0	6.8	7.2	5.8	6.8
Capital expenditures	25.7	8.7	9.0	21.7	20.6	15.6	10.5	14.9	14.8	12.5	11.5
Investments	2.9	.2.1	2.0	2.0	1.6	1.2	1.6	2.5	1.5	0.7	1.2
Financial investments	4.4	2.9	4.2	16.4	14.2	9.8	1.8	3.3	3.1	2.6	2.4
Amortisation of debt	18.6	3.7	2.8	3.3	4.8	4.6	7.1	9.1	10.2	9.2	7.9
Amortisation refinancing	24.3	36.1	38.0	34.5	39.2	46.0	48.9	36.3	35.0	43.4	40.1
TOTAL	100.0	100.0	100.0	100.0	100.0	100.0	100.0	100.0	100.0	100.0	100.0

Source: Minsterio da Fazenda, Tesouro Nacional.

Despite improvements in the external balance the Brazilian authorities — to bear down on inflation and maintain support for the real — have been obliged to maintain high real interest rates and to achieve a large primary surplus.[20] Two results of these high interest rates are high debt servicing costs and restricted growth. Thus, discretionary expenditures suffer as the result of a pincer movement comprising of weak revenue generation (the result of low growth) and high debt servicing obligations.

The dilemma discussed above is represented in concrete terms in Table 6.5. The table gives a summary view of Brazil's federal government expenditures. It will be noted that expenditures on amortisation and amortisation refinancing in 2004 amounted to no less than 48 per cent of total government spending.

The data also reveal the limited extent to which amortisation prevails relative to amortisation refinancing. The burden of amortisation refinancing (at 40.1 per cent of total government spending) is, of course, highly sensitive to movements in interest rates. For this reason, it is clearly to the government's advantage to embark on a path of lower real interest rates. However, given the need to adhere to the inflation-targeting framework and to maintain the external valuation of the currency, there are tight limits to the pursuit of such an attractive policy option. Despite reductions in the SELIC benchmark interest rate between 2003 and 2006, Brazil's real interest rates remain very high by international standards.

Turning to current expenditures, it will be noted that public sector debt service, social security spending and transfers to state and local governments are classified as constituting non-discretionary categories of expenditures. Taken together, these spending categories account for 31.8 per cent of total public spending. Combining the relevant items from current and capital expenditures, it will be observed that total non-discretionary spending in 2004 accounted for 79.8 per cent of total expenditure. By contrast, in 1995 (the year after the real was launched) non-discretionary expenditures stood at just 69.7 per cent of the total. Thus, it becomes clear that the government's relative scope for discretionary expenditures narrowed sharply over a relatively short period. Against this background, the constraints which shackle much-needed investment in social programmes become all the clearer.

As mentioned above, it should not blithely be assumed that the imposition of tight, discretionary spending-limiting fiscal policy automatically damages the interests of the poor. It is perfectly possible that, if there were a substantial reordering of priorities within the government's expenditure programme, the poor could benefit while orthodox fiscal policies remained in place. In the case of Brazil, as we have shown, such a reordering has not occurred to any significant extent. Due to institutional and political constraints, the government has been unable to divert resources from the coveted programmes of its congressional backers into areas of social spending such as health and education. To add to these difficulties, we have shown that the design of key poverty reduction initiatives preceding the Bolsa Família was flawed. Moreover, there is evidence to suggest that, for a variety of reasons, several programmes have not spent their full budget allocations.[21]

Having analysed the nature of the government's macroeconomic strategy — that is, the imposition of strict orthodox measures, which would win approval of the international financial community and multilateral agencies — it becomes clear that, at least in the short term, there is only quite limited scope for combining orthodoxy with social development, especially given the unwillingness of the government to switch discretionary spending priorities.

The only forces that might increase growth and allow a breakout from the trap described above are structural reforms, which eventually might be expected to lead to higher growth and accelerated revenue generation for the government. Both of these conditions would provide a favourable environment for redistribution, not least through the enhanced ability of the government to raise discretionary expenditures. Unfortunately, so far progress on the structural reform agenda has been very limited (especially on the spending side),[22] thus impeding enhanced growth performance.

Is Orthodoxy Compatible with Redistribution? The Long Term

We have shown that it has only been possible to a limited extent in Brazil to combine macroeconomic orthodoxy with greater social equity in the short run. This is because of the inevitable policy lags, the direct impacts of restricted growth on the poor, the limited scope for discretionary spending that exists and the failure of the authorities to reallocate spending within existing fiscal parameters. Still, it might be argued that an orthodox set of policies, though not redistributive in the short run, nevertheless may provide the foundations for greater equity over the longer term. We suspect that, for Brazil at least, this may not automatically be the case. The reason for this has to do with the impacts of orthodox policies on long-term growth and, by extension, on the feasibility of redistribution.

The pursuit of income redistribution over the long term will require that Brazil embark on a path of sustained accelerated growth. The reasons for this are twofold. In the first place, it can be argued that higher growth is necessary in order to mop up unemployed labour and to increase the real wages of the poor. Second, the realisation of income redistribution over the long term is likely to be far more fiscally practical and politically feasible within the context of high rates of economic growth. As we have seen, it has proven extremely difficult in Brazil to reorder government discretionary spending priorities within the current straitened fiscal context. If growth accelerated and public revenue rose, the scope for discretionary social investment would increase. On the tax side, a sustained rebound in economic growth would make the pursuit of a redistributive agenda more palatable to those on higher incomes: it is far easier to alter shares in an expanding pie.[23]

However, due to the low rates of public investment in infrastructure and education and private investment in productive capacity,[24] the conditions for sustained future higher rates of growth have not so far been created. As we have shown above, private sector investment has failed to accelerate strongly despite a favourable policy climate, at least in terms of price and exchange rate stability and in terms of the enforcement of property rights.[25] At the same time, we have shown how public sector investment has been severely constrained by the adoption of ambitious fiscal targets. Unless reversed this may seriously compromise the country's future economic growth. More specifically, Brazil's capacity to engage in export-led growth is currently being held in check by chronic under-investment in port and highway infrastructure as well as in electricity generation, transmission and distribution.[26]

To its credit, these profound difficulties have been acknowledged by the Lula administration, the consequence being that in its second term it has announced an ambitious range of schemes designed to bolster infrastructural investment. This package, termed the Programa Aceleração de Crescimento (PAC), aims to promote investment worth R$503.9 billion between 2007 and 2010. In stimulating investment, the emphasis has been placed on the provision of tax incentives to the private sector. Still, some increases in direct public sector expenditure on investment are envisaged. Were the programme to succeed in enabling Brazil to grow at consistently higher rates, the implications for equity in the long run could be quite favourable. However, at the time of writing, great uncertainty surrounded the eventual growth impacts of the PAC.

A particularly serious shortcoming of the present configuration of public spending is the consistent failure to accelerate spending on education and training. This has two implications. First, through its negative impact on productivity growth, educational under-investment constrains potential output growth and international competitiveness. As we have argued, this will hamper efforts to redistribute income. Second, under-investment in education and training has very direct distributional consequences in that, increasingly in a service-led economy, income flows to individuals will be determined by the amount of human capital embodied in each.

So far it has been argued that, in the case of Brazil, the pursuit of orthodox policies has constrained investment, and as a result the future potential for growth and redistribution. Is it, however, always the case that orthodox policies have such effects? While the case of Ghana, for example, lends support to this conclusion, the experience of Chile shows that, under certain circumstances, the pursuit of orthodoxy can provide a springboard for a subsequent acceleration in growth. In explaining the more favourable experience of Chile, it is worth noting that, while fiscal and monetary orthodoxy were the order of the day, there were also substantial structural supply-side reforms (Marcel and Solimano, 1994). These embraced labor market deregulation,[27] thorough reform of capital markets and encouragement of higher domestic savings through the partial privatisation of pension provision. These developments, which have yet to occur in Brazil, contributed to a surge in private sector investment and economic growth. It is also worth noting that Chile has long — pre- and post-orthodoxy — offered more comprehensive access to education than Brazil.

Conclusions: The Continuing Dilemma

In January 2003, President Lula came to power with two goals: the pursuit of social justice and a commitment to economic orthodoxy. Over the course of this chapter, we have argued that, so far at least, these two objectives have only proved partially compatible. While the government has done a credible job of continuing the market-based policies it inherited from the previous administration (and thus earned high marks with the international financial community), this has been at the cost of not achieving marked improvements in key social objectives, such as higher real wages and greater equity in the distribution of income and assets. Of course, it may be argued that the adoption of an orthodox macroeconomic stance forms a necessary foundation upon which future attempts to tackle Brazil's deep-rooted social problems can be based.

However, we have shown that the impact of tight fiscal and monetary policy in practical terms is to constrain the authorities' scope to expand discretionary expenditures that might favour the poor. While structural reforms have the potential to counter this tendency, thus far they have been limited in scale and even, according to their proponents, are expected only to have a limited — and delayed — effect. More fundamentally, it should be recognised that fiscal and monetary orthodox, to the extent that they restrict investment in infrastructure and human capital, will inevitably limit the growth potential of the economy. Thus, the notion that orthodoxy in macroeconomic policy represents a necessary precondition for accelerated growth in some future period, needs at least some critical re-evaluation. In other words, Brazil runs the risk of being caught in a trap in which social problems remain under-addressed despite ostensibly sound macro-economic and fiscal performance.

It should also be noted that a high rate of economic growth does not automatically result in an improvement in a country's income distribution. For instance, in the miracle high-growth years of the Brazilian economy (1968–73), the income distribution did not even out to any extent. Indeed, there was evidence of increased concentration (Baer, 2001, pp. 78–81). In the case of the Mexican economy, it is also clear that the high concentration of income has persisted throughout periods of both stagnation and high growth (Lustig, 1998). However, it is undoubtedly the case that attempts to redistribute income will be politically more palatable in an economy experiencing sustained high growth. We have argued that the failure of such growth to materialise in contemporary Brazil — or for the foundations for such growth so far to be laid — means that the resolution of the distributional question remains a distant prospect.

Therefore, as the Lula government advances towards the conclusion of its mandate, it remains faced with a fundamental dilemma: the need to simultaneously maintain economic respectability within a globalised international financial system, while attempting to remedy the country's grave socio-economic disparities. Of course, it should not be pretended that redistribution is impossible in a situation where orthodox policies are followed and modest growth prevails. However, to repeat our point, attempts to redistribute under these circumstances will probably be far more challenging since they are more likely to involve some groups in society losing out in absolute terms. In order for redistribution to occur in this context, considerable political will is necessary — but this has seemed lacking throughout the Lula government's term.

References

E. Amann and W. Baer (2003), 'Anchors Away: The Costs and Benefits of Brazil's Devaluation', *World Development*, June.

E. Amann and W. Baer (2006) 'Economic Orthodoxy Versus Social Development? The Dilemmas Facing Brazil's Labour Government', *Oxford Development Studies*, vol. 34, no. 2, pp 219–41.

E. Amann and W. Baer (2007) 'The Macro-economic Record of the Lula Administration, the Roots of Brazil's Inequality and Attempts to Overcome Them', paper presented at the 2007 Congress of the Latin American Studies Association, Montréal, Canada, 5–8 September.

J.L. Bachtold (2004) 'Os lucros dos bancos', *CMI Brasil*, 18 February, available from www.mediaindependente.org.

W. Baer (2001) *The Brazilian Economy: Growth and Development*, 5th ed. (Westport, CT: Praeger).

Banco Central do Brasil (2003) 'Social Security Reform', *Focus*, 18 December.

Banco Central do Brasil (2004) *Boletim*, February.

Bloomberg (2004) 'Brazil Bankruptcy Law Could Increase Bank Lending', 28 June.

D. Cruz (2004) 'Primeiro Ano de Governo Lula aprofunda desemprego,' *CMI Brasil*, 1 January.

O Estado de São Paulo (2003) 'Lula lança Bolsa-Família com verba indefinida', 21 October.

Economist Intelligence Unit (2004) *Brazil Country Report*, 1st Quarter.

Exame (2005) 'Para dar um novo salto', Julho, p. 40–43.

IPEA (2003) *Boletim de Conjuntura,* Dezembro.

IPEA (2004) *Boletim de Conjuntura,* Março.

F. Giambiagi (2004), 'A procura de uma nova agenda', *Conjuntura Econômica,* Janeiro.

F. Giambiagi (2005) 'Estabilização, reformas e desequilíbrios macroeconómicos: Os anos FHC', in F. Giambiagi et al. (eds.), E*conomia Brasileira Contemporânea (1945–2004)* (Rio de Janeiro: Editora Campus).

C. Kassis and A. Girolami (2004) 'Brazil's Challenge', *Latin Finance,* October.

S. Kuznets (1971) *Economic Growth of Nations: Total Output and Production Structure* (Cambridge, MA: Harvard University Press).

N. Lustig (1998) *Mexico: The Remaking of an Economy,* 2nd ed. (Washington, DC: The Brookings Institution).

M. Marcel and A. Solimano (1994) 'The Distribution of Income and Economic Adjustment', in B. Bosworth (ed.), *The Chilean Economy: Policy Lessons and Challenges* (Washington DC: The Brookings Institution).

A. Minella, P. Springer de Freitas, I. Goldfajn and M. Murinhos (2003) *Inflation Targeting in Brazil: Constructing Credibility Under Exchange Rate Volatility* (Brasília: Banco Central do Brasil).

O Globo (2005) 22 de Junho.

R. Pães de Barros et al. (2007). *A Importância da Queda Recente da Desigualdade na Redução da Pobreza,* IPEA Texto para Discussão no. 1256.

Partido dos Trabalhadores (2002) *Programa de Governo 2002.*

Programa Fome Zero (2003) *Balanço de 2003.*

M. Rands (2003) 'Brazil Under the Government of President Lula — Social Security Reform: Will It Work?' mimeo (Brasília: Brazilian National Congress).

F. Rezende and A. Cunha (2002) *Contribuites e Cidadãos: Compreendendo o Orçamento_Federal* (Rio de Janeiro: Fundação Getulio Vargas).

A. Steffen (2003) 'Fome Zero', in *World Changing: Another World Is Here,* 4 December, available from www.worldchanging.com/archives/000168. htm.

R. Thorp (1998) *Progress, Poverty and Exclussion: An Economic History of Latin American in the Twentieth Century* (Washington: Inter-American Development Bank).

Vej (2005) 29 de Junho, p. 58.

Notes

[1] We would like to thank Leonard A. Abbey, Jorge Paulo Lemann, Peri Silva and two anonymous referees for valuable help and comments. Edmund Amann would like to acknowledge the financial support of the Leverhulme Trust. An earlier version of this chapter originally appeared as 'Economic Orthodoxy Versus Social Development? The Dilemmas Facing Brazil's Labour Government', *Oxford Development Studies*, vol. 34, no. 2 (2006).

[2] The equity-efficiency trade-offs are best demonstrated in the works of Simon Kuznets: see, for instance, Kuznets (1971).

[3] Partido dos Trabalahadores or Labor Party.

[4] The document explicitly criticises previous governments for the fragmented and clientalistic nature of their anti-poverty programmes: 4 December, Partido dos Trabalhadores (2003, p. 39).

[5] For more detailed information on *fome zero*, see Programa Fome Zero: Balanço de 2003.

[6] A policy which has become known as the 'Bolsa-Familia' (family grant). This is supposed to provide R$50 to each family whose monthly income falls below R$50 plus R$15 for each child less than 15 years old. Families whose monthly income lies between R$50 and R$100 are simply to receive R$15 per child under the age of 15. *O Estado de Sâo Paulo*, 21 October 2003.

[7] *O Estado de Sâo Paulo*, 21 October 2003, p. 13 and Banco Central do Brasil, *Boletim*.

[8] For more details on the January 1999 devaluation and its consequences, see Amann and Baer (2003).

[9] IPEA (December 2003).

[10] For more information, see Amann and Baer (2003).

[11] *The Economist*, 14 August 2003.

[12] *Banco Central do Brasil Focus*, 'Social Security Reform', 18 December 2003.

[13] In June 2004, the Lula government used all of its political power to force through Congress an increase in the minimum wage of only R$260 in opposition to substantial pressure from across the political spectrum for an increase to R$275.

[14] *IPEA Boletim de Conjuntura*, 2004 (March), p. 58.

[15] ICMS (Imposto sobre Operações Relativas á Circulação de Mercadorias e sobre Serviços — Tax on Goods and Services). This is a state-based sales tax.

[16] CPMF (Contribuicâo Provisório nos Movimentos Financeiros — Provisional Tax

on Financial Movements). This is a federal tax on financial transactions popularly known as the 'check tax'.

[17] Cofins (Contribuição para o Financiamento da Seguridade Social — Tax for Financing Social Security).

[18] For greater detail, see Gustavo Rangel, *Barclays Capital Research*, 15 August 2003.

[19] The key problem here is the lack of appropriate inter-governmental transfer mechanisms to compensate states for lost revenues.

[20] It will be recalled that the inflation-targeting framework severely limits the discretion of the authorities to pursue a more lax monetary policy in the event that inflationary pressures are rising. Such a scenario may well (and has) come to pass after an episode of currency weakness.

[21] This was not due to the anxiety of individual ministries to behave in a fiscally responsible way, but rather to the politics of PT ministers making expenditure decisions.

[22] Especially reforms that would prioritise social investment ahead of pandering to special interest groups.

[23] Within the context of rapid economic growth, there can be redistribution without making anyone worse off in absolute terms.

[24] Brazilian investment as a portion of GDP has remained subdued, oscillating around the 19% mark. In China, by contrast, the rate of investment is currently around 40% of GDP (*Exame*, Julho 2005, p. 40). In the case of Brazilian industrial investment, this declined from 18.8% of value-added in 1998 to 15.2% in 2003 (*O Globo*, 22 June 2005).

[25] However, regulatory uncertainty, most especially in the electricity sector, can be argued to be hampering investment.

[26] Many structural bottlenecks will have to be overcome: 80% of Brazil's highways were classified as 'deficient', 'bad' or 'terrible' by a government commission; railroads, which carry only 24% of Brazil's cargo with 28,000 kilometres of tracks, needed dramatic improvements in infrastructure. Seaports are also notoriously expensive and inefficient compared to their East Asian counterparts. Average port costs are estimated for Brazil at US$41 per ton versus US$18 for the United States. In Santos, Latin America's largest port, 30 containers can be loaded in one hour versus 100 in Singapore. To deal with such deficiencies, the government in December 2004 instituted a public private partnership (PPP) programme. This allows for the private provision of infrastructure services under contract to the government, which in turn guarantees the purchase of such services for a specific time period and for a specific price. The advantage of this arrangement is that investment can take place (financed by the private sector) without the need to resort to scarce public sector capital investment funds (*Latin Finance*, October 2004).

[27] Chile's natural resource-based export sectors were particular beneficiaries of labour market reforms and became magnets for FDI.

PART III

TAX REFORMS AND OTHER POLICY ISSUES

7

THE STRUGGLE FOR TAX REFORM IN CENTRAL AMERICA[1]

Manuel R. Agosin, Roberto Machado and Aaron Schneider

Weak Economic Growth

Much like the bigger countries of Latin America and the Caribbean, during the 1950s and 1960s economic growth in the five countries that comprise the Central American Common Market (CACM) — Costa Rica, El Salvador, Guatemala, Honduras, and Nicaragua) — had been quite brisk and certainly faster than in the industrial countries. The initial switch from a growth process led by integration into the world economy producing mainly foodstuffs (with coffee, bananas, meat and sugar predominating) to import substitution on the basis of national markets gave way in the 1960s to an emphasis on regional integration as the main impulse to economic growth. This forward movement peaked during the 1970s. Disputes of various kinds among the members of CACM, and the beginning of long-lived civil wars and armed conflicts, caused the integration process to grind to a halt. So did economic growth. While regional integration was later taken up again as a policy objective with the advent of peace in the 1990s, it was a half-hearted affair, with only modest progress toward the adoption of a common external tariff and the removal of other barriers to regional trade, such as the removal of internal customs.

Growth has been lacklustre since 1990, a watershed year with the advent of peace in the region and the consolidation of market-oriented reforms.[2] In fact, with the partial exception of Costa Rica, the region has continued to diverge from the levels of income of the industrial countries. This can be seen in Table 7.1, which shows the levels of per capital GDP in purchasing power parity as a share of the same in the United States. While Costa Rica has kept pace with the industrial leaders, the other countries in the region have continued to fall behind.

As can be seen in Table 7.2, the rates of growth of GDP per capital have been very modest since 1990, and substantially slower than during the heyday

Table 7.1: Per Capita GDP in CACM Countries, Relative to that of the United States, 1975–2006 (in US current PPP dollars)

	1975	1980	1990	2000	2006
Costa Rica	29	28	22	24	25
El Salvador	23	18	13	13	13
Guatemala	17	17	12	12	11
Honduras	12	13	10	8	8
Nicaragua	30	18	10	9	9

Source: World Bank, World Development Indicators Online.

Table 7.2: Per Capita Growth of GDP in CACM Countries, 1960–2006 (average annual percentage rate)

	1961–70	1971–80	1981–90	1991–2006
Costa Rica	2.8	3.0	–0.2	2.7
El Salvador	2.2	–0.2	–1.5	1.8
Guatemala	2.7	3.0	–1.5	1.3
Honduras	1.5	2.1	–0.7	0.9
Nicaragua	3.4	–2.8	–3.8	1.5

Source: World Bank, World Development Indicators Online.

of import substitution. In other words, in spite of substantial liberalisation of their economies (including the lowering of external tariffs, the liberalisation of banking and finance, and the privatisation of numerous state enterprises), these countries have failed to even replicate their growth performance during a period (1960–80) marked by considerably more government intervention.

There are, of course many reasons for this unsatisfactory performance. But one of them is undoubtedly the inability of governments to provide basic public goods needed for the private sector to respond more positively to the stimuli emanating from the international economy. The region remains backward with respect to infrastructure, education and health. Indicators in these areas are considerably poorer than what one could expect for these countries' level of development.

The countries of Central America urgently need to increase public investment and social spending. This is the only way to accelerate growth, generate employment and reduce poverty, yet the governments of the region fail to mobilise the necessary resources and apply them well. Tax revenues are among the lowest in the hemisphere, providing scant resources to assist the poor and promote growth. This situation calls for the design and implementation of comprehensive fiscal reforms, which would address deficiencies in tax legislation and administration.

Unfortunately, these reforms have only partly advanced. Despite important changes in each of the countries of the region, there is still much work to be done. Two challenges need to be highlighted. First, the countries of the region need to make strides towards harmonising fiscal systems within the region and with international markets, to ease what inevitably will be a difficult deepening of market integration as a result of free trade agreements. Second, international actors need to resist the temptation to press for short-term fiscal bargains. Tax competition and loosened social regulations are two of the typical sweeteners sought by investors, yet a wiser strategy would take a longer term perspective of sustainable investment and social change backed by reasonable tax contributions.

The paragraphs that follow describe some of the pressing needs for comprehensive reforms, will outline some of the recent steps taken by governments in the region to mobilise greater resources and point out the shortcomings that remain to be addressed.

The Pressing Need for Reform

It will be difficult for Central American countries to grow at a more rapid rate without significantly increasing their tax burdens and their spending as a proportion of GDP.

Tax revenue in Central America absorbs between 10 and 14 per cent of GDP, with public expenditure between 10 and 18 per cent.[3] These rates are low compared with what would be expected in economies with the structural characteristics of Central American countries.

Table 7.3: Fiscal Deficit and Public Debt, 2001–05 (% of GDP)

	Fiscal Deficit					*External Debt*	*Internal Debt*
	2001	*2002*	*2003*	*2004*	*2005*[a]	*2005*[ab]	*2005*[ab]
Costa Rica	2.9	4.3	2.9	2.8	2.8	18.6	36.0
El Salvador	3.6	3.1	2.7	1.1	2.9	33.1	13.1
Guatemala	1.9	1.0	2.3	1.0	1.4	13.5	4.3
Honduras	6.0	5.3	5.6	3.1	3.0	61.6	4.1
Nicaragua	7.5	2.5	2.8	2.2	2.0	61.3	26.3

[a] Preliminary data.

[b] As of 31 December 2005.

Source: CEPAL, International Monetary Fund, and official sources.

In addition to the need for greater social spending and public investment, there are two reasons to mobilise greater resources in Central America. First, in recent years most countries of the region have presented chronic fiscal deficits, producing a significant and dangerous increase in public debt (Table 7.3).

With the exception of Guatemala, all of the countries have built public debts above 45 per cent of GDP, well above widely accepted thresholds for small, open economies like those in Central America. Estimates by the Inter-American Development Bank (IADB) suggest that only Guatemala has a sustainable level of debt.

There are essentially two routes to improved debt sustainability, and they both lead through fiscal balance and macroeconomic stability. Interestingly, one route calls for low taxes and low spending, securing debt sustainability but limiting developmental change. The second route applies similar taxes and spending to secure debt sustainability but at higher levels, which provide fiscal room for investment, social protection and development. There are obviously limits to the ceiling of public revenues and spending before they crowd out private activity, but with average revenues around 12 per cent of GDP, none of the countries of Central America is even close.

Guatemala is perhaps the typical example of the low tax-low spend route to debt sustainability. Its government presents the lowest fiscal deficits in the region and its public debt has remained the lowest in the region, less than 20 per cent of GDP. This has been sustained with a tax burden that is among the lowest in the region and the world (along with Panama), oscillating between 9 and 10 per cent of GDP. The inadequacy of this model for long-term development is evidenced by the persistence of extreme poverty, weak infrastructure, and vulnerability to shocks such as those presented by natural disasters, like Hurricane Stan during 2005. The tax system simply generates too few resources.

All of the countries in the region require comprehensive fiscal reform, and this urgency has only increased with the impending fiscal loss associated with the inauguration of the Central American Free Trade Agreement (CAFTA). In those countries that have passed complementary legislation, the treaty has already entered into force, implying losses from trade taxes estimated between 0.3 and 0.7 per cent of GDP in 2010 (see Barreix et al., 2004).

To address these losses, the countries of the region will need to seek additional resources from other tax bases. Yet domestic tax handles are typically difficult to seize, especially in the context of states that are widely considered to make poor use of citizens' resources. This environment of mistrust is aggravated by the lack of transparency and accountability in public finance institutions in each of the countries. In the following paragraphs, attention will be paid to the degree to which the countries of CACM have met these challenges.

Table 7.4: Tax Revenues, 2004 (% of GDP and proportion of total revenue)

| | Revenues (% GDP) | | Proportion of the Total | | | | | | | | | |
| | | | Income | | VAT | | Excise | | Trade | | Other[b] | |
	2004	2005	2004	2005	2004	2005	2004	2005	2004	2005	2004	2005
Costa Rica	13.0	13.2	28.5	28.8	36.6	36.4	24.0	24.0	8.2	8.3	2.7	2.5
El Salvador	11.5	12.6	25.5	27.7	45.4	45.7	3.5	3.9	8.4	7.5	15.0	15.2
Guatemala	10.1	9.5	26.0	27.9	46.6	45.1	11.6	6.6	11.6	16.4	4.2	4.0
Honduras[a]	10.1		21.8		33.3		27.6		7.8		9.5	
Nicaragua[a]	14.5	15.0	23.1	23.6	33.3	33.9	20.4	19.5	5.0	5.4	18.2	17.6

[a] Corrected for under-estimation of GDP.

[b] Includes smaller taxes that vary by country.

Source: Authors' calculations, based on studies done for the Inter-American Development Bank.

Tax Systems in the Region

As shown in Table 7.4, tax revenue in Central America absorbs between 10 and 14 per cent of GDP. Tax burdens — as well as total expenditures and expenditures on health and education as a share of GDP — are low compared with what would be expected in economies with the structural characteristics of Central American countries.

This statement is the result of an econometric analysis of tax revenue, total public expenditure and public expenditure on education and health care throughout the world as a proportion of GDP, and the relative ranking of the countries of the region. All variables were measured in the late 1990s, but the situation has hardly changed since then. The differences between countries in terms of tax revenue and public expenditure are explained by the variation in GDP per capita (measured in purchasing power parity) and by the income distribution as measured by the Gini coefficient. As per capita income rises, so does the tax burden and public expenditure, because the higher a country's income, the greater its capacity to finance public expenditure and basic social spending. It is also reasonable to expect that the demand for public expenditure by the population will vary in direct relation to per capita income and inversely with income inequality. The latter hypothesis assumes that the more egalitarian the distribution of income, the greater the influence of the middle income segments in economic and social policy decision-making — and it is precisely these latter groups that demand social public services.[4]

The results support these hypotheses. In the estimated model, the fiscal variables normalised on GDP are adequately explained by GDP per capita and the income distribution variable (Gini coefficient). Two hypotheses were expounded in the text: tax revenue and public expenditure as a proportion of

GDP vary both directly with per capita income, and inversely with inequality in income distribution. The results, calculated for the late 1990s using World Bank (2004) data, can be summarised as follows:

$$T/Y = \underset{(0,18)}{1,45} + \underset{(5,20)^{**}}{3,97\log YPC} - \underset{(-4.93)^{**}}{0,36\ GINI} \qquad (1)$$

Adjusted R^2 = 0.469; Number of observations = 95. Figures in parentheses correspond to the t-statistic; an asterisk indicates that the coefficient in question is statistically significant at the 5 per cent confidence level, and two asterisks indicate significance at the 1 per cent level.

$$G/Y = \underset{(2,42)^*}{19,50} + \underset{(3,57)^{**}}{2,66\log YPC} - \underset{(-4,42)^{**}}{0,36\ GINI} \qquad (2)$$

Adjusted R^2 = 0.307; Number of observations = 120.

$$GSAL/Y = \underset{(-3,54)^{**}}{-4,36} + \underset{(9,67)^{**}}{1,10\log YPC} - \underset{(-3,19)^{**}}{0,039\ GINI} \qquad (3)$$

Adjusted R^2 = 0.555; Number of observations = 121.

$$GED/Y = \underset{(0,44)}{0,74} + \underset{(3,49)^{**}}{0,54\log YPC} \underset{(-1,12)}{-0,02\ GINI} \qquad (4)$$

Adjusted R^2 = 0.138; Number of observations = 120.

The variables are defined as follows:

T/Y	=	tax revenues as a proportion of GDP (Y)
YPC	=	GDP per capita
$GINI$	=	Gini coefficient of income distribution
G/Y	=	total public expenditure as a proportion of GDP
$GSAL/$	=	public expenditure on health as a proportion of GDP
GED/Y	=	public expenditure on education as a proportion of GDP

In all equations, GDP per capita appears as highly significant in explaining the behaviour of fiscal variables. The Gini coefficient is also significant in all equations except (4), which explains the variations between countries in public expenditure on education. Naturally, this model is extremely parsimonious. An attempt was also made to include a variable that would measure natural resource wealth (exports of minerals as a proportion of total exports), but this

*Figure 7.1: Central American Countries: Expected and Observed Tax Revenue,
Late 1990s (% of GDP*

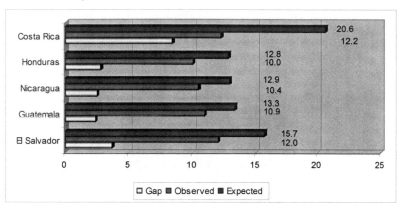

Source: World Bank, World Development Indicators, official national figures and authors'
       calculations.

proved not to be significant. The possible endogeneity of the Gini coefficient
with respect to GDP per capita (as suggested by Kuznets' inverted-U) does not
cause problems of multicollinearity that invalidate the results obtained.

The comparison between observed tax burdens and the tax burdens
that would result from these countries' income levels and Gini distribution
coefficients are shown in Figure 7.1. The 'expected' levels of tax burdens, of
course, assume that the econometric model from which they are derived is
the 'correct' one. However crude these calculations may be, they do provide a
fair indication that these countries do need to raise the level of tax revenue to
GDP.

Using the same methodology, it is easily shown that Central American
countries spend too little on health and education. As is shown in Figures 7.2
and 7.3, with the exception of Costa Rica in the case of health expenditures,
all other countries in the region have observed levels of social spending that are
considerably lower than those that can be predicted by plugging into equations
(3) and (4) the values for their per capita GDPs (in PPP terms) and their Gini
income distribution ratio.

To attend to social spending and public investment needs, these levels of
collection are insufficient, and there is significant room to expand revenues.
In fact, revenue expansion is highly feasible without creating new taxes or
increasing rates. A recent IADB publication estimates that tax collection in
Central America could increase by three to four percentage points of GDP
simply by expanding the tax base (see Agosin et al., 2005).

Figure 7.2: Education Expenditures as a Share of GDP, Observed and Expected, c. 2000 (%)

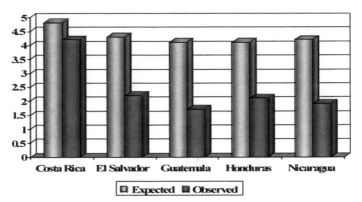

Source: Authors' calculations, based on World Bank, *World Development Indicators Online.*

Figure 7.3: Health Expenditures as a Share of GDP, Observed and Expected, c. 2000 (%)

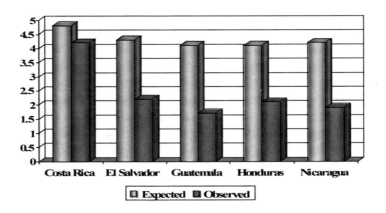

Source: Authors' calculations, based on World Bank, *World Development Indicators Online.*

The most important taxes are the income tax, value-added tax (VAT), excise taxes (referred to as "selective consumption taxes") and trade taxes. In the case of excises, their importance to overall revenue is principally related to the tax on fuels.[5]

With respect to trade taxes, the 1990s has seen a consistent reduction in their importance as a result of trade liberalisation in almost all countries of the region. This reduction will be accentuated by the coming into effect of the CAFTA. The only country that has not yet ratified CAFTA is Costa Rica; in the other four countries, tariff reductions mandated by CAFTA are already being implemented.

Over the past two decades, the reduction in revenue brought about by trade liberalisation was compensated for by significant increases in VAT. VAT rates have risen from between 5 and 10 per cent to around 12 and 15 per cent. While there is some further room for increasing VAT rates, that room is rapidly diminishing. As we shall argue below, any further revenue from VAT ought to come from broadening its base rather than raising rates.

Given the declining role of trade taxes and heavy reliance on excises, most advisable tax reforms should concentrate on the other two important taxes: income and VAT. In general, the personal income tax (PIT) is not unified and has different schedules for each type of income. In addition, there exist a large number of exemptions according to income source (insurance, interest, dividends and other financial income and capital income). In practice, this creates significant room for tax avoidance (and evasion) and complicates the task of tax authorities. In effect, almost the entirety of the income tax burden falls on salaried workers within the formal sector, greatly distorting vertical and horizontal equity and weakening revenue effectiveness.[6]

In addition, personal income is defined on a territorial basis, such that income generated outside national borders is not taxed. Though international income is difficult to trace, it is increasingly relevant as income flows across ever more fluid borders. The principle of worldwide income would close current avenues of evasion and allow greater instruments of control to revenue authorities.

The tax on corporate income (CIT) also presents a slew of subjective exonerations for protected or favoured sectors, such as agriculture or tourism, and for foreign firms installed in tax-free zones. An additional characteristic of CIT in several countries is the presence of accelerated depreciation

Table 7.5: Corporate income tax rates, 1986–2004 (% of gross profits)

	1986		1992		July 2004	
	Min.	Max.	Min.	Max.	Min.	Max.
Costa Rica	0	50	30	30	30	30
El Salvador	0	30	0	30	25	25
Guatemala	0	42	12	34	25	25
Honduras	0	55	0	40	15	25
Nicaragua	0	45	0	35	25	25

Note: Minimum rates exclude tax exemptions given for development purposes.
Source: Gómez Sabaini (2005).

regimes.[7] Such an instrument is appropriate only in particular circumstances as an incentive to investment, and therefore calls for only a temporary status. When accelerated depreciation becomes permanent, as has occurred in several countries, it loses its utility as an attraction for investment and becomes simply a ruse for lowering tax rates.

As elsewhere in the world, legal corporate income tax rates have been coming down in Central America. As can be seen from Table 7.5, they are now between 25 and 30 per cent of gross corporate income. This is probably still on the high side for countries that do need investment. However, very few firms pay these legal rates. The large number of exemptions for 'development' purposes — for firms in export processing zones and for firms engaged in tourism, and so on — implies that tax rates could be considerably lower if all firms paid them. Not only could countries garner more revenue by lowering rates and eliminating exemptions, horizontal equity would also improve, since those who are able to obtain exemptions are usually the larger and better connected firms.

As a result of current privileges, taxable net income from declared PIT and CIT obligations is significantly lower than gross income. This provides evidence of the appreciable erosion in the tax base that implies significant revenue losses. Further, the porous and unequal income tax regime is partly responsible for low levels of revenue in the region.

With respect to the VAT, erosion of tax bases, economic distortions, inequality and the complication of administration result from two problems characteristic of the region: excessive exemptions and the use of the zero rate.[8]

Several goods and services are commonly exempt from VAT, such as products in the basket of basic consumption goods, transportation, medical and educational services, financial and insurance transactions and energy and

Figure 7.4: VAT Yields in Central America and Chile, Early 2000s (%)

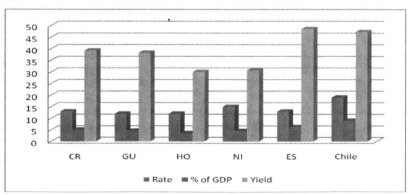

Source: Gomez Sabaini (2005).

fuel. As occurs for income tax, aside from these universal exemptions applicable to all, there are also particular exonerations for specific categories of agents (NGOs, cooperatives, non-profits, etc.), the agricultural sector and firms in tax-free zones.

These exemptions create distortions as a result of abuse by those with access to exempt goods as well as the complications created for tax administration. In addition, these problems are worsened by the application of the zero rate to goods produced for the domestic market. For exports, a zero-rated VAT makes sense to avoid prejudicing domestic producer competitiveness, against the exports of other countries. On the other hand, when the zero rate is applied to goods consumed domestically, it both erodes the tax base and creates an important avenue for tax evasion.

As a result of these practices, VAT yields (estimated as the share of revenues from VAT to GDP divided by the legal rate) are very low in Central America. A reasonable VAT yield is around 50 per cent. As shown in Figure 7.4, the only country that is close to that benchmark is El Salvador. Interestingly, only El Salvador has a flat rate with no exemptions or zero-rated items. El Salvador's VAT yield is almost the same as Chile's, which also has a flat rate applicable to all goods with very few exceptions.

The point of this discussion has been to suggest that the tax systems of the region share some basic deficiencies: they have too many loopholes, which create incentives for taxpayers to avoid payment and complicate administration, so that countries fail to mobilise sufficient revenue. There are national particularities, but the basic story is the same. The basic story of reform efforts over the last few years is also basically the same — each country has taken some important steps, but these are far from sufficient and frequently followed by backsliding and reversal.

Recent Reforms

In recent years, several countries have implemented partial tax reforms that, in general, have pointed in a positive direction. In Costa Rica, an ambitious fiscal reform project, which had been in discussion in the Legislative Assembly since 2002, was approved by the Legislative Assembly in February 2006. However, it was declared unconstitutional by the Supreme Court in March due to non-compliance with some legal procedures in passing the law. Currently, the law is being presented again for parliamentary approval but divided in parts. The main tax components of the law move towards broadening existing tax bases, such as extending VAT to services, and introducing principles of worldwide income and global income. Corporate income tax exemptions in export processing zones would be eliminated and tax rates unified for all business firms, with few exceptions allowed for firms proving they are adding to the country's productive potential. But these would be temporary and not permanent as previously. And these exceptions would take the form of lower rates rather than outright exemptions. The estimated impact of such a reform would be an increased collection of 1.5–2 per cent of GDP.[9]

In El Salvador in October 2004, a series of tax measures were approved, fundamentally aimed towards combating evasion and smuggling through strengthening mechanisms of control and tax compliance.[10] The measures also reduced the range of admissible deductions to income tax and increased the rates of excise on alcoholic beverages and cigarettes. In 2005, these measures generated one percentage point of increased tax as a percentage of GDP, increasing tax collection to 13.2 per cent of GDP. Significant increases were recorded in revenues from excise taxes (27.4 per cent with respect to 2004) and from income taxes (23.7 per cent).

In June 2004, a series of measures were also approved in Guatemala; the main elements were the modification of the corporate income tax and the reintroduction of excise tax on alcoholic beverages. The measures also introduced the Extraordinary and Temporary Tax to Support the Peace Accords (IETAAP in Spanish); this substituted for the Tax on Merchant and Agribusiness Firms (IEMA in Spanish), which was declared unconstitutional by the Supreme Court at the start of this year. Both taxes operated as a minimum payment for the corporate income tax based on the gross assets of firms. This is not a bad idea in countries with weak accounting standards, where corporate income is anything the firm wishes to declare. In fact, many firms report losses for years on end — a fact that is, of course, impossible if they are still in business. The IEMA attempted to close this loophole. However, one problem that made it unpopular with business firms was its very high rate. The rates of the IETAAP are substantially lower than of the IEMA, and they are applied temporarily and decreasing with time.[11] In 2005, tax collection had slightly reduced as a proportion of GDP, bottoming at 9.9 per cent. In 2006, legislation increasing penalties and strengthening monitoring and auditing powers of the tax administration were passed, though their impact has not yet been felt.

In Honduras, the Tax Equity Law (LET in Spanish) was passed in 2003, which modified the income tax, VAT and excise structure.In the case of income tax, the law expanded the definition of taxable income by limiting deductions for bonuses and business expenses, and incorporating as income the common end-of-year bonus payments for the 13th and 14th months of wages that are higher than 10 minimum salaries in taxable income. In addition, a tax was introduced at the rate of 1 per cent of gross assets as an anticipated minimum payment on the corporate income tax, except in those firms with assets lower than L\$3 million (approximately US\$165,000), firms in export processing zones, and firms exempt from payment of corporate income tax (mining and tourism). In the case of the VAT, the taxable base was broadened to those goods and services that had been exempt. Finally, the rates of excise paid on cigarettes was raised from 32.25 to 45 per cent (and to 47.5 per cent at the start of 2004), tax on fuels (overturning the excise and import tax) was consolidated to a per gallon price, and was earmarked to social programmes and road maintenance. These measures generated an increase in collection of 1.5 per cent of GDP between 2002 and 2004. In 2005, tax collection had reached 17.7 per cent of GDP, 0.3 percentage points higher than in 2004.

In May 2003, the Fiscal Equity Law (LEF in Spanish) was passed in Nicaragua, limiting the use of zero-rated items on the VAT (previously labelled the General Sales Tax) to exports and 57 goods included in the basic consumption basket. In addition, the law broadened the application of VAT to services in general. At the same time, the reforms broadened the base for the calculation of personal taxable income and introduced a 1 per cent tax on gross assets of firms as a minimum payment towards the corporate income tax. Between 2002 and 2004, tax collections increased from 13.5 to 15.5 per cent of GDP, and by 2005 had reached 16 per cent. Unfortunately, many of these advances have gradually been eroded by the penchant of the Legislative Assembly, with the connivance of the executive, to continue to grant new business tax exemptions. One of the latest is a new law to promote tourism, by which reinvested profits in tourism industries are exempted from tax. Not only are such tourism industries defined rather broadly but the very existence of this incentive is a huge loophole and lends itself to abuse.

To summarise, each of the countries has undertaken some measures of tax reform that generally point in the same direction. Reforms simplify rates and bases, and mobilise revenues mostly by expanding the tax base. In only a few cases have increased rates been used to mobilise greater revenue. Further, in each country there has been some slippage from original proposals. Increases in revenues have been modest so far, and in some cases, like Guatemala, they have been quickly eroded by legal challenges from key sectors.

What Needs to Be Done

This discussion has focused on the current status of tax systems in Central America. The region continues to be characterised by governments that mobilise paltry resources and, as a result, have little to spend on social investment and infrastructure. Most of the discussion has highlighted the confusing and distorting system of incentives, bases and rates that apply to income tax, consumption tax and excise taxes. In the context of increasing integration and the prospect of continued decline in trade taxes, the inefficiencies in the tax regime for other bases will have to be addressed. Each country has taken some positive steps, but in many cases advances have been limited and/or rolled back. In short, there is need for significant and comprehensive reform in all of the countries of the region.

The following basic outlines seem appropriate:

- Introduce the concept of global personal income by taxing financial income and capital income in a manner similar to the tax on salary income.
- Introduce the concept of worldwide income by taxing income independently of where income was generated.
- Introduce limits on admissible deductions from personal income tax such as medical, educational and other expenses.
- Eliminate corporate income tax exemptions and other preferential treatments.
- Unify corporate income taxes across the economy, ensuring that the resulting rate is reasonable.
- Introduce systems to track transfer prices and enter double-taxation treaties with countries that provide foreign direct investment.
- Eliminate accelerated depreciation regimes and introduce criteria for weak capitalisation.
- Eliminate use of the zero rate for value-added tax, except in the case of exports.
- Restrict value-added tax exemptions to basic needs goods.

A few of these measures have been introduced already, but several are particularly difficult. The introduction of corporate income tax in export-processing zones and the tracking of transfer prices are two examples. Introducing corporate income tax, effectively eliminating current exemptions, would have to be undertaken in a coordinated fashion by all the countries at once. Failure to do so would create opportunities for investors to switch to free trade zones in countries that maintain the exemptions, creating an incentive to each country to back out of any agreement to coordinate their corporate income tax rates. The result has not only been a maintenance of exemptions, but an even more perverse pattern of interstate competition, in which countries race to the bottom by providing ever greater subsidies, weakening regulations such as labour and environmental legislation and its enforcement, and continuing with exemptions. On the other hand, an impetus to greater cooperation has emerged as the result of a World Trade Organization determination that all countries will have to eliminate preferential treatment on corporate income tax by 2009.

In the case of transfer pricing, the difficulties arise mostly because of the complexity of the task. Training for tax administrations in modern techniques of accounting as well as business practice is necessary to manage oversight of transfer pricing practices. Further, effective information sharing with countries of origin of foreign direct investment is necessary to verify claims of transfer pricing and agree upon measures to avoid double taxation.

In both cases, responsibility for improvement lies in several camps. First, and most obviously, the tax administrations of the countries of the region have to improve. Without the administrative capacity to implement these regulations, legal changes are meaningless. Second, the tax laws have to be simplified and made more effective, to weaken the incentives to avoid and evade payment and to ease the work of tax administration. Finally, international investors, and the governments of the countries from which they hail, need to work harder at promoting an investment and development climate in Central America. Pursuit of immediate tax holidays, incentives and exemptions may serve profit in the short run, but they starve governments of needed resources and weaken the environment for long-term investments and growth.

References

M. R. Agosin and A. Barreix y R. Machado (eds.) (2005) *Recaudar para crecer. Bases para la reforma tributaria en Centroamérica* (Washington, DC: Inter-American Development Bank).

A. Alesina and D. Rodrik (1994) 'Distributive Politics and Economic Growth', *The Quarterly Journal of Economics*, vol. 109, no. 2, pp. 465–90.

A. Barreix, J. Roca and L. Villela (2004) 'Impacto fiscal de la liberalización comercial en América', *Integración y comercio en América. Nota Periódica* (Washington, DC: Inter-American Development Bank).

J. C. Gómez Sabaini (2005) 'Evolución y situación tributaria actual en América Latina: Una serie de temas para la discusión', paper prepared for the UN Economic Commission for Latin America, September, Santiago, Chile, unpublished.

Notes

[1]   The authors are, respectively, Professor of Economics, Universidad de Chile; Economic Affairs Officer, United Nations Economic Commission for Latin America and the Caribbean; Assistant Professor of Politics, Tulane University.

[2]   The peace agreements came in stages. While the major regional peace accords were signed in 1988 at the initiative of President Oscar Arias of Costa Rica, El Salvador achieved a lasting peace only in 1992, and Guatemala's formal Peace Accords had to wait until 1996.

[3]   Correcting for the underestimate of GDP in Nicaragua and Honduras — a phenomenon that is well known by specialists in the subregion. For a discussion of this underestimate in Honduras, see UNDP (2000, Ch. 3). Estimations made

by one of the authors of this article, based on an analysis of all existing data, show that GDP in Honduras and Nicaragua would have to be corrected by at least 40% and 70%, in that order, to bring it close to its real level. After several years of work, the Central Bank of Nicaragua raised its GDP estimate by 63% in the national accounts revisions of 2003. The Central Bank of Honduras has not yet published its revisions.

4   Note that this theoretical outline contradicts the influential model developed by Alesina and Rodrik (1994), which postulates that tax revenue is greater the more unequal is the income distribution. Those authors use a median-voter model that finds a correlation between voter preference for higher taxes and smaller stocks of physical and human capital among the majority of the population (precisely where the income distribution is most unequal). The statistical data do not support this theory, however. On the contrary, they are consistent with our theoretical approach.

5   For example, in Honduras taxes on fuels represented 67% in Honduras of the total excise taxes in 2004.

6   Horizontal equity implies that contributors with similar ability to pay contribute equally. Vertical equity implies that those with higher incomes pay proportionally more.

7   The allowance for accelerated depreciation allows firms to discount from their taxable income by the corporate income tax all amounts above the normal depreciation of capital goods, recuperating more quickly their original investment.

8   The application of the zero rate operates by returning the VAT paid on inputs to producers of tax-exempted goods.

9   The original proposal would have generated from 3–3.5% of GDP, but several modifications to the original project have diluted its impact. These include maintaining VAT exemptions for some goods that are not in the basic consumption basket, reducing the rate of the VAT applicable to professional services from 10 to 6%, and the maintenance of lower rates on income tax for favoured sectors.

10   The measures approved included a more precise definition in the penal code of tax crimes, the increase in penalties for such crimes, access by authorities to the bank accounts of individuals under investigation, and the increase in the power of customs officers, among others.

11   The IETAAP applies a rate of 2.5% on the assets or gross sales of firms, whichever is greater. The rate is set to fall to 1.25% in 2005, to 1% in 2006 and 2007 and to zero from 2008. The rates of IEMA, by contrast, were 3.5% of assets or 2.25% of sales, depending on the choice of the firm.

8

SOCIO-ECONOMIC CHANGE AND FISCAL CHALLENGES IN CENTRAL AMERICA: GLOBALISATION, DEMOCRATISATION AND THE POLITICS OF REFORM

Aaron Schneider

Paradoxically, as globalisation and liberalisation free factors of production from national constraints, territorially bounded states have become more important than ever. Where governments fail to adapt to changing circumstances, they are overwhelmed, and a growing category of failed, rogue and narco-states have emerged. Of particular interest, therefore, is the way the end of the twentieth and beginning of the twenty-first century have seen countries rearticulate to the global economy in a region once assumed failed. That region is Central America, where civil war and economic crisis in the 1980s have been followed by a new outwardly oriented development model, the emergence of social groups associated with that model, and new democratic political regimes (Oxhorn and Starr, 1999, p. 10).

To sustain themselves, the governments of the region must find ways to tap into new sources of wealth, but they must ensure that the amount extracted and the way it is extracted do not stifle economic actors. This requires technically sound fiscal policies. Often overlooked, however, is the fact technical strategies must also be politically viable. Governments will be unable to mobilise resources from emerging sectors if they cannot also politically incorporate also emerging economic and social actors. Yet, political incorporation is no easy task, as already established actors frequently crowd the political arena, long excluded citizens seek entry, and scarce resources intensify the struggle for access.

This paper explores the way in which political institutions of the five Central American countries have evolved to mediate changing socio-economic circumstances. The countries are undergoing similar socio-economic patterns, but their political systems vary from the relatively stable, 100-year old party system in Honduras to the chaotic, fragmented party system in Guatemala, in which parties emerge and disappear in the space of an election. Based on a political economy analysis, the paper explores the options for fiscal reform in each country, focusing on options to coax revenue from potentially conflicting social groups.

The relationship between politics and public finance will be teased out below. The first section discusses the twin challenges of globalisation and democratisation as they are translated into political life, with a close look at the party systems of each country as an indicator of the way these two fundamental structural challenges are filtered by local political context. Close analysis of party systems offers a window into the nature of political confrontation and political alliance in each country, thereby setting the boundaries to potential reforms. The reforms of interest here are discussed with respect to the current fiscal systems in the region, which evolved over time to fit prior patterns of global integration, and are now inadequate to new processes of accumulation. Finally, the paper uses the political economy analysis of each context to describe the obstacles to reform as well as to interpret successful episodes of reform in each country.

The Central American Model of Globalisation

In the past decade, economic actors in Central America reoriented themselves to productive relations that spread across borders. This was expressed in the rising economic weight of several sectors: manufacturing assembly, non-traditional agricultural exports, tourism, natural resource extraction, and remittances.

Two trends bear this out. First, the countries of the region have expanded their exports significantly. Export earnings in Costa Rica increased by 3.97 times, in El Salvador by 5.83 times, in Guatemala by 3.22 times, in Nicaragua

Table 8.1: Composition of Export in Goods, Value Added, US$ million

	Traditional		Non-traditional		Maquila		Tourism	
	1990	1999	1990	1999	1990	1999	1990	1999
Costa Rica	33.8	18.6	46.5	40	5.7	22.5	14	18.9
El Salvador	47.4	17.9	46.2	50.8	3.5	18.9	2.9	12.3
Guatemala	41	30.8	43.1	43.3	2.6	8.7	13.4	17.2
Honduras	72.7	20.7	20.5	41.2	3.5	29.3	3.3	8.8
Nicaragua	76.4	47.3	20.1	28.6	0	8.5	3.5	15.7

Traditional exports by country: Costa Rica — banana, coffee, meat, sugar; El Salvador — coffee, sugar, shrimp; Guatemala: banana, coffee, cardamom, sugar, oil; Honduras — banana, coffee, wood, packaged meat, silver, lead, zinc, sugar; Nicaragua — coffee, cotton, sesame, sugar, meat, shrimp, banana, gold, silver.

Source: Agosín et al. (2004, p. 45).

by 4.75 times, and in Honduras by 2.96 times. The amounts are impressive; Costa Rica now exports goods valued at US$7012 million, El Salvador US$3394 million, Guatemala US$3805, Honduras US$3114, and Nicaragua US$1862.

Second, the countries of the region have shifted their export profiles. According to Agosín, Machado, and Nazal (2004), the value added in exports rose during the 1990s in El Salvador, Honduras, and Nicaragua. The *maquila* sector boomed everywhere, providing $29.3 million in Honduras, and tourism rose everywhere, providing $18.9 million in Costa Rica. Table 8.1 shows increases in the main categories of exports during the 1990s.

What is most relevant about these newly emerging sectors is that their expansion changes the way in which people work and live. As truly internationalised chains of value, they extract, transform and market materials in the sites that provide the greatest returns, regardless of geographical location. For all citizens, the greatest gains to their livelihoods are to be made by tapping into these production chains. For those with physical and human capital, they can act as providers and intermediaries to these transnational chains, acting as local counterparts to finance and produce goods destined for the United States. For many more, it means leaving the countryside and entering cities or migrating to the United States, where their labour provides far greater returns. Others who largely existed on the margins of national economic life, such as women and indigenous groups, now find their land and lives rapidly absorbed into these chains of value.

For example, women accounted for over 80 per cent of *maquila* workers in the early 1990s. This has increased their participation in the labour force from a low of 12 per cent in Guatemala and Honduras in 1950 to 36 and 40 per cent in the same countries in 2000. The greatest increases occurred during the 1990s, when women's labour force participation jumped by 15 percentage

Figure 8.1: Women's Labour Force Particpation (% of EAP)

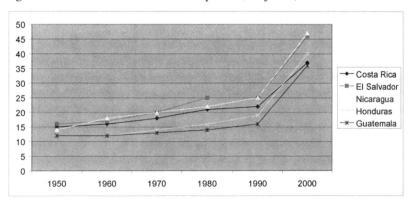

points in Costa Rica, 21 in El Salvador, 22 in Nicaragua, 28 in Honduras and 24 in Guatemala. As a result of their new insertion into formal sector economic activity, women's issues — long ignored — have gained political import as women's organisations, social movements and non-traditional labour organisations now constitute important actors within the urban context. The same can be said for long-excluded indigenous groups in Guatemala, and other excluded populations newly integrating to market processes.

These changes in economic structure and social formation pose multiple challenges to the states of the region, in which they must both mobilise resources from newly emerging economic sectors and politically incorporate newly emerging social actors.

Political Divisions in Central America

These challenges are being met by newly democratic regimes. Globalisation presents relatively similar challenges to each country: all have to deal with the rise of economic sectors associated with globalisation, and all have to deal with the nature of political incorporation in democratic societies. Still, the two challenges appear with different intensities; they are interpreted in different ways; the legacies of prior incorporations differ; sequences vary; and the strategic choices of social actors receive local twists. As a result, the precise nature of political conflict varies across countries.

There is a rich literature that attempts to link social and economic change to patterns that ossify in national politics (Lipset and Rokkan, 1990, p. 14; Lijphart, 1984). In terms of the twin crises facing Central America in the 1990s, two of the patterns identified by Herbert Kitschelt (1992) in Eastern Europe are the most similar. Like Central America, Eastern Europe was a peripheral region undergoing simultaneous economic opening and political transition. Kitschelt suggests that partisan conflict in Eastern Europe during the 1990s could be understood as a multidimensional conflict over inclusive versus exclusive citizenship and market versus political distribution of resources (1992, pp. 12–13).[1]

The first of these dimensions, the nature of liberal citizenship, has long been an issue in Central America (Booth and Seligson, 1989). The fall of authoritarian regimes opened a host of local and national spaces for contestation, and in the process excited individual and social movement activism (Escobar and Alvarez, 1992). In day-to-day politics, this cleavage is expressed in concerns about corruption, human rights, minority civil rights, military involvement in politics, and democratic participation in public life. For the purpose of the current discussion, this cleavage will be referred to as the inclusiveness of democracy, in which citizens divide in preferences for more inclusive and more exclusive practices.

The second cleavage is an attempt to come to terms with market relations under globalisation. This cleavage is familiar to those who have studied Central America in the past, in which groups identify with more or less market orientation in economic affairs and thereby divide along a left–right cleavage (Yashar, 1997; Mahoney, 2001; Reuschemeyer et al., 1992).

The existence of two dimensions of significant political importance opens room for a variety of different political combinations (Roemer, 2001). As the dimensions of cleavage get expressed and perceived, and as ideological positions get defined, seemingly opposed groups may find themselves allies. Structural processes set in motion changes to political systems, but within these structural constraints there is room for agency by political elites and social actors to influence the way incorporation occurs (Mahoney and Snyder, 1999).

A great deal of literature has explored party systems to understand the way structural and political cleavages are translated into divisions among the political elite, and thereby into the political system. What is at stake here is how differently structured political elites affect the process of policy-making, presenting obstacles to the adoption of reforms that will sustain state administrations in the face of challenges posed by democratisation and globalisation. Implicitly, the project works with a theory of state-building, in which sustaining the state requires political elites to enter into binding agreements with emerging actors, coaxing revenues from them in exchange for access to policy and provision of public services (Levi, 1988; Moore, 2004). Where the political elite is fragmented, polarised or otherwise unstable, it will be unable to establish lasting linkages to key sectors of society.

In highly unequal societies like Central America, the task of state-building is even more complicated. Where rising groups can gain access to the state, they tend to be loath to contribute revenues, preferring to use the state to repress demands for public services, especially if those services target underprivileged groups. This calls for a theory of state-building that is not solely based on exchange — pay for what you receive — but rather based on countervailing power (Galbraith, 1952). Rising groups need to be politically incorporated if the state is to fund itself, but they cannot be granted sole power over policy-making. They need to be wrapped into coalitions with under-privileged and marginalised groups, creating a balance in which rising elites accept their responsibility to pay for the privilege of prosperity, while under-privileged and marginalised groups accept access to policy in exchange for membership in the coalition (Lieberman, 2003).

Most attempts to promote policy change do not incorporate such political analysis, and they tend to fail. Reformers bring in world-class experts and devise sophisticated reform plans. Yet the best laid technical solutions and the highest paid consultants are worth nothing, as they usually do not tailor their advice to local political circumstances (Easterly, 2006), nor do they understand the challenge of cross-class coalition-building.[2]

Central American Party Systems

Data on the parties of Central America are scarce, but the Instituto de Estudios de Iberoamerica and Portugal of the University of Salamanca, Spain has provided a database of political elites (Sáez, 1998). The survey was carried out in 1998, and it includes a sample of 17 national legislatures, among them the legislatures of Central America.

The survey applies a questionnaire of 260 questions to national legislatures, with 49 legislators surveyed in Costa Rica, 64 in El Salvador, 70 in Nicaragua, 71 in Honduras and 79 in Guatemala. The sample includes all the major parties from each of the countries.[3]

From the survey, 10 questions were selected as particularly useful indicators of opinions on the two dimensions of cleavage. The exact questions can be found in the Appendix. As a way of aggregating these questions and deriving scales to position the parties on each dimension of political competition, the project conducted factor analysis on the data from each country.[4]

For three reasons, the project identifies scores for each party on the left–right and exclusive–inclusive dimensions. First, there are strong theoretical reasons to suggest these are the two dimensions most relevant to current politics in the region; second, the 10 questions were selected as indicators of these two dimensions; and third, we are most interested in the different ways party systems translate these two issues for local contexts. Factor loadings for each question on each dimension are reported in the Appendix.

In all five countries, two factors appear to organise the data best: Left–Right Polarisation and Inclusive–Exclusive Democracy. The score of each party on each dimension can be obtained by aggregating multiple measures and creating factor scores, the average score of legislator responses from each party weighted according to factor loadings of the variables. For ease of comparison, the scores have been rescaled on a scale from zero to 10 that indicates where each party positions itself.[5]

Further, based on the standard deviation of responses for legislators from each party, we can generate a measure of the diversity across legislators from a single party. Thus, we can map both the party position and how disciplined its members are in holding that position, at least in their survey responses. Finally, we can make use of the size of each partisan delegation to gauge its relative weight within the political system.

In the graphs below, the size of the circles reflect the average proportion of seats held by parties over the last three elections. To indicate party position, circles have been centred at the factor score of each party on each dimension, in which parties farther to the left are leftist and to the right are rightist. Parties located lower are inclusive and those located higher are exclusive.

The standard deviation of legislator responses along each dimension is indicated using the cross-hatch. Wider and taller cross-hatches indicate more diversity among the responses of legislators within a party; narrower and shorter cross-hatches indicate more cohesion. The sections below discuss the results for each country, supplemented with qualitative detail to help describe each country context.

El Salvador

El Salvador has settled into a system of stable but polarised conservatism (Stanley, 1996; Paige, 1997). The main left party, the Farabundo Marti National Liberation Party (FMLN), and the right-wing Republic National Alliance (ARENA) dominate the party system, while fringe parties such as the Christian Democrats (PDC), Democratic Convergence (CD) and National Conciliation Party (PCN) occupy minor positions of pressure and patronage.

These patterns are borne out in the responses to the legislator survey (see Figure 8.2). On average, FMLN representatives had a score of 1.65 on the left–right scale, far from their ARENA colleagues, who averaged 8.13. In terms of inclusive–exclusive democracy, the FMLN was slightly more exclusive (4.90 vs. 3.64). Looking within parties at the standard deviation of the responses, the spread of legislator responses in the cross-hatch was fairly broad along both dimensions, though the standard deviation of responses on the left–

Figure 8.2: El Salvador

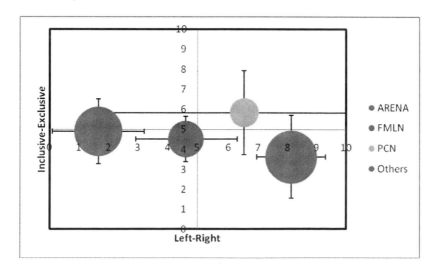

right dimension still did not extend very close to the centre for either party. These measures confirm the impression of El Salvador as a highly polarised environment in which the chief political opponents are consistent in their ideological conflict. On average, ARENA claimed close to 40 per cent of the seats and the FMLN close to 35 per cent, leaving only 25 per cent or so to be divided among additional parties.

Among these additional parties, the PCN located itself right of centre on economic issues and was more exclusive in its orientation towards democracy. It held a not-insignificant proportion of seats, gaining around 11 per cent on average, and it makes sense to consider this party slightly less right wing than ARENA, as it has traditionally been more interested in the trappings of power and patronage than the ideological project of market liberalism.

The traditional foil to the PCN was always the Christian Democrat party, the PDC (Baloyra-Herp, 1983, pp. 295–319), but unfortunately the data from the Christian Democrats (PDC) and the Democratic Convergence (CD) were absorbed into the 'Others' category. As a result, it is difficult to know exactly how much each contributed to the position of the final bubble. Based on what we know more generally about these two parties, one might surmise that CD, as a group that splintered from the FMLN over issues of democratic participation and ideological moderation, might be located slightly to the right and be more inclusive than the FMLN on the graph, while the PDC, which opposed the PCN but was not unwilling to ally with the military during the 1980s, would be located to the left of the PCN but probably close to the same in terms of exclusiveness. The data allow us to map only an average position, which appears between these two positions.

In sum, Salvadoran conservative hegemony confronts a polarised and organised Leftist opposition. Neither side is particularly inclusive, and the right advances its programme by adopting an exclusive approach to democracy in alliance with patronage-oriented elites from smaller parties.

Nicaragua

In Nicaragua, the legacy of 50 years of patrimonial, dynastic rule under the Somoza family and a decade of socialist experimentation under the Sandinistas bequeathed a legacy of exclusive democracy, in which left–right polarisation, while intense, takes a back seat to jockeying for power.

For most of the 1990s, the two main parties, the Liberal Constitutionalists (PLC) and the Sandinistas (FSLN), dominated the party system. Smaller parties, such as the Sandinista Renovation Movement (MRS), occupy a small but important number of legislative seats (Cué, 2001), and a number of upstarts have attempted to draw on the original coalition that defeated the Sandinistas in 1990, such as the PCN, PRONAL and UNO-96. The current

Figure 8.3: Nicaragua

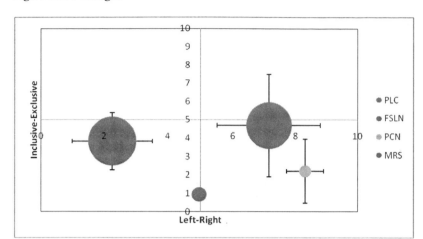

Left-Right

split within the PLC was driven by the National Liberal Alliance (ALN), a reformist movement that came in second in the 2006 elections.

The legislator survey offers a useful illustration of some of these patterns (see Figure 8.3). On average, FSLN representatives had a score of 2.25 on the left–right scale, far from their PLC colleagues, who averaged 7.16. In terms of inclusive–exclusive democracy, PLC representatives offered slightly more exclusive responses (4.69 vs. 3.83), though neither party was particularly inclusive. This reflects the patronage orientation to which both parties have gravitated over time, driven by their leaders, and helps explain how two supposedly polarised parties could form a governance pact in which they would agree to divide the institutions and spoils of government.

Looking within parties, both show a significant spread among the responses of representatives, though two interesting observations can be made. First, the PLC is extremely diverse internally, with standard deviations of 1.65 on left–right issues and 2.80 on inclusive–exclusive issues. The FSLN also shows a wide spread, and it is noteworthy that the spread was somewhat broader on inclusive-exclusive issues.

The wide spread on the inclusive–exclusive dimension suggests one of the reasons the MRS splintered from the FSLN. Many of the deputies from the MRS emerged within the ranks of the FSLN and split off when they saw their colleagues operating to support patronage networks. The MRS scores extremely inclusive at 0.94, though its left–right position is directly in the centre, at 4.96.

Unfortunately, the ALN did not have representation during the 1998 and 2002 legislatures, as the party emerged entirely from within the PLC. In the data, one might conclude that the ALN effectively split the PLC bubble in two along the vertical axis. Those right-wing actors who favoured a more inclusive democracy turned to the ALN, and those associated with patronage networks stayed with the PLC. For the current legislature, which is essentially divided into three between the ALN, PLC and FSLN, one can expect continued confrontation between the ALN and PLC over the right-wing mantle. The FSLN will surely continue its practice of allying with one, then the other, in an attempt to keep them divided.

In sum, Nicaragua displays a high degree of left–right polarisation, but both major parties are well towards the exclusive end of the spectrum. As a result, they are able to enter into agreements to share the spoils of office, and the left has won the presidency by playing its alliance strategy to split the right into two camps.

Honduras

In Honduras, the two main parties, the Liberal (PL) and the Nationalists (PN), are over 100 years old and occupy fairly similar centre right ideological positions. Both include elements of more inclusive, citizenship-oriented leadership, but both continue to draw their greatest support from exclusive clientelist bases tied to the parties through particularist benefits. The system prevents significant polarisation or fragmentation as parties moderate their left–right ideological positions. At the same time, the tendency towards clientelist appeals and exclusive democratic practice weakens any attempt to deepen democracy or undertake significant reforms. To fill some of the policy space left open by the large parties, smaller parties have emerged, but they do not garner enough support to weigh heavily in legislative votes or to shift the policy debate.

These tendencies are borne out in the responses to the survey (see Figure 8.4). On average, Liberal Party representatives had a score of 4.20 on the left-right scale, not far from their National Party colleagues, who averaged 6.51. In terms of inclusive–exclusive democracy, the two parties were virtually identical (5.20 vs. 5.48). Looking within parties at the standard deviation of the responses, the spread of legislator responses in the cross-hatch was fairly broad along both dimensions, suggesting that the parties do not concentrate their political appeal, nor do they hold their legislators to particular policy preferences. The relatively large size of both the PL and PN circles indicates their basic duopoly over representation, together accounting for over 94 per cent of the seats.

The responses of legislators from the smaller parties place them extremely close to the ideological positions of the major parties. The Christian Democrats (PDCH) and the Social Democrats (PINU-SD) both scored slightly to the left of the traditional parties, 2.93 and 2.71. The PINU-SD was equally exclusive

Figure 8.4: Honduras

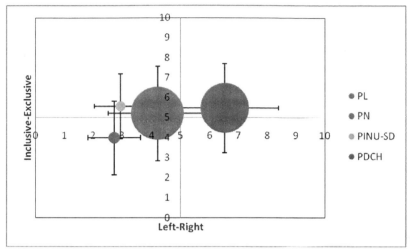

(5.55), and the PDCH emerged as slightly more inclusive (3.98), though the ideological spread of both parties was significant, suggesting a poor ability to articulate a coherent ideological message. The one party whose legislators have presented a coherent ideological message, the Democratic Unity Party (PUD), was unfortunately absent from the survey. Had its representatives been included, one might expect them to occupy a position towards the bottom left of the issue space.

In Honduras, the two traditional parties have continually shared the centre of the left–right spectrum, and both maintain patronage networks that allow them to govern unspectacularly while fending off satellite parties, mostly challengers from the left.

Guatemala

The chief characteristic of the Guatemalan political system is fragmentation and volatility (Castañeda, 1990). New social forces have been unable to displace actors established under prior political and economic models, and the degree of democracy and the nature of economic liberalisation remain highly insecure (McCleary, 1999). In terms of party system dynamics, the most obvious tendency is towards cycling majorities. No social sector or political elite enjoys dominance, and each attempt by one group to define the nature of democratisation and globalisation for Guatemala is met by the seemingly coordinated efforts of the rest of the political elite to drag the system back to a fragmented and frozen status quo.

This chaos makes it difficult to use survey statistics to characterise the two critical dimensions of democratisation and economic issues, yet several patterns emerge (see Figure 8.5). First, multiple parties occupy similar ideological positions. On average, representatives from ANN and UNE both occupied slightly centre left positions (3.82 and 3.65) and FRG and PAN occupied slightly centre right positions (6.17 and 6.18). The PP appeared somewhat in the middle of these two groupings, at 4.59, but it too was clustered with the rest. Only the URNG, the revolutionary movement turned political party, deviated significantly from the rest, occupying a position at the extreme left of the spectrum, though its small size meant it remained somewhat marginalised.

A second observation is that there was an extremely limited range of responses on the inclusive–exclusive dimension. This could produce certain anomalies in measurement, such as the ANN legislators favouring more exclusive democracy than the patronage-oriented FRG. In addition, it offers evidence that none of the parties is particularly inclusive, perhaps a signal that none has attempted in any significant way to address the chief element of exclusion in the Guatemalan polity: the failure to effectively incorporate the indigenous majority.

Looking within the parties, a few tendencies emerge. The spread of legislator positions on the inclusive–exclusive dimension was wide for all the parties, suggesting a range of opinions and lack of definition for any party. On economic issues, there was a similar amount of deviation within parties for most cases, though it would appear that the UNE is fairly disciplined internally in occupying a centre left position. The one party that showed the least internal deviation was the URNG, perhaps because of the legacy of military hierarchy,

Figure 8.5: Guatemala

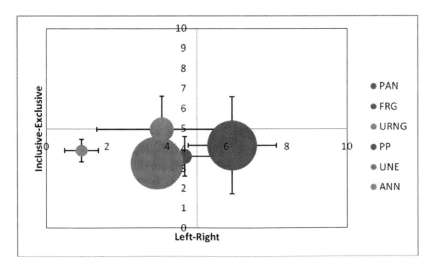

and perhaps because many of its members who might have considered deviating have long since left their ranks for the ANN and UNE.

In Guatemala, the end of civil war has generated a cycling majority, in which alternative alliances of leftist, centrist and rightist groups compete for dominance, but each ends up facing a coalition of the rest and fragmenting internally.

Costa Rica

In Costa Rica, a stable two-party system has undergone a radical realignment in recent years. Since the civil war of 1948, the country has enjoyed the longest unbroken period of democratic rule in Latin America. The main party to emerge from that civil war, the PLN, occupied the centre left of the party system and established a welfare state that incorporated formal sector workers and middle sectors in both the urban and rural sectors. This coalition dominated the party system until 1982, winning every presidential election except two, and controlling the legislature. Opposition parties generally remained split between several centrist and leftist options, but coalesced behind the rightist social Christian platform of the PUSC, and a two-party system operated until 2006. During this period, the PUSC and the PLN averaged close to 80 per cent of legislative seats (Sanchez, 2003, p. 126).

Facing off against the PUSC, the PLN moved rightward and the PUSC won consecutive presidential victories in 1997 and 2001. Yet governance proved destructive for the PUSC, as its leaders moved in a more exclusive direction, closing decision-making and falling prey to corruption. The party practically disappeared in 2006. Its legislative representation fell to five seats, and its presidential candidate polled a distant third to the winning PLN candidate and a new centre left partisan force, the PAC.

It is unfortunate that the survey results are not available from the current legislature. Such responses would evidence the severe decline of the PUSC, and its replacement by a left of centre and inclusive option in the PAC. Essentially, the PAC absorbed support from both the PUSC and the PLN, occupying the space indicated in the graph by the FD. The overall pattern from the Costa Rica figures is consistent with the nature of the two-party system that consolidated from 1982 until 2005, with an opening for an inclusive and centre-left PAC (see Figure 8.6).

First, there is a clear position of the PLN and PUSC clustered around the centre of the ideological spectrum. Each occupies a sizeable portion of the legislature, between 30 and 40 per cent, and each occupies a similarly moderate position on both economic and political issues. PUSC was farther to the right on economic issues (6.07 versus 3.67), but they were approximately the same on democratic issues (5.60 and 5.29). If the survey had been taken later, two

Figure 8.6: Costa Rica

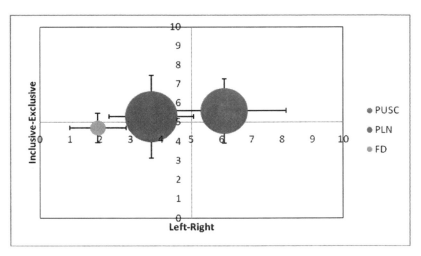

things would have been evident. First, the PUSC would have been much smaller, shrinking almost to nothing in the most recent elections. Second, the PUSC rapidly and inexorably moved towards a more exclusive democracy during its two administrations in power, from 1998 to 2005. Both administrations were wracked by corruption, as the party was unable to manage governing and accepting more transparent and democratic oversight.

As the PUSC declined, the PAC emerged to take its seats in the legislature. Interestingly, the PAC did not simply fill the vacated PUSC space to the right of centre. Instead, the PAC has absorbed most of the support for the small leftist parties, some of the more inclusive and left centre elements of the PLN, and the more inclusive elements within the PUSC. As a result, the PAC takes the position that the FD, PALA and PIN occupied in the lower left quadrant of the ideological space. As a result, any survey of current legislators would surely show the PAC averaging the positions of the FD, PALA and PIN on the left–right dimension (between 1.91 and 4.65) and the inclusive–exclusive dimension (between 0.00 and 4.70).

In Costa Rica, the centrist two-party stability of the last decades has disappeared, as the centrist parties have moved rightwards and in a more exclusive direction. This has opened room for a significant opposition on the left favouring more inclusive democracy.

Obstacles to Fiscal Reform in Central America

How can countries with vastly different political contexts respond to structural and fiscal challenges that are remarkably similar? The answer can only be generated if we understand the nature of the obstacles to reform in each country. Economic and structural shifts in the countries are largely similar, driven by globalisation and democratisation. The fiscal challenges to the region are also largely similar, as all countries have to adjust fiscal systems that were adequate to statist development strategies but are inadequate for a liberalised, export-oriented model.

Yet each country displays a unique political context. Local conflict reflects the broad structural conflicts posed by democratisation and globalisation, in which national contexts filter the specific confrontations, coalitions and patterns of conflict. Beyond the technical obstacles to fiscal reform, daunting in each case to be sure, national political systems present obstacles that are relatively unique to each country. Each national reality will require a reform strategy that is tailored to the local actors and institutions.

Understanding the political systems makes it possible to devise strategies that can overcome the obstacles to fiscal reform. If this is to happen, one must first consider the difficulty of reform. Fiscal reforms vary in their degree of difficulty; some imply a bigger change of a more drastic nature with more complex details, while others are simpler, more gradual and more limited (Haggard and Nelson, 2005, p. 473). Expanding an existing programme — such as extending pension benefits to rural workers once urban workers have already been covered — might be expensive, but it hardly implies an inherently difficult process. The administrative mechanisms exist and the political agreements are established; they just need to be expanded. Similarly, other reforms can be undertaken with minimal difficulty, such as adding projects to an existing programme, extending a programme from one region to another, or moving an established policy from one level of government to another.

Slightly more difficult, creating a new agency requires greater tact and timing. A new bureaucracy has to be created, and its relationship to other actors has to be negotiated. More difficult still is when a reform implies a change in the fundamental rules of governance. Altering the way bureaucracies and interest groups do their business is likely to engender outright opposition. The reform has to be more thought out, and the strategy of implementation better designed, as some are likely to object to relearning their responsibilities.

Even more difficult are reforms that impose new costs. Raising taxes, either by expanding bases or raising rates, implies a new set of costs for political and social actors to negotiate. Those who must pay new costs will oppose such reforms, and that opposition must be overcome.

Retracting benefits that have already been granted represents perhaps the most difficult reform. Once benefits are extended, interests form around defending them; people join organisations, establish institutions and codify laws; they then come to identify with them — perhaps even perceive them as rights. Any attempt to withdraw the benefits implies an attack not only on material interests but on core moral identities.

These differences in the level of difficulty of reform have to be kept in mind as one devises a reform strategy. At certain moments, it may be possible to undertake large and difficult changes, such as immediately after an election, when political capital is high and citizens are willing to grant government certain time to implement new policies.

In Central America, some of the fiscal reforms imply large changes, imposing a new cost on actors who have never paid such costs in the past. Property taxes, which are negligible in all the countries, have been pressed by USAID, the IMF and other international donors, but arouse vehement opposition each time they are considered.

In Guatemala in 2006, the government faced a choice between a difficult set of reforms that would have raised rates, expanded bases and established new sources of revenue, or a more limited administrative reform that would increase the penalties for tax evasion and improve the bureaucratic capacity of tax administration. Pressure to pursue one or both of these measures increased as Hurricane Stan revealed corruption and incompetence in government responsiveness to social needs and reconstruction expenses opened a gaping hole in public finance. Complicating matters, tax receipts fell below 10 per cent of GDP, far below the measly 12 per cent that had been agreed at the 1996 Peace Agreement that ended the civil war and the 2000 Fiscal Pact.

Yet the government found its authority rapidly deteriorating. Popular sectors were outraged at the weak government response to natural disaster, and they staged a mounting cycle of protest to express social demands. Legislative allies deserted the governing coalition, in part out of anger at weak government performance, and in part as potential candidates prepared for a presidential run in elections to be held the following year. Simply put, government was making a choice about a fiscal response in a moment of particular weakness.

Under these conditions, one could not be surprised to see the government opt for simple reforms that would strengthen the legislation around revenues and improve bureaucratic capacity, but would do little to change the underlying structure of the fiscal system. Indeed, this was exactly what happened, and a reform of the administration and legal framework was passed in May 2006. The reforms have produced moderate results, and tax revenues would appear to have risen above 10 per cent, though there appears little hope of any deeper structural changes that might bring tax revenues to a level that might ensure fiscal sustainability.

Kinds of Obstacle

The difficulty of reform is one aspect that must be considered before offering policy advice, but the degree of difficulty is not the only consideration. In addition to their degree of difficulty, reforms vary in terms of the type of obstacle that must be overcome. Rather than a continuous gradation of more or less, such differences can be characterised qualitatively, with the difference one of kind. Strategies for reform should consider both the intensity of obstacles (more or less) and also the type of obstacle (difference in kind).

Kinds of obstacle are set apart by the actors and institutions involved. Actors are social actors, operating on the basis of interests, who come together in coalition behind reforms or stand off in opposition against them. Institutions are the organisations and rules that establish incentives to bound the behaviour of different actors. Institutions define who is included in political debate and sets limits on the available options. Institutions can be formal and legal rules and organisations, or they can be informal practices and norms that constrain behaviour (Levitsky and Helmke, 2006). Four variations are discussed below.

Strong and Concentrated Opposition

In many cases, opposition to reform is strong and concentrated. This opposition can come from organised groups, powerful business interests, members of the political elite and actors within the bureaucracy. They are powerful because of their economic, social and political resources or their institutional positions, each of which gives them a degree of veto over reform. Relative to such opponents, those who favour reform are weak. To a certain degree, there is a vicious circle: to enhance state capacity, reformers require autonomy and power, but autonomy and power require state capacity.

Many have described 'first-generation' reforms in these terms. Macroeconomic adjustment, privatisation, liberalising trade and markets have been characterised as reforms in which governments faced great challenges, but were weak in the face of opponents (Nelson, 1989; Haggard and Kaufman, 1992; Haggard and Webb, 1994; Williamson and Haggard, 1994).[6]

The strategy promoted by many was an immediate, comprehensive and direct attack. Jeffrey Sachs (1993), reflecting on his experiences in Poland, Russia and Bolivia, promoted a 'Big Bang' approach, 'rapid, comprehensive, and extensive reforms to implement normal capitalist relations'. The comprehensiveness of reform was linked to its timing. New governments that were recently elected and held a surplus of political capital were encouraged to undertake reform before opposition could organise. Similarly, governments that suffered a crisis, natural disaster or other shock could take advantage of disruptions that demobilised opposition and united supporters (Bates and Krueger, 1993).[7]

There are few governments in Central America that are likely to enjoy the kind of political capital Solidarity had earned. On the other hand, none of the Central American countries must attempt a wholesale transition from a socialist to a capitalist economy in the way that Poland did.

Guatemala could be characterised by a powerful, concentrated and well-connected opposition to reform. These opponents are located in sectors that stand to lose much from a fiscal model adequate to globalisation. Such sectors are protected oligopolies within industry, commerce and finance, which are largely outside the formal tax net, and they act to prevent the formation of a reformist coalition. Their competitive advantage is the weakness of the state, and their accumulation is based on the inability of the state to charge taxes, regulate their activities or monitor their products. These groups dominate the main business association of Guatemala, CACIF, and they prevent the rise of sectors more aligned with an alternative model of public finance.

Rather than attempt a Big Bang approach in Guatemala, government attempted to reach a social pact around fiscal reform, including negotiations between business, social sectors and government (Fuentes and Cabrera, 2005). As Fuentes and Cabrera note, no sooner had the pact been agreed than actors turned to the courts to declare elements of the pact unconstitutional. In the three years after the pact, there were 60 cases of unconstitutionality in which business, partisan and social sectors overturned tax increases through legal recourse (Fuentes and Cabrera, 2005: 18).

With powerful and concentrated opposition, there is little room for slow negotiation. Reform requires a 'Big Bang' comprehensive set of reforms. Only such a shock can sufficiently strengthen the reform credentials of a government and buy the time necessary to demonstrate the viability of reform. This will force social actors to change their strategies of economic activity in a direction that complements, rather than contradicts, a fiscal model adequate to globalisation.

Collective Action

The 'Big Bang' is not appropriate in all places and all times. A related, but not identical, challenge is posed by collective action problems (Olsen, 1966).[8] This shifts attention from the opponents to the beneficiaries of reform, who are often weak, dispersed and difficult to organise.

The nature of the collective action problem is that certain goods, such as mobilisation in support of reform, are public, in the sense of being 'non-excludable and non-rivalrous'. Non-excludable means that, once provided, nobody can be excluded from enjoying the fruits of the public good, and non-rivalrous means that the fact that one actor benefits takes nothing away from another. Providing public goods is notoriously difficult, and support for fiscal reform is no different. Supporters may want the reform to occur, but all would rather wait for someone else to take the risk and pay the costs of organising, rather than making the effort themselves.

To confront collective action problems, it is necessary to change the incentives facing potential bases of support. Potential beneficiaries offer little support because they have little incentive to do so. If they can be offered selective incentives, such as economic, political or moral benefits, their support becomes more likely. Alternatively, they can be offered sanctions, such as social pressure, disciplinary actions or coercion, which make them more likely to support reform. Mancur Olson (1966), in observing processes of overcoming collective action constraints, argued that the presence of a larger, more powerful actor, with the resources and will to promote organisation, could pay the costs of offering selective incentives or imposing sanctions.

There is frequently a relationship between the first and second obstacles, strong and concentrated opponents, and supporters confronted with collective action constraints. In this situation, the 'Big Bang' approach mentioned before is only part of the solution. A frontal attack may be necessary, but only after collective action constraints have been overcome to create a coalition of supporters. Once a government offers selective incentives and negative sanctions to patch together a coalition of support, it can then take on powerful opponents.

Many of the reforms characterised as 'second generation' have operated according to this logic (Corrales, 1999; Graham et al., 1998; Weyland, 1996). The 'second generation' label is generally used to refer to civil service reforms, electoral reforms, decentralisation or other reforms that attack the structures of incentives and boundaries of inclusion of the modern state. These reforms require institutional changes, even cultural changes, in the way in which the state functions, and frequently include both collective action constraints on supporters as well as a powerful and well-ensconced opposition.

The difficulties in building a coalition of support and taking on opponents can be profound, especially when it comes to fiscal reforms. Distinct from the 'Big Bang' approach, a government can only move cohesively and rapidly after a medium-term period of preparing a coalition, by punishing opponents and offering incentives to allies.

In Central America, there are numerous examples of building such coalitions, though their expansive nature has limited the extent of the reforms attempted. In El Salvador, for example, a series of tax measures were approved in October of 2004. These aimed to combat evasion and contraband through strengthening mechanisms of control and tax compliance, including a more precise definition for the penal code of tax crimes, an increase in penalties for such crimes, access by authorities to the bank accounts of individuals under investigation, and the increase in the power of customs officers, among others (Agosín et al., 2006). The measures also reduced the range of admissible deductions to income tax and increased the rates of excise on alcoholic beverages and cigarettes.

The reforms were discussed extensively within the Assembly. The centre left opposition, generally opposed to more regressive taxes such as the excise, was willing to acquiesce to efforts that closed loopholes in income taxes. Their votes, combined with the votes of government party deputies and those of conservative satellite parties, were sufficient to pass the reforms. The effect was limited, though not insignificant: a one percentage point increase in tax as a percentage of GDP, taking tax collection to 13.2 per cent of GDP, with particular gains with respect to 2004 made in excise (27.4 per cent) and income tax (23.7 per cent).

In Nicaragua, a similar elite agreement produced limited reform. Like El Salvador, it was during a moment of truce between two seemingly polarised parties. In Nicaragua, however, the truce was solidified by a pact between the governing rightist party and its chief leftist opposition. Their pact ensured a continued monopoly on administrative, legislative and judicial posts, as well as effective impunity for violations that occurred during their efforts to build patronage organisations.

When tax legislation came before the Nicaraguan Congress in 2003, legislators from the two main parties, responding to the coordinated dictates of their party leaders, passed the Fiscal Equity Law. The law limited the use of zero rates on the VAT to exports and a few special cases and broadened the base of the VAT to services. It also reduced the number of exempt goods included in the basic consumption basket. At the same time, the reforms increased the taxable income base and introduced a 1 per cent tax on gross assets of firms as a minimum payment towards the corporate income tax. As a result, between 2002 and 2004, tax collection increased from 13.5 to 15.5 per cent of GDP, and by 2005 had reached 16 per cent.[9]

The first obstacles to reform considered here were concentrated and powerful opposition and collective action constraints among supporters. Both are obstacles related to the nature of social and political actors in favour or opposed to reforms, and both can be overcome with some artful politicking. The same is true of the third and fourth type of obstacle, though the focus is the institutional context of reform rather than actors.

Information Problems

Unlike the prior examples, in which all actors were clear in terms of their support or opposition, benefits and costs of reform, in examples of information problems actors are faced with an uncertain set of payoffs. Some actors may benefit, others may suffer costs, but none can be sure what the future holds.

Fiscal reform frequently has this characteristic. This is particularly the case for indirect taxes, which levy consumption, exchange or transport, instead of directly targeting ability to pay. In response to indirect levies, unexpected changes can occur as economic actors change their behaviour, patterns of growth shift, and the ultimate impact on any individual and sector is not clear until long after reform has been implemented.

Much has been written on the topic of imperfect information within economics, and Joseph Stiglitz won a Nobel prize for his insights (e.g. Stiglitz, 1985). The economics literature makes the point that uncertainty can produce sub-optimal outcomes as a result of the cost of risk to the actors involved.[10] To confront these situations, economists look for ways to increase the information available.

In the case of fiscal reform, there can be a similar dilemma. Certain groups may benefit from a reform, but they do not know if they will benefit and by how much. Some may benefit more than others; some may benefit immediately others after a certain amount of time. These uncertainties mean that individuals will be cautious about the reforms on offer, and government may be unwilling to offer the best possible reform packages for fear they will not be supported. All sectors may acknowledge that a reform is needed, but none can be sure how many of the costs they will have to pay and how many of the benefits they will receive.[11]

In policy environments characterised by problems of imperfect information, some have noticed reforms occurring by stealth or platforms.[12] Each step in the process of fiscal reform can be seen as a new platform, in which state and social actors can evaluate the impact of changes and decide whether and how to proceed. As each reform advances, greater information becomes available, and benefits and costs are revealed. With each platform, new beneficiaries can be identified and brought into support, and more platforms become reachable.

An episode of platforms appears to be unfolding in Costa Rica. Originally, an ambitious fiscal reform project was presented for discussion in the Legislative Assembly in 2002. Despite widespread agreement among both government and opposition that the reform was necessary, it sat in committee discussion for four years before being approved. Further, only a few months after approval, the law was promptly declared unconstitutional by the Supreme Court, and a newly elected government was forced to begin discussions from scratch in 2006.

The problem with the reform was not that it was poorly designed. It included almost all the elements of a fiscal system adequate to globalisation. It redefined income on a global rather than national basis, and established a universal basis for income rather than differentiating according to income base. It eliminated unnecessary tax exemptions, and widened the value added tax to include most products and services. It strengthened tax administration and introduced reasonable excise and property taxes. In short, it was a comprehensive reform based on the finest current understanding of fiscal issues (Agosín et al., 2006).

Yet the reform touched too many interests and created too many uncertainties. While legislators from all the major parties advocated for a fiscal reform, none was completely sure how the sweeping changes would affect its constituents. They slowed the process as much as possible to debate each particularity and introduce their preferred amendments. Further, the Supreme Court found multiple errors and contradictions in the law, each of which would require constitutional debate rather than sweeping change through normal legislation.

Faced with the almost immediate repudiation of the legislation, the newly elected government in 2006 began an alternative process of fiscal reform. This time, the reform would be passed in stages, in which individual elements would be introduced in sequence, gaining support, convincing doubters, and gradually moving the fiscal system in a direction more adequate to a liberalised model.

The first proposals to broaden existing tax bases, such as extending VAT to services, have been discussed and passed during 2006. Proposals to introduce principles of worldwide income on universal bases are next for consideration.

Attempts at a comprehensive and sweeping fiscal reform in the years after 2002 were unsuccessful in Costa Rica. They were difficult changes, important interests surely opposed them, and a coalition of support had not been built. But these were not the primary obstacles. The main obstacle was a lack of information. All the parties basically agreed that a reform was necessary, but they were not entirely sure how each change would impact upon their supporters. Instead of a comprehensive Big Bang approach to reform, the current government has adopted a gradual and incremental approach. Each reform will garner new resources and clarify the direction of change, and each reform will thereby expand potential support for new stages of reform. This is the essence of a platform approach to reform and, though slow, it is most appropriate in the context of uncertainty and doubt surrounding reform.

Transaction Costs

The final obstacle discussed here is transaction costs. These costs are similar to those that characterise imperfect information in the sense that they complicate the institutional environment and prevent optimal policy choices. In the case of fiscal reform, transaction costs are the costs of shifting from one set of policies to another. Even if the new policies are pareto superior, such as replacing cascading taxes with value-added taxes, the gains of reform will be illusory if nobody is willing to pay the costs of making the shift.

Literature on transaction costs was also the subject of a Nobel prize, in this case for Oliver Williamson. Williamson (e.g. 1975, 1985) demonstrated that markets can reach sub-optimal equilibriums because of transaction costs. Transactions require transfers of value, but the possibility of converting assets into a liquid form that can be exchanged has a cost, in which simply making an exchange is costly. To confront this problem, contracts specify the way in which the costs of the transaction will be distributed, should that be necessary.[13]

For different types of transaction, with different problems of imperfect information, varieties of contract have been described. These include barter, market, firm and government. What sets each apart are the ways in which they specify values to be exchanged and how they distribute the costs of the transaction (Alchian and Demsetz, 1972; Coase, 1960).[14]

In the case of fiscal reform, there can be significant transaction costs. This does not necessarily refer to the costs of making an exchange, but rather the costs of shifting relationships between state and society, especially actors within the private sector. Especially in the context of newly emerging economic sectors, establishing new, more efficient tax handles to replace old, inefficient ones may be in everyone's interest, but it is still difficult to attain. Simply switching over implies costs, and how to distribute those costs is unclear. Further, fiscal changes imply new relationships of power, responsibility and rights, in which new economic categories are defined, responsibilities to the state established, and benefits under the law agreed. Establishing these arrangements requires clarity of contract, such as the amount of tax a micro-enterprise will have to pay in exchange for legal recognition or other state services.

One example of the use of contracts within reform processes is the use of social pacts, consultations and consensus (CEPAL, 1998; Kaufman and Nelson, 2005). The idea of these compacts is to establish a reform through prior agreement of all actors, including a distribution of the costs associated with the transaction. Once agreed, the reform can proceed. In cases in which fiscal reform has included an explicit change in the relative power and responsibilities of different actors, such as decentralising reforms, such prior negotiation is particularly useful.

Another useful strategy is linking difficult reforms with policies that have already achieved a degree of consensus. The process of reaching consensus — for example, through a poverty reduction strategy — establishes a degree of trust among state representatives, society and international donors. This establishes a degree of trust that can be mobilised to support additional reforms without having to establish entirely new agreements. In Chile, for example, the consensus that was built around the transition to democracy served as glue to hold together a coalition that could also discuss the terms of expanding social spending and increased taxes to pay for that spending (Marfan, 2001; Boylan, 1996).

The point of establishing a social pact around reform prior to attempting any policy change is that a pact sets the terms of debate, the actors involved and the rules by which they will negotiate. Such prior negotiation is particularly important when the actors involved are new or in the process of being incorporated into the political system, the changes they require imply costs, and there is limited political agreement as to how those costs ought to be distributed. In this context, it is first necessary to set the rules of engagement before deciding how to proceed. Only then can actors create a broad coalition and agree on reforms.

Such an agreement cannot be pursued in every context, however. If actors are significantly polarised, hold obdurate positions, or are otherwise unwilling or unable to reach agreements, there can be little hope of different groups reaching an agreement about the rules by which they should operate. The potential gains from a broad pact may be great, but there are some transaction costs that are simply too large for any process of negotiation to overcome.

This has been the case in Guatemala. While widespread optimism surrounded the achievement of a fiscal pact in 2000, there has been little optimism since. The exercise in pacting an agreement around fiscal issues was an important part of the post-civil war peace process that began with the peace agreement of 1996, but the fiscal pact was not an exercise which could bring polarised and fragmented interests to an agreement on how to share the costs and benefits of a new fiscal model (Fuentes and Cabrera, 2005). The Guatemalan party system is fragmented and volatile, making major social and political actors wary of any long-term commitments. They prefer to sabotage existing agreements in the hope that they can do better in another or simply maintain the status quo.

Instead of broad and far-reaching measures, the Guatemalan political system has only been able to enact temporary stop-gaps. In June 2004, a series of measures modified the corporate income tax and reintroduced excise taxes on alcoholic beverages. The measures also introduced an Extraordinary and Temporary Tax to Support the Peace Accords (IETAAP in Spanish). This tax operates as a minimum payment towards the corporate income tax, though it had to be set at rates lower than taxes that it replaced, and was also set with a time limit to decline over time and expire at the end of the current government mandate (Agosín et al., 2006).

The Guatemalan experience stands in contrast to what happened in Honduras. Honduras has a two-party system that has lasted for decades; the two major parties occupy centrist ideological positions; they secure over 90 per cent of the vote; and they have established stable bases of political support through patronage mechanisms. This is very different from the fragmented and volatile Guatemalan political system, and it allows room for negotiating far-reaching pacts among political groups that essentially agree on fundamental aspects of democratic practice and economic policy.

The first such pact emerged prior to the 2001 elections. Both parties agreed on basic reforms to the fiscal system, and both candidates committed to supporting the reforms regardless of the winner. As a result, the Tax Equity Law (LET in Spanish) was passed in 2003, which modified the income tax, VAT and excise structure.

In the case of income tax, the law expanded the definition of taxable income by limiting deductions for bonuses and business expenses, and incorporating as income end-of-year bonus payments above a certain level. In addition, a tax was introduced at the rate of 1 per cent of net assets as an anticipated minimum payment on the corporate income tax, except in those firms with assets lower than a certain level, firms in tax-free zones and firms exempt from payment of corporate income tax (mining and tourism). In the case of the VAT, the taxable base was extended to those goods and services that had been exempt. Also, the rate of excise paid on cigarettes was raised from 32.25 to 45 per cent (and to 47.5 per cent at the start of 2004). Finally, the highly lucrative tax on fuels was consolidated to a per gallon price and earmarked to social programmes and road maintenance, overturning the excise and import tax on fuels. These measures generated an increase in collection of 1.5 per cent of GDP between 2002 and 2004. In 2005, tax collection had reached 17.7 per cent of GDP, 0.3 percentage points higher than 2004.

The Honduran political elite enjoyed a degree of fundamental agreement about the nature of a desirable fiscal regime. This agreement allowed them to negotiate over the nature of costs and benefits to be distributed in any fiscal reform, and to agree on how and when to implement the reforms. The process of negotiation was elitist and narrow, and the reforms themselves remain incomplete. Still, the process of reform in Honduras is one of overcoming transaction costs, in which the obstacle is not a high degree of political polarisation or fragmentation, but rather the difficult process of negotiating how costs and benefits are to be distributed.

The four types of obstacle discussed above can be organised according to whether they focus on actors or on institutions (see Table 8.2).

Each obstacle to fiscal reform calls for a distinct political strategy, most significantly in terms of the timing and speed of reform. For obvious reasons, Big Bang strategies can be expected in early moments of a government winning election and taking power. Occasionally, mid-term elections or crises can generate new peaks of political capital, but rarely is a government as strong as it is at the very start. Once the Big Bang begins, however, it is likely to be short lived. The episode of reform lasts only a short time, and is over once the political capital is spent.

Collective action problems suggest a similarly short timeframe for reform. Overcoming collective action takes time, however, as potential allies have to be

Table 8.2: Reform Types and Responses

Actors	Institutions
I. Strong and concentrated opposition call for a 'Big Bang', a rapid and comprehensive fiscal reform undertaken during peaks of political capital.	III. Information problems require gradual and incremental approach to attain new platforms of reform.
II. Collective action problems among supporters require offering selective incentives and sanctions to enhance cooperative behaviour.	IV. When faced with transaction costs, can be overcome through a social pact to establish the rules of the game.

convinced or coopted, through the extension of selective benefits and sanction. This means that overcoming collective action constraints is unlikely to occur at the start of a government. Also, building a coalition cannot occur too late in a mandate. Governments will be wary of mobilising a coalition for reform so close to an election. Once a coalition is established, it does not necessarily remain intact for long, and forming a coalition too late forces governments to decide whether to use the coalition to win the next election or pass the reform. Reforms that require overcoming collective action constraints are therefore likely to occur towards the middle of the electoral cycle.

Information problems suggest a much longer and more gradual process. Under information problems, small reforms proceed incrementally, and there is no fast-paced and rapid burst comparable to the Big Bang approach. Instead, a slow progression from easy reforms to harder ones, smaller ones to bigger ones, is the likely pattern. Ideally, this builds throughout a governmental period, in which early easy victories pick 'low-hanging fruit' and lead to continual progress throughout the mandate.

Finally, transaction costs imply a need for a long, drawn-out process of building consensus about the nature of distributing costs and benefits of reform. The danger that a reform too close to an election will threaten incumbents is absent in this case because the reform is the fruit of a consensus decision; in other words, no actor can secure electoral gain by opposing it. If anything, reform after a social pact favours incumbents, by allowing them to claim the credit for gains from reform.

Conclusion

So what are the implications of these political analyses for reform? The analysis studies episodes of reform as evidence of different types of obstacles being overcome. Quite obviously, the strategies to overcome these obstacles have to be tailored, depending on the type of obstacle faced and the degree of difficulty of the reform being attempted.

A final word is appropriate here about the nature of reforms more generally. This has been the focus of detailed discussion elsewhere (Agosín et al. 2005). Still, it is relevant to reiterate that what makes fiscal reform important at the current juncture is the fact that states that were never particularly good at mobilising revenue and serving citizens now find that their most dynamic economic actors are more difficult to tax and more unwilling to contribute than ever before. At the same time, citizens who have long been excluded are increasingly incorporated in processes of accumulation and finding new opportunities to mobilise in democratic systems.

A political economy interpretation of challenges to reform provides greater clarity in considering the structural changes in the region and the obstacles to putting reforms in place. The reforms and the structural changes are similar across countries: all countries require fiscal systems adequate to a globalised pattern of accumulation; all countries face structural changes associated with the rise of transnational actors. The question facing each country is how to tailor their reform strategy to the specific obstacles produced by the political economy of actors and institutions in their territory.

References

M.R. Agosín, R. Machado and P. Nazal (2003) *Pequenas Economías, Grandes Desafíos* (Washington: BID).

M.R. Agosín, A. Schneider and R. Machado (2006) 'Two Steps Forward, One Step Back: Tax Reform and Fiscal Capacity in Central America', *Tax Notes International* Fall.

M. Alcántra Sáez (1998) 'Elites parlamentarias en América Latina', survey financed by Programa Nacional de Estudios Sociales, Económicos y Culturales del Plan Nacional de I+D.

A.A. Alchian and H. Demsetz (1972) 'Production, Information Costs and Economic Organisation', *American Economic Review*, no. 62, pp. 777–95.

E. Baloyra-Herp (1983) 'Reactionary Despotism in Central America', *Journal of Latin American Studies*, vol. 15, no. 2 (November), pp. 295–319.

R. Bates and A.O. Krueger (eds.) (1993) *Political and Economic Interactions in Economic Policy Reform: Evidence from Eight Countries* (Cambridge: Blackwell).

J.A. Booth and M. Seligson (eds.) (1989) *Elections and Democracy in Central America* (Chapel Hill, NC: University of North Carolina Press).

K. Bowman, F. Lehoucq and J. Mahoney (2005) 'Measuring Political Democracy: Case Expertise, Data Adequacy, and Central America', *Comparative Political Studies*, vol. 38, no. 8, pp. 939–70

D.M. Boylan (1996) 'Taxation and Transition: The Politics of the 1990 Chilean Tax Reform', *Latin American Research Review*, vol. 31, no. 1, pp. 7–31.

V. Bulmer-Thomas (1987) *The Political Economy of Central America Since 1920* (Cambridge: Cambridge University Press).

J. Castañeda (1990) 'Is Squeaky Clean Squeaky Fair?' *Los Angeles Times*, 18 November.

M.A. Centeno (1996) *Democracy Within Reason: Technocratic Revolution in Mexico.* (University Park, PA: Pennsylvania State University Press).

CEPAL (1998) *El Pacto Fiscal: Fortalezas, Debilidades, Desafíos* (Santiago: Economic Commission for Latin America).

R.H. Coase (1960) 'The Problem of Social Cost', *Journal of Law and Economics* no. 3, pp. 1–44.

D. Collier and R. Berins Collier (1991) *Shaping the Political Arena: Critical Junctures, the Labour Movement, and Regime Dynamics in Latin America* (Princeton: Princeton University Press).

Corrales, Javier (1999) 'The Politics of Education Reform Implementation: Bolstering the Supply and Demand, Countering Institutional Blocks', *Umbarl 2000*, p. 1.

S.S. Cué (2001) 'La incompleta Transformación del FSLN', *America Latina Hoy*, no. 27, pp. 89–122.

O.A. Davis, M. Hinich and P.C. Ordeshook (1970) 'An Expository Development of a Mathematical Model of the Electoral Process', *American Political Science Review*, no. 64, pp. 426–48.

P. Dricken (2006) *Global Shift: Transforming the World Economy* (London: Sage).

W. Easterly (2006) *The White Man's Burden: Why the West's Efforts to Aid the Rest Have Done So Much Ill and So Little Good* (New York: Penguin).

A. Escobar and S. Alvarez (eds.) (1992) *The Making of Social Movements in Latin America: Identity, Strategy, and Democracy* (Boulder, CO: Westview).

J.A. Fuentes and M. Cabrera (2005) 'El Pacto Fiscal de Guatemala: una oportunidad perdida', presentation to 17th Regional Seminal on Fiscal Policy, CEPAL, Santiago.

J.K. Galbraith (1952) *American Capitalism: The Concept of Countervailing Power* (Boston: Houghton Mifflin).

C. Graham et al. (eds.) (1998) *Beyond Tradeoffs: Market Reforms and Equitable Growth in Latin America* (Washington, DC: Brookings Institution).

M. Grindle (2004) *Despite the Odds: Contentious Politics and Education Reform* (Princeton, NJ: Princeton University Press).

S. Haggard and R.R. Kaufman (eds.) (1992) *The Politics of Economic Adjustment: International Constraints, Distributive Conflicts, and the State* (Princeton, NJ: Princeton University Press).

S. Haggard and S.B. Webb (eds.) (1994) *Voting for Reform: Democracy, Political Liberalisation, and Economic Adjustment* (Washington, DC: World Bank and Oxford University Press).

J.T. Jackson (2005) *The Globalizers: Development Workers in Action* (Baltimore, MD: Johns Hopkins University Press).

R. Jenkins (1999) *Democratic Politics and Economic Reform in India* (Cambridge, MA: Cambridge University Press).

R.R. Kaufman and J.M. Nelson (eds.) (2005) *Crucial Needs, Weak Incentives: Social Sector Reform, Democratisation, and Globalisation in Latin America* (Baltimore, MD: Johns Hopkins University Press).

J.O. Kim and C.W. Mueller (1978) *Introduction to Factor Analysis* (Beverly Hills, CA: Sage).

H. Kitschelt (1992) 'The Formation of Party Systems in East Central Europe', *Politics and Society*, vol. 20, no. 1, pp. 7–50.

M. Laakso and R. Taagepera (1979) 'Effective Number of Parties: A Measure with Application to West Europe', *Comparative Political Studies* vol. 12, no. 1 (January), pp. 3–27.

D. Lal (1987) 'The Political Economy of Economic Liberalisation', *The World Bank Economic Review*, no. 1, p. 2.

M. Levi (1988) *Of Rule and Revenue* (Berkeley: University of California Press).

S. Levitsky and G. Helmke (2006) *Informal Institutions and Democracy: Lessons from Latin. America* (Baltimore: Johns Hopkins University Press).

E.S. Lieberman (2003) *Race and Regionalism in the Politics of Taxation in Brazil and South Africa* (Cambridge: Cambridge University Press).

A. Lijphart (1984) *Democracies: Patterns of Majoritarian and Consensus Government in Twenty-One Countries* (New Haven: Yale University Press).

S.M. Lipset and S. Rokkan (eds.) (1990 [1967]) 'Cleavage Structures, Party Systems, and Voter Alignments: An Introduction', in P. Mair (ed.), *The West European Party System* (Oxford: Oxford University Press).

J. Mahoney (2001). *The Legacies of Liberalism: Path Dependence and Political Regimes in Central America* (Baltimore: Johns Hopkins University Press).

J. Mahoney and R. Snyder (1999) 'Rethinking Agency and Structure in the Study of Regime Change', *Studies in Comparative International Development*, vol. 34, no. 2 (April–June), pp. 3–32.

S. Mainwaring (1999) *Rethinking Party Systems in the Third Wave of Democratisation: The Case of Brazil* (Stanford, CA: Stanford University Press).

S. Mainwaring and T.R. Scully (1995) *Building Democratic Institutions: Party Systems in Latin America* (Stanford: Stanford University Press).

M. Marfan (2001) 'The Chilean Tax Reform of 1990: A Success Story', *Notes* (Santiago: Inter-American Development Bank, Sustainable Development Department, Poverty and Inequality Unit).

R. McCleary (1999) *Dictating Democracy: Guatemala and the End of Violent Revolution* (Gainesville, FL: University Press of Florida).

M. Moore (2004) 'Revenues, State Formation, and the Quality of Governance in Developing Countries', *International Political Science Review*, vol. 25, no. 3, pp. 297–319.

G.L. Munck and J. Verkuilen (2002) 'Conceptualizing and Measuring Democracy: Evaluating Alternative Indices', *Comparative Political Studies*, vol. 35, no. 1 (February), pp. 5–34.

M. Naim (2005) *Illicit: How Smugglers, Traffickers, and Copycats are Hijacking the Global Economy* (New York: Doubleday).

J.M. Nelson et al. (1989) *Fragile Coalitions: The Politics of Economic Adjustment* (New Brunswick: Transaction Books).

M. Olson (1966) *The Logic of Collective Action* (Cambridge: Harvard University Press).

E. Ostrom (1990) *Governing the Commons: The Evolution of Institutions for Collective Action* (New York: Cambridge University Press).

P. Oxhorn and P.K. Starr (eds.) (1999) *Markets and Democracy in Latin America: Conflict or Convergence?* (Boulder, CO: Lynne Rienner).

J. Paige (1997) *Coffee and Power: Revolution and the Rise of Democracy in Central America* (Cambridge, MA: Harvard University Press).

A. Przeworski (1985) *Capitalism and Social Democracy* (Cambridge, MA: Cambridge University Press).

J. Puches and F. Torres (2000) *Las finanzas públicas y la política fiscal en las economías de Centroamérica durante los años noventa y perspectivas de corto y mediano plazo* (Santiago: CEPAL).

D. Reuschemeyer, E. Stephens and J. Stephens (1992) *Capitalist Development and Democracy* (Chicago: University of Chicago Press).

W. Robinson (2003) *Transnational Conflicts: Central America, Social Change, and Globalisation* (London: Verso).

J.E. Roemer (2001) *Political Competition: Theory and Application* (Cambridge: Harvard University Press).

J. Sachs (1993) *Poland's Jump to the Market Economy* (Cambridge, MA: MIT Press).

F. Sanchez (2003) 'Cambio en la Dinámica Electoral en Costa Rica: Un Caso de desalineamiento', *América Latin Hoy*, no. 35 (December), pp. 115–46.

A. Segovia (2005) *Integración real y grupos de poder económico en América Central: Implicaciones para el desarrollo y la democracia de la región* (San José: Friedich Ebert Foundation).

W. Stanley (1996) *The Protection Racket State: Elite Politics, Military Extortion, and Civil War in El Salvador* (Philadelphia, PA: Temple University Press).

J.E. Stiglitz (1986) 'Economics of Information and the Theory of Economic Development', NBER Working Papers no. 1566 (Boston: National Bureau of Economic Research, Inc).

D. Stokes (1966) 'Spatial Models of Party Competition', in A. Campbell (ed.), *Elections and the Political Order* (New York: Wiley).

E. Torres Rivas (1993) *Crisis del Poder en Centroamérica* (San José: EDUCA).

K. Weyland (1996) *Democracy Without Equity: Failures of Reform in Brazil* (Pittsburgh: University of Pittsburgh Press).

J. Williamson and S. Haggard (1994) 'The Political Conditions for Economic Reform', in J. Williamson (ed.), *The Political Economy of Policy Reform* (Washington, DC: Institute for International Economics).

O.E. Williamson (1985) *The Economic Institutions of Capitalism: Firms, Markets, Relational Contracting* (New York: The Free Press).

O.E. Williamson (1975) *Markets and Hierarchies: Analysis and Antitrust Implications* (New York: Macmillan).

World Bank (2006) *DR-CAFTA: Challenges and Opportunities for Central America* (Washington: Central American Department and Office of the Chief Economist, Latin America and Caribbean Regions).

World Development Indicators, online at www.worldbank.org/data various years.

D.J. Yashar (1997) *Demanding Democracy: Reform and Reaction in Costa Rica and Guatemala, 1870s–1950s* (Stanford, CA: Stanford University Press).

E. Zoco (2006) 'Legislators' Positions and Party System Competition in Central America: A Comparative Analysis', *Party Politics* no. 12, pp. 257–80.

Appendix: Factor Loadings and Questions

Factor Loadings

	Costa Rica		El Salvador		Guatemala		Nicaragua		Honduras	
	Econ	Pol	Econ	Pol	Econ	Pol	Econ	Pol	Econ	Pol
Self Place	**.82**	.01	**.98**	-.05	**.68**	.02	**.85**	.14	**.87**	.01
Party Place	**.88**	.06	**.94**	-.15	**.69**	-.07	**.84**	.10	**.89**	.06
Trst Bus/Un	**.26**	-.01	**.63**	-.03	**.54**	.01	**.66**	.17	**.20**	-.01
Impt. Unem	**.44**	-.15	**.37**	.19	**.33**	-.14	**.54**	-.17	**.38**	.01
Stat v. Mkt	**.55**	-.23	**.70**	-.07			**.69**	.17	**.36**	.20
Democ pref	-.10	**.23**	.17	**.26**	-.10	**.55**	.10	**.20**		
Impt. Rights	.07	**.67**	-.37	**.59**	.34	**.38**	.26	**.45**	.07	**.73**
Public Life	-.01	**.70**	-.16	**.50**			.15	**.63**	.04	**.73**
Corruption	-.05	**.29**	-.53	**.21**	-.24	**.30**	.25	**.57**	-.23	**.25**

Left–right Dimension

With respect to the following people, groups, and institutions, I would like to know how much confidence — high, some, little, or none — you think they deserve for their contribution to public life?

1) Trust Business Associations
2) Trust Unions

In a moment, I am going to name a series of common problems to many countries. Can you tell me, for each one, the degree of importance today in Guatemala: high, some, little or none?

3) Importance of unemployment and under-employment

As you know, when we speak about politics, normally we use the terms 'left' and 'right'. On this card are a series of boxes that go from left to right. In which box would you place yourself?

4) Self-placement
5) Party-placement

As you know, in many countries on the continent, there is currently a debate between statist positions and neoliberal positions. With respect to these issues, could you tell me if you are more in favour of an economy regulated by the state or by the market?

6) State versus market

Inclusive–Exclusive Dimension:

7) With which of the following sentences do you most agree?
    (a) Democracy is preferable to all other forms of government.
    (b) In contexts of economic crisis and political instability, an authoritarian government can be preferable to a democratic one.

In a moment, I am going to name a series of common problems to many countries. Can you tell me, for each one, the degree of importance today in Guatemala: high, some, little or none?
    8) Importance of human rights or minority and ethnic rights?
    9) Importance of corruption?
    10) Importance of the democratisation of public life and institutions?

Notes

[1]   He also identified authoritarian versus libertarian modes of decision-making and authority, a conflict that has been settled in favour of democratisation in Central America, at least for now.

[2]   In the face of failure, international consultants attempt to shift blame by invoking a failure of national political will. This is both too easy and not usually the case. Most political leaders would like to improve their governance, promote growth, combat inequality and poverty and improve development. Their problem is not a lack of will; rather, reforms fail because there are too many political wills, working at cross purposes, which therefore cannot reach agreement. A sophisticated approach to politics understands that it is about overcoming opposing wills, coordinating competing wills, educating and mobilising wills that have yet to be formed, and constructing national wills out of personal, ethnic, class-based, sectoral, regional and partisan divisions.

[3]   Especially in countries like those in Central America, it is often useful to combine qualitative and quantitative insights to accurately characterise cases (Bowman et al., 2005).

[4]   Factor analysis is a useful way to aggregate multiple variables measured on different scales. Instead of arbitrarily rescaling and aggregating variables, factor analysis offers an algorithm to aggregate variables based on the empirical relationship between variables and underlying dimensions (Munck and Verkuilen, 2002). Simply put, variables that more closely tap into underlying dimensions should be given more weight than variables that relate only somewhat to the underlying dimension. The technique applied, principal factor analysis, makes use of the squared multiple correlations among variables to estimate their commonality along dimensions. A varimax rotation of factors maximises the variance of the squared loading and the variance of the factors, providing

consistent results. The method is a way to efficiently make use of the information in the survey by weighting the importance of survey responses in terms of their construct validity with respect to underlying dimensions (Kim and Mueller, 1978).

[5]   Eigenvalues suggest how much more of the data could be explained by adding another dimension. As general practice, eigenvalues above one are considered evidence that dimensions usefully organise the data (Kim and Mueller, 1978). As seen in the table below, eigenvalues for two dimensions organise the data best in Honduras and Costa Rica. In Nicaragua, El Salvador and Guatemala, the second dimension obtains an eigenvalue slightly less than one, but still helps explain a reasonable amount of the variance, and more than any additional dimensions.

Eigenvalues

Factor	Honduras	El Salvador	Nicaragua	Guatemala	Costa Rica
Left–right	2.0	3.5	3.0	1.3	2.1
Inclusive–Exclusive	1.1	.7	.8	.8	1.1
3	.3	.3	.4	.4	.5
4	.3	.2	.2	–	.3
5	–	.1	.2	–	.1

[6]   These types of problems are particularly vexing under democratic regimes (Lal, 1987). New democracies inherited the macroeconomic crises of authoritarian regimes, but did not possess the hierarchical and disciplined institutional processes that characterise dictatorship. In the early 1990s, as countries faced the double transition of authoritarianism to democracy and macroeconomic adjustment, it was particularly difficult to imagine how weak governments could advance difficult reforms in the face of newly mobilised and invigorated social actors (Centeno, 1996).

[7]   Sachs uses the example of Poland after the election of Solidarity to justify his support for a Big Bang approach. In Poland, Solidarity won all but one of the Senate seats in 1989. The Communist Party, which ran unopposed for 35 seats in the lower house, actually lost two seats, as people turned in blank ballots rather than cast a vote to give the Communist Party candidate 50% (Sachs, 1993, p. 38). The result was a resounding victory for Solidarity, and an unprecedented legitimacy for the incoming government. It proceeded to pursue drastic reforms in rapid succession: 'liberalisation, stabilisation, privatisation, creation of a social safety net' (Sachs, 1993, p. 79). The government reduced tariffs, freed prices and opened trade to the West, especially the European Union, which it would

    eventually join. Stabilisation focused first and foremost on the reduction of subsidies, raising revenues and balancing of the budget.

[8]   Collective action problems are related to common-pool problems, though in the case of common-pool, goods are non-excludable, but rivalrous: use by one individual depletes the total available for others (Ostrom, 1990).

[9]   Several commonalities are typical of reforms that must overcome collective action problems, and were evident in the Nicaraguan and Salvadoran cases. First, such reforms emerge only after seemingly polarised elites found a way to negotiate a compromise. Second, such reforms are very limited in nature. Reaching an agreement among opposing forces required compromise, and compromise required all parties to restrain their demands. Also, the reforms were negotiated and agreed at the level of elites, within the leadership of political parties and mostly within the legislature, far from the animus of popular pressure, and therefore limited in their ambition and their impact.

[10]   There are two typical cases. The first is the case of moral hazard, in which information asymmetries make it possible for actors with information to take advantage of those without. A related case is the case of adverse selection, in which entire markets are characterised by limited information, creating distortions in which products on offer are low quality or overpriced or assumed to be that way. As an example, information problems frequently characterise insurance markets, such as medical insurance, in which individuals know they are sickly but insurers do not, leading to insufficient or too expensive care.

[11]   Merilee Grindle (2004) has explored these patterns for the case of education reforms. To provide greater information and secure broader support, governments seek slow changes, marginal improvements and incremental steps. If they can secure 'low hanging fruit', they can then proceed to more challenging tasks. By moving slowly, governments disseminate greater understanding of the nature of change and the full costs and benefits, and citizens can evaluate whether and how much they will benefit.

[12]   By pursuing reforms that are so small as to be almost imperceptible, Jenkins (1999) argues that India has made significant progress in liberalising key economic sectors. Once the benefits of these reforms became evident, it was possible to disseminate successes and pursue greater changes. In addition, the federal structure of India offered an additional advantage, the presence of multiple state and local jurisdictions. Piecemeal reforms could be experimented and advanced in distinct districts and thereby increase the amount of knowledge about reform processes while lowering the sense of risk. Once success was evident at the local level, reforms could be scaled up to the state and national levels. Further, if a reform failed to have the desired effects, the damage was limited.

[13]   Further, contracts resolve information problems related to transaction costs. Some assets have value in forms that are difficult to transfer, such as physical property.

It is difficult to know exactly how much a property is worth, and contracts offer a guarantee to parties to a transaction that the values being exchanged are equal and transferable.

14   One example of using contracts to deal with transaction costs is the case of labour. In a typical labour contract, the employer offers a wage and receives the work of the labourer. Yet the work of the labourer has a specific form, impossible to separate from the person of the labourer, and for this reason difficult to exchange without a well-specified contract. This example also suggests information asymmetries, in which the employer cannot be sure if the worker is using all of her effort or skill when she enters into the contract. To resolve these transaction costs, labour markets are characterised by many forms of contract, including open markets, collective bargaining agreements between firms and unions, and government regulations on the terms of contracts, such as minimum wage legislation. The point is that transactions that might otherwise be prohibitively costly to undertake and enforce are made possible through contracts.

9

EQUITY, GROWTH AND BALANCED BUDGETS: TAX POLICY IN THE UNITED STATES

Dennis S. Ippolito

On 7 June 2001, President George W. Bush signed into law one of the largest tax cuts in the history of the United States. The Economic Growth and Tax Relief Reconciliation Act of 2001 contained an estimated $1.4 trillion in tax cuts, primarily individual income tax reductions, over 10 years (Congressional Budget Office, 2001, p. 5). Additional tax cuts for individuals, and to a lesser extent corporations, were enacted each year from 2002–06. Since budget deficits over this period averaged more than $300 billion annually, the Bush tax programme has been widely criticised as fiscally irresponsible. But with Democratic control of the Congress for the final two years of his presidency, most of the Bush tax cuts will likely be allowed to expire after 2010.[1] As a result, structural tax policy will revert to pre-Bush parameters, baseline revenue levels will climb accordingly, and baseline deficits will shrink or disappear (Congressional Budget Office, 2007a, p. 2).

The fiscal impact of the Bush presidency, then, may prove limited.[2] There is, however, another dimension of the Bush tax programme that illuminates deep and long-standing divisions in American politics. The individual income tax cuts of the past several years, especially the reductions in marginal rates, have reinforced partisan differences over progressivity versus economic efficiency. Democrats have charged that broad-based tax cuts disproportionately benefit high-income taxpayers and reduce the equity or fairness of the tax system. Republicans have countered that tax burdens have actually become more progressive as marginal rates have declined and, more importantly, that low rates promote economic growth.

The debate over marginal tax rates has been a central feature of American politics since the New Deal of the 1930s. From this perspective, the Bush presidency is simply the latest skirmish in an ongoing partisan battle over equity and progressivity. And again, since marginal rate reductions for high-income taxpayers will probably disappear in a few years, Bush's success in reshaping tax policy may prove short lived.

The reality, however, is more complex when it comes to assessing the tax policy legacy of the Bush administration or other administrations. Tax policy in the United States cannot be divorced from broader issues about budget policy — whether and how budgets should be balanced; the appropriate composition of spending policy; and the size and role of government. This last issue is particularly important in analysing the politics of tax policy in the United States. Over the past several decades, federal revenue-GDP levels have averaged slightly more than 18 per cent (Congressional Budget Office, 2007a, p. 77). Spending-GDP levels have been higher — averaging above 20 per cent — and more volatile. The rarity of balanced budgets — only eight over the past half-century — demonstrates the intractability of political divisions over whether to balance budgets at high or low revenue levels.[3]

In addition, as the budget has shifted from discretionary spending, particularly on defence, to mandatory spending for social welfare entitlements, spending controllability has weakened and deficit control has become more difficult. This budget policy context, then, is key to understanding the goals and significance of the Bush administration's tax programme and the types of tax policy challenges future administrations will face.

Modern Tax Policy: The Stable Era

The 1970s was a pivotal decade with respect to tax policy and to budget policy generally. From the end of World War II until the 1970s, tax policy was relatively stable, constrained by a bipartisan consensus on Cold War defence spending and on the balanced-budget rule. But the shift in spending policy from defence to social welfare initiated by the Johnson administration's Great Society programmes shattered this consensus and exacerbated partisan stakes over tax policy.

Balanced-budget Stability

The post-World War II administrations of Harry S. Truman and Dwight D. Eisenhower subordinated tax policy to spending requirements. As a result, budgets were balanced three times during the late 1940s and four times between 1950 and 1960. From 1961 until the late 1990s, by comparison, there was only one balanced budget, in 1969, and deficit-GDP levels climbed steadily over much of this latter period.

The balanced-budget priority of the Truman and Eisenhower administrations required high revenue levels, which precluded major changes in tax policy (Witte, 1985, p. 153). Individual income tax rates changed very little under Truman, and the top marginal rate remained above 90 per cent under

Eisenhower (Steuerle, 2004, p. 48). Corporate tax rates were lowered very little over this period, and a number of World War II excise taxes were repeatedly extended as well.

In effect, the mass tax system put into place to finance World War II was left largely intact thereafter. During 1944 and 1945, revenue-GDP levels averaged approximately 20.5 per cent, with nearly 80 per cent of these revenues generated by individual and corporate income taxes (US Government, 2007, pp. 31–33). Over the next 15 years, revenue-GDP levels averaged 17 per cent, with the individual income tax supplying nearly half of these revenues.

The paucity of major tax law changes over such an extended period obscures some intense partisan battles over tax policy. In 1947 and 1948, for example, the Republican-controlled Congress repeatedly challenged Truman over tax cuts. Truman successfully vetoed two early versions of what he called the 'wrong kind of tax reduction at the wrong time', with one of his objections being the disproportionate allocation of tax cuts to upper-income taxpayers (Ippolito, 1990, p. 36). A third Truman veto just prior to the 1948 election was overridden, in part because of bipartisan congressional support for a less regressive measure (Ippolito, 1990, p. 36).

With a Democratic-controlled Congress during Truman's second term, the pressure for additional tax cuts lessened. At the same time, Truman's efforts to reverse the 1948 tax cuts were unsuccessful. Not until the outbreak of the Korean War did Congress agree to a tax increase, which sharply raised revenue-GDP levels.[4]

The Eisenhower administration took office in 1953 and launched a comprehensive revision of the federal income tax code. In addition to numerous technical changes, a variety of tax preferences were instituted, but the net revenue loss from the final 1954 Bill was minimal. Moreover, and despite Republican control of the House and Senate, the 1954 tax Bill made only minor reduction in marginal rates — the lowest rate was lowered from 22.2 to 20 per cent, while the top rate went from 92 to 91 per cent.

In 1955, facing a Democratic Congress, Eisenhower blocked any tax cut. During his second term, with Democrats continuing to control the House and Senate, Eisenhower agreed to minor adjustments in corporation, payroll and excise taxes, but individual income tax policy was preserved intact. At the end of his presidency, Eisenhower called for any immediate surpluses to be used for debt reduction, with his successor and future Congresses exercising 'the choice they should rightly have in deciding between reductions in the public debt and lightening of the tax burden, or both' (US Government 1960, p. M8).

The Eisenhower tax programme, then, was governed by spending requirements, which were driven primarily by Cold War defence budgets. As shown in Table 9.1, defence-GDP levels nearly tripled during the Korean War and averaged approximately 10 per cent annually for the remainder of the 1950s. The defence percentage of total federal outlays, which peaked at nearly 70 per cent during Korea, remained well above 50 per cent through 1961.

Table 9.1: Defence Budget Shares and Percentage of GDP, 1950–61

| Fiscal Year | Defence Percentage of | |
	Total Outlays	GDP
1950	32.2%	5.0%
1951	51.8	7.4
1952	68.1	13.2
1953	69.4	14.2
1954	69.5	13.1
1955	62.4	10.8
1956	60.2	10.0
1957	59.3	10.1
1958	56.8	10.2
1959	53.2	10.0
1960	52.2	9.3
1961	50.8	9.3

Source: US Government 2007, pp. 119-20.

An important, if frequently overlooked, aspect of these unprecedented 'peacetime' defence spending levels was the extent to which Eisenhower resisted pressures from the military and from Congress for even higher defence budgets. On fiscal and social policy grounds, Eisenhower insisted that defence spending had to be kept within sustainable ceilings, and his defence budget requests to Congress reflected this approach (Ippolito, 1990, pp. 104–05). In the end, Congress generally acceded. The post-Korea defence budgets that Eisenhower proposed were nearly identical to the appropriations enacted by Congress (Ippolito, 1990, p. 106).

The Great Society Transition

The Kennedy–Johnson years produced important changes in spending policy that eventually undermined the stability of tax policy. The Revenue Act of 1964, signed by Lyndon B. Johnson but initiated by John F. Kennedy, provided large, broad-based and permanent tax cuts for individuals. It also marked a significant departure in revenue policy, subordinating balanced-budget concerns to economic growth. Four years later, the Revenue and Expenditure Control Act increased individual income tax-GDP revenues to their highest level since World War II. In between, spending was increased for the Vietnam War and for the Great Society's domestic programmes. The spending impact of the former began to diminish after 1968, but outlays for domestic programmes greatly accelerated. As spending policy shifted from defence to social welfare, deficit-control problems began to mount.

When President Kennedy sent his tax cut proposal to Congress in 1963, he stated that: 'Our present choice is not between a tax cut and a balanced budget ... [but] rather, is between chronic deficits arising out of a slow rate of economic growth, and temporary deficits stemming from a tax programme designed to promote a fuller use of our resources and more rapid economic growth' (US Government, 1963, pp. 10–11). The centrepiece of this new tax programme was a lower marginal rate structure for individuals that would remove 'the checkrein of taxes on private spending and productive incentive' (US Government, 1963, p. 9). To replace the 20–91 per cent rates then in effect, Kennedy proposed a lower and narrower set of brackets from 14–65 per cent.

Congress ultimately approved marginal rate reductions that were reasonably close to the original proposals. The lowest bracket was lowered to 14 per cent, but the top rate was set at 70 per cent and intermediate brackets were adjusted accordingly. A new minimum standard deduction was added to reduce further the tax liability of low-income taxpayers, but cuts were large and roughly proportional for middle-income taxpayers (Ippolito, 1990, p. 42). When rate changes and structural reforms were taken into account, high-income taxpayers had their existing tax liabilities reduced by almost 15 per cent (Ippolito, 1990, p. 42).

Progressivity, then, was not a major consideration in the 1964 tax law changes. In addition, the Kennedy tax cut introduced a new fiscal policy approach in which economic growth took primacy over a balanced budget. In establishing a credible precedent for large, across-the-board tax cuts to promote economic growth, Kennedy set the stage for an even more ambitious tax-cut programme by the Reagan administration two decades later.

Initially, the 1964 tax cuts helped fuel the economic expansion of the mid-1960s and, because spending growth was modest in 1963 and 1964, deficits were much smaller than expected (Ippolito, 1990, p. 43). When defence and domestic spending growth then began to climb, President Johnson conceded that additional revenues would be needed to keep deficits under control. But Johnson was reluctant to increase taxes for individuals, particularly in advance of the 1966 mid-term elections. Instead, Johnson proposed and Congress approved the Tax Adjustment Act of 1966 that mandated graduated withholding for individuals and accelerated tax payments for corporations. Congress also enacted a second tax Bill that suspended corporate investment credits.

These revenue measures proved insufficient, as defence and domestic spending growth generated outlay-GDP levels that were comparable to those of the Korean War, albeit with a smaller defence share. In FY1968, for example, outlays were 20.6 per cent of GDP, with defence accounting for 45 per cent of total spending. In 1953, when outlays were 20.4 per cent of GDP, defence was 70 per cent of total spending. And unlike Korea, when taxes were raised sharply at the outset to finance the war, major Vietnam War tax increases were delayed. As a result, the FY1968 deficit of 2.9 per cent of GDP was well above the Korean War peaks.

In August 1967, Johnson finally sent Congress specific proposals to increase taxes on individuals and corporations. When Congress passed the Revenue and Expenditure Control Act the following June, a 6 per cent surcharge on individual and corporate tax liabilities was instituted. Congress also forced the administration to accept domestic spending cuts. The combined effect was a FY1969 surplus, the first balanced budget in a decade.[5]

Nevertheless, the Johnson presidency had put in place a domestic programme base that would require high revenue levels even as Vietnam War spending declined. The Kennedy–Johnson era also altered tax burdens in ways that would make it more difficult to maintain these high revenue levels. In the early 1960s, almost 90 per cent of taxpayers were facing marginal rates of approximately 20 per cent (Congressional Budget Office, 1983, p. 9). By 1969, nearly two-thirds of taxpayers were in higher brackets. Despite the 1964 tax cut, average tax rates for individuals had increased, while FY1969 individual income tax-GDP revenues were 9.2 per cent, the highest level since World War II. And to complicate the politics of tax policy even further, social security taxes and state and local taxes were rising as well.

Modern Tax Policy: The Reagan Effect

The presidency of Ronald Reagan had an enormous impact on the politics of tax policy. Under Reagan, the largest individual income tax cut since World War II was enacted in 1981 (Jones and Williams, 2008, pp. 10–11). And in 1986, the Tax Reform Act lowered the top marginal rate on individual income to 28 per cent, the lowest rate in half a century. Reagan's presidency also produced huge deficits of course, which makes his tax cut accomplishments even more remarkable. But in order to understand Reagan's fiscal approach and priorities, it is necessary to take into account the confused and confusing course that tax policy, and budget policy generally, took during the 1970s.

Tax Policy in Disarray

During the Nixon, Ford and Carter administrations, tax law changes were frequent, and tax policy was erratic. A series of tax 'reform' measures did little to improve the revenue productivity or fairness of the tax code. Indeed, tax preferences — exclusions, deductions and credits that reduced 'normal' tax liabilities — proliferated, even as promises to improve equity were advanced by large and increasingly liberal Democratic majorities in Congress. And, despite the steep defence cuts after the Vietnam War, deficit-GDP levels were much higher in the 1970s than in the preceding decade. Finally, the economy performed poorly, with high levels of inflation and unemployment. It is always difficult for tax policy to reconcile the competing demands of equity, economic efficiency and revenue sufficiency. In the 1970s, however, it appeared that none of these requirements was being satisfied.

Nixon–Ford

Before leaving office, Lyndon Johnson had proposed several deficit-control tax increases, and his Treasury Department had recommended major reforms in structural tax policy to curb tax avoidance by the wealthy. The Tax Reform Act that Richard M. Nixon signed in 1969 incorporated many of these reforms — a new minimum tax on preference income, increased capital gains levies, higher exemptions and standard deductions for low- and middle-income taxpayers — and provided for net increases in individual and corporate taxes. The structural reforms in the 1969 tax Bill broadened the tax base, and the redistribution of tax burdens improved the progressivity of the income tax (Ippolito, 1990, p. 48). But this reformist impulse proved short lived.

In 1970, Nixon's budget message to Congress recommended payroll tax increases (for social security), along with excise tax extensions and new user fees for special government services. Congress rejected most of Nixon's tax programme, and the excise tax extension it finally approved also cut back the minimum tax requirements enacted in 1969. The following year, Nixon initially pursued a similar course but, with the economy weakening and deficits increasing, he announced an economic recovery programme that included individual and corporate tax cuts. The Revenue Act of 1971, cleared by Congress in December, generally conformed to Nixon's recommendations. Higher personal exemptions and standard deductions for individuals were instituted, investment tax credits were reinstated and tax preferences for corporations were expanded. The size of the tax cut, an estimated $25.9 billion over three years, was relatively small, but additional tax reductions, both permanent and temporary, were enacted in 1975, 1976, 1977 and 1978.

While Nixon and the Democratic-controlled Congress could agree on stimulative tax cuts, their battles over spending ceilings — and deficits — were intensifying. In 1972, for example, Nixon vetoed a number of spending bills, as he tried to force Congress to adopt an overall limit on spending. And while he achieved some tactical success in 1972, the level and composition of spending policy was moving in a decidedly Democratic direction. Over the FY1969–75 period, Congress cut defence-GDP levels from 8.7 to 5.6 per cent (US Government 2007, p. 136). Over the same period, spending for social welfare programmes increased from 5.7 per cent of GDP to 9.7 per cent, and discretionary domestic spending-GDP levels increased as well. By FY1975, defence outlays had dropped to about one-fourth of total spending, and that budget share would fall even further in the later 1970s.

On the tax side, Nixon's attempts to broaden the tax base and reduce tax preferences were blocked by Congress. Indeed, in 1974 Congress significantly expanded tax preferences by creating tax-free treatment of retirement savings and pension plans. And in 1974 Congress also adopted a new budget process designed to counter more effectively executive branch influence over tax and spending policy (Ippolito, 1981, pp. 37–38).

When Nixon resigned in August 1974, Gerald Ford became president. Two months later, Ford sent to Congress an income tax surcharge proposal coupled with tax relief for low- and middle-income taxpayers and business tax cuts. Congress took no action on Ford's tax programme and ignored much of the remainder of his economic recovery agenda. During 1975, as the economy continued to deteriorate, Ford recommended a tax cut, which Congress then used as a vehicle for new spending and tax preferences as well as the straightforward rebates Ford had proposed. Later in the year, Ford vetoed a tax-cut extension, and forced Congress to include spending reductions and an overall spending ceiling in the measure he ultimately signed.

Ford's broader effort to revive the structural reform focus of the 1969 Tax Reform Act made very little headway in Congress. By the time Congress completed action on the Tax Reform Act of 1976, most of Ford's comprehensive tax programme had disappeared. In addition, the permanent individual and corporate tax cuts contained in the Bill greatly outweighed its reform provisions (Ippolito, 1990, p. 50).

The Carter Presidency

The absence of clear direction in tax policy continued under Jimmy Carter. Early in 1997, Congress passed the Tax Reduction and Simplification Act, yet another in a series of economic stimulus tax cuts. Having failed to define the scope and substance of that legislation, Carter attempted to regain the initiative on budget policy with a comprehensive tax package in 1978. In this instance, Carter proposed curbing or eliminating major tax preferences to help offset the cost of individual and corporate tax cuts. For individuals, Carter called for a two percentage point reduction in all tax brackets. Carter also recommended that investment tax credits for corporations be permanently extended.

The Revenue Act of 1978 bore little resemblance to the Carter plans for tax reform. The most dramatic difference was with respect to capital gains. Carter had called for tightening the tax treatment of capital gains for upper-income taxpayers, as part of a broader effort to increase the progressivity of the income tax. Instead, Congress raised the capital gains exclusion from 50 to 60 per cent and weakened the existing alternative minimum tax treatment of capital gains (Ippolito, 1990, p. 51). Congress also scaled back the individual tax cuts Carter had recommended, leaving the marginal rates untouched, while widening brackets and providing roughly proportional reductions in tax liabilities for all but the lowest income group (Ippolito, 1990, p. 51).

While the Carter administration did manage to persuade Congress to limit the total revenue losses under the 1978 Revenue Act, neither serious tax reform nor increased progressivity was achieved. Moreover, Congress passed additional legislation to prevent Carter's Treasury Department from issuing proposed new rules affecting the tax treatment of fringe benefits, making even clearer its aversion to serious tax reform. That prohibition was extended the following year. Congress did agree to minor tax increases as part of a fiscal 1981 budget reconciliation Bill, including limits on the use of tax-free bonds by state and local governments and stricter rules on capital gains from foreign real estate investments, but the Carter presidency had very little impact on structural tax policy during its one term.

Tax legislation during the 1970s, then, eviscerated the principled coherence of the Tax Reform Act of 1969. The proliferation of tax preferences during the 1970s was truly remarkable. By FY1981, there were more than 100 tax preferences, roughly double the number 10 years earlier, and their combined revenue loss had increased from less than 25 per cent of total budget receipts to nearly 40 per cent (Ippolito, 1990, p. 54). Since the reduction in tax liabilities was roughly proportional for the vast majority of taxpayers, the tax preference system meant less progressive individual taxation, despite the steep marginal rate structure that remained in effect.

Progressivity was also adversely affected by inflation-induced 'bracket creep', in which taxpayers faced higher tax brackets without equivalent increases in real income, and by rapidly escalating social security taxes. When the 1978 tax cut was passed, for example, estimates showed that inflation-generated tax increases and the social security tax increase approved the previous year would offset scheduled income tax cuts for virtually all income groups (Ippolito, 1990, p. 54).

When Ronald Reagan ran for president, income tax and social security tax burdens for individuals had been rising sharply, the economy was anaemic, and the budget had been in deficit for 11 consecutive years. The Reagan tax-cut programme did not disavow the importance of balanced budgets. Supply-side theories, which claimed that tax cuts would eventually lead to increased revenues because of incentive-driven economic growth, were embraced by Reagan to reconcile his commitment both to tax cuts and balanced budgets. But the 1970s had weakened the political importance of and economic justification for balanced budgets, which meant that tax policy was ripe for a drastic overhaul.

Taxes, Defence and Deficits

The Reagan administration's tax programme was designed to provide immediate economic stimulus and, over the long term, to reduce the size and redefine the role of the federal government. Ronald Reagan's overriding priorities were tax cuts and defence budget increases. Reagan was also committed, however, to major domestic policy retrenchments, including cutbacks in social welfare programmes such as social security and Medicare. The strategy of pursuing tax cuts in advance of offsetting spending reductions was set forth in the president's 1982 economic report, which explained 'that it will take some time to achieve the desired level of deficits' and to enforce 'a trend toward a balanced budget … necessary to restrain the growth of government' (Tobin and Weidenbaum, 1988, p. 420).

Reagan's agenda was only partly successful. Tax cuts were achieved in 1981, which also marked the beginning of a sustained buildup in defence spending and, over time, Reagan managed to reverse the growth of discretionary domestic programmes. Outlay-GDP levels for these programmes had nearly doubled over the preceding two decades; by the late 1980s, these levels were close to where they had been before the Great Society expansion. On social welfare, however, significant cutbacks were not realised. As a result, overall spending-GDP levels remained high, and deficits exploded. By FY1986, when the 1981 tax cuts were fully phased in, their estimated revenue loss was about $210 billion, and the budget deficit was over $220 billion (Ippolito, 1990, p. 65).

The 1981 tax cut was only part of a more complicated Reagan tax record. In 1982 and 1984, for example, election-year tax increases were enacted that curbed or eliminated some of the corporate tax loss provisions from 1981. In 1983, social security payroll taxes were raised, and social security benefits became taxable for high-income recipients. Most important, the Tax Reform Act of 1986 marked the most far-reaching and arguably most progressive tax reform since World War II. The 1986 Bill established a modified flat tax for individuals and corporations, but it also shifted tax burdens from individuals to corporations, eliminated billions of dollars in tax preferences, and eliminated all income-tax liabilities for millions of low-income taxpayers. It was also, in intent and largely in effect, deficit-neutral.

The 1981 Tax Bill

By the time Congress completed action on the 1981 Economic Recovery Tax Act, its five-year cost had risen to an estimated $750 billion in individual and corporate tax cuts, larger by far than any previous tax cut and well above Reagan's original proposal. But the 1981 Bill clearly embodied Reagan's philosophy about tax policy. The focus was economic growth through enhanced individual incentives for work, savings and investment, as well as investment and productivity tax incentives for business. Individual incentives were, in Reagan's view, tied to marginal tax rates, and the final version of the 1981 Bill reduced marginal tax rates for individuals by 23 per cent over three years and cut the top marginal rate from 70 to 50 per cent. In addition, tax brackets, standard deductions and personal exemptions were indexed to eliminate inflation-generated tax increases.

On the corporate side, lower rates were put in place, along with liberalised tax treatment of investments in plant and equipment and some two dozen new or expanded tax preferences. These business tax cuts were estimated at about $150 billion over five years, approximately 20 per cent of the projected revenue loss from the overall Bill (Ippolito, 1990, p. 59). A number of these business tax preferences were scaled back or eliminated, however, in 1982 and 1984.

While the 1981 tax cut exacerbated the deficit problem, the economic stimulus it provided eventually yielded impressive results. By the end of Reagan's first term, the signs of economic recovery were unmistakable, as was the diminution of the inflation problems of the late 1970s. As economic growth persisted despite high deficits, Republicans became less willing to sacrifice low revenue levels in order to balance the budget. Democrats were equally unwilling to sacrifice social welfare spending. The inevitable result was a partisan standoff on budget policy even as both sides pledged allegiance to a balanced budget.

In addition, the 1981 tax cuts complicated the debate over fairness. The 1981 Democratic critiques of the president's tax plan featured the predictable theme of 'tax cuts for the rich', and these critiques continued throughout the Reagan presidency. As tax return data for 1982 and 1983 became available, however, it was apparent that tax revenues and the shares of total income taxes paid by upper-income groups were increasing significantly, while low-income middle-income shares were declining (Internal Revenue Service, 1985, pp. 80–81). Despite lower marginal rates for all taxpayers, tax burdens had shifted to high-income taxpayers and especially to the top 1 per cent.

The central importance that Reagan assigned to marginal rates on individual income was underscored by the deficit-reduction tax increases in 1982 and 1984. The Tax Equity and Fiscal Responsibility Act of 1982 reduced the short-term revenue losses for the 1981 tax cut by more than 25 per cent through 'revenue enhancers' — that is, scaled-back tax preferences, especially for business — but made no changes in Reagan's individual tax policies (Ippolito, 1990, p. 67). The Deficit Reduction Act of 1984 targeted tax preferences once again, and also contained excise tax extensions and increases, but individual tax rates were unaffected.

The 1984 election presented a sharp contrast on tax policy. The Democratic platform pledged to 'cap the effect of the Reagan tax cuts for wealthy Americans and enhance the progressivity of the tax code' (*Congressional Quarterly*, 1985, p. 28-B). The Republican platform was quintessential Reaganism, calling for the outright elimination of 'the incentive-destroying effects of graduated tax rates' (*Congressional Quarterly*, 1985, p. 42-B). With Reagan's landslide re-election, that goal no longer seemed far fetched.

The Tax Relief Act of 1986 was a milestone in federal tax policy, establishing a flat tax for high-income taxpayers (with a maximum effective rate of 28 per cent), making wholesale reductions in tax preferences, and eliminating all income liability for an estimated six million low-income taxpayers through higher personal exemptions and standard deductions (*Congressional Quarterly*, 1987, p. 524). This last provision was hailed by the Democratic Speaker of the House, Thomas P. O'Neill, as 'the best anti-poverty bill in this House for at least half a dozen years' (*Congressional Quarterly*, 1987, p. 524). That the lowest marginal rate structure since the 1920s was widely perceived as 'fair' meant that tax burdens, not rates, were now being viewed by many as the more meaningful measure of progressivity. And since the Tax Reform Act of 1986 explicitly transferred tax burdens from low- and middle-income taxpayers to high-income taxpayers, and also from individuals to corporations, it attracted bipartisan support in Congress and widespread approval from economists and tax experts.

What the 1986 tax Bill did not do, however, was reduce deficits. Designed to be revenue-neutral in its net revenue impact on individuals and corporations, the measure actually increased short-term deficits slightly (Ippolito, 1990, p. 86). Taking into account the 1981 tax cut, the 1986 tax reform measure and all of the offsetting tax increases adopted during Reagan's presidency, revenues were lower than they would have been if pre-Reagan tax law had remained in effect. It is important to note, however, that revenue-GDP levels under Reagan were still relatively high — indeed, average annual levels for the 1980s were higher than those for the preceding three decades, with individual income tax-GDP levels significantly higher (see Table 9.2). Total spending-GDP levels for the 1980s were above 22 per cent, by far the highest for the period, but domestic programmes — notably social welfare entitlements — rather than defence were driving this spending. The extremely high deficits of the 1980s, then, demonstrate the deep divisions over how to finance expanded domestic spending commitments. The Reagan administration had hoped, in the beginning, to retrench those commitments and, over time, balance the budget. When Congress blocked these social welfare retrenchments, the administration refused to abandon its tax programme and settled for deficits. Thus, when Reagan left office, the question was whether that refusal would continue or be abandoned in favour of deficit reduction.

Table 9.2: Revenues, Spending and Deficits, Fiscal Years 1950–89

	Revenues		Spending		
Fiscal Years	*Individual Income*	*Total*	*Defence*	*Total*	*Deficits*
1950–59	7.4%	17.2%	10.4%	17.6%	0.4%
1960–69	7.8	17.9	8.7	18.7	0.8
1970–79	8.1	8.0	5.9	20.0	2.1
1980–89	8.5	18.3	5.8	22.2	3.9

Source: US Government 2007, pp. 25, 33, 47-52.

Balanced Budgets vs. Tax Cuts

The 1990s produced a remarkable shift in budget policy. The decade began with deficits that climbed to nearly $300 billion and ended with large and growing surpluses. A high level of economic growth in the United States for most of the decade contributed significantly to this dramatic improvement in the nation's fiscal outlook. But major changes in spending policy, particularly defence cuts, and tax policy, notably individual income tax increases, were necessary in order to eliminate structural deficits and bring deficits into balance.

No New Taxes

The first step in fiscal consolidation took place under George H.W. Bush. In 1988, Bush had campaigned for the presidency with a firm commitment to the Reagan priorities on defence and taxes. On the former, Bush pledged to support defence increases for strategic and conventional force modernisation (Ippolito, 2003, p. 243). The tax pledge, highlighted in his acceptance speech at the Republican convention, was unambiguous: 'Read my lips. No new taxes.' Two years later, Bush signed a multi-year, $500 billion deficit-reduction Bill that curbed defence budgets and raised taxes.

While the end of the Cold War shielded Bush from criticism over his defence programme, the tax increase was another matter entirely. Bush had very little support from congressional Republicans as a deficit-reduction package was negotiated during the spring and summer of 1990. The higher tax rates (and related cutbacks in deductions and exemptions for high-income taxpayers) included in the reconciliation Bill he eventually signed positively enraged many conservatives in his party.

The political price that Bush paid for breaking his tax pledge might seem excessive, given the fiscal situation he faced. In 1985 and 1987, Reagan and Congress had agreed on statutory deficit ceilings to force a balanced budget over six years — either through negotiated deficit-reduction programmes or automatic cuts in spending programmes. The deficit ceilings that Reagan faced were sufficiently high that he was able to avoid hard choices on taxes or defence, and Bush's first year in office benefited from a similarly favourable fiscal outlook. On 29 January 1991, when Bush submitted his FY1991 budget to Congress, he stated that the deficit ceiling ($64 billion in 1991) would be met without any 'major legislative action' (US Government, 1990, p. 9). In 1993, he reported that the budget would be balanced without any new taxes.

This optimistic outlook soon evaporated as the economy abruptly weakened. By March, the Congressional Budget Office (CBO) was reporting that the Bush budget had seriously overestimated revenues and underestimated spending (Congressional Budget Office, 1990a, pp. 1–10). The CBO projected the FY1991 deficit would be $130 billion, more than double the allowable deficit ceiling. By June, as the economy deteriorated further, the CBO estimate had climbed to $230 billion, and the out-year deficit estimates were even higher (Congressional Budget Office, 1990b, p. xiii). With deficits of this magnitude, automatic spending cuts were not a feasible option. In FY1991, for example, even $100 billion in spending cuts (or sequesters) would have required a 25 per cent reduction in defence and a 40 per cent reduction in discretionary domestic programmes (Congressional Budget Office, 1990b, p. 56). Additional cuts would then be needed to meet the deficit ceilings for 1992 and 1993.

Faced with these unyielding realities, Bush called for congressional leaders to negotiate with administration officials a comprehensive, multi-year deficit-reduction programme. The Democratic leaders of the House and Senate agreed to participate in a 'budget summit', but insisted that Bush would first have to renounce his 'no new taxes' pledge. When he did so, conceding that the 'size of the deficit problem' made 'tax revenue increases' necessary, the negotiations finally began (*Congressional Quarterly*, 1991, p. 130).

The budget summit of 1990 lasted nearly five months, and the original agreement between administration and congressional representatives contained an estimated $500 billion in deficit earnings over five years. The ratio of spending cuts to tax increases was approximately 2:1, as Democrats agreed to entitlement cutbacks and administration representatives accepted defence cuts. On the tax side, higher energy taxes, Medicare payroll taxes and individual income taxes were included, but there was no change to marginal tax rates. Instead, White House negotiators agreed to raise tax liabilities for upper-income taxpayers by limiting their itemised deductions.

Bush's efforts to rally support for the deficit-reduction agreement made little headway. The Iraqi invasion of Kuwait in August had led to a mass deployment of US troops to the Persian Gulf, and Bush hoped that congressional Republicans would rally behind him accordingly. Instead, a majority of House Republicans joined with liberal Democrats in rejecting the budget agreement. This unusual alliance was forged as Republican conservatives rejected any compromise on taxes, and Democratic liberals deserted their leaders on entitlement reductions.

The ironic result, at least for Republicans, was a new budget plan that relied even more heavily on tax increases, and in particular raised the top marginal rate to 31 per cent. Passed without Republican support and signed by Bush under duress, the 1990 Omnibus Budget Reconciliation Act (OBRA 1990) was a clear-cut policy victory for congressional Democrats. What the Bush administration was able to salvage came in the form of new budget process controls — multiyear limits or caps on discretionary spending and pay-as-you-go (or Paygo) restrictions on tax cuts and entitlement programme increases — that would protect deficit-reduction savings through FY1995.

While the 1990 budget Act would eventually begin to narrow the deficit gap, its immediate effects were negated by continuing weakness in the economy. The impact on revenues was particularly pronounced. OBRA 1990 was expected to raise revenue-GDP levels to approximately 19.5 per cent from 1991–95; actual revenues for the period averaged less than 18 per cent (Ippolito, 2003, p. 285). As a result, deficits remained high. Bush had paid a heavy political cost for raising taxes, and he had very little to show for it in terms of deficit reduction. Bill Clinton, by comparison, managed not only to balance the budget but to do so while advancing Democratic priorities.

The 1993 Budget Agreement

When the Clinton administration took office in 1993, deficit projections were actually worsening. According to Clinton, the budget he inherited would, if left unchanged, generate a $635 billion deficit by 2000, with sharp escalations in debt levels and interest costs (*Congressional Quarterly*, 1994, p. 10-D). The nearly $500 billion in deficit reduction he then proposed to Congress still left the projected deficit at $240 billion by 1998, despite tax increases that were much larger than those Bush had approved.

The Omnibus Budget Reconciliation Act of 1993 barely made it through the Democratic-controlled Congress — Republican opposition was unanimous, Democratic defections brought the House margin down to two votes and, in the Senate, the Vice President was forced to break a 50–50 tie. While there were controversies over virtually all of the major elements of the 1993 budget agreement, the most intense disputes centred around tax policy. For example, the Clinton administration failed to gain congressional support for a new energy tax. It did succeed, however, in raising marginal rates and overall tax burdens for high-income taxpayers.

In comparing the 1990 and 1993 deficit-reduction agreements, the latter was much more reliant on tax increases. Of an estimated $240 billion in additional revenues over five years, nearly half came from raising top marginal rates from 31 per cent to 39.6 per cent (Congressional Budget Office, 1993, p. 20). High-income taxpayers were also targeted for higher Medicare payroll taxes and additional taxes on Social Security benefits. In sum, about 80 per cent of the tax increases under OBRA 1993 affected only high-income taxpayers. To push this redistribution of tax burdens even further, OBRA 1993 expanded the earned-income tax credit for low-income families. With this expansion, effective tax rates (income and payroll) for low-income workers were expected to drop to the lowest levels in two decades (Ippolito, 2003, p. 263).

In addition to reversing the marginal rate cuts of the 1980s, OBRA 1993 took aim at Reagan's cutbacks in discretionary domestic spending. The discretionary spending caps in the 1993 budget Act were extremely tight and expected to yield substantial deficit savings. Clinton and congressional Democrats assumed that they would nevertheless be able to provide real growth in domestic programmes by cutting defence, an assumption that proved to be correct.

The Balanced-budget Battle

The 1994 mid-term elections gave Republicans control of both houses of Congress for the first time in 50 years. Before long, the Clinton administration and the Republican congressional leadership were locked in a bitter fight over budget policy, and especially taxes. After Republicans failed to pass a constitutional balanced-budget amendment (and send it to the states for ratification), they moved forward with an ambitious plan to eliminate deficits by 2002. This deficit-reduction programme was very different from the 1990 and 1993 efforts, however. The Republican road to balanced budgets began with tax cuts totalling an estimated $245 billion, roughly equivalent to the 1993 tax increase (*Congressional Quarterly*, 1996, pp. 2–44). In order to pay for these tax cuts and to eliminate deficits, Republicans proposed massive cutbacks in entitlement programmes — notably Medicare and Medicaid — and in discretionary domestic spending. Projected spending cuts for all domestic programmes totaled nearly $900 billion over seven years.

As this reconciliation legislation was moving through Congress, Republican leaders also challenged Clinton by making immediate cuts in domestic appropriations Bills. When Clinton was presented with spending Bills well below levels he had recommended, he vetoed them, triggering a government shutdown of affected agencies in November. After nearly a week, a continuing resolution was worked out to provide funding through mid-December. Before that deadline was reached, Clinton vetoed the Republicans' reconciliation Bill. He also vetoed three appropriations Bills on 18 December, leading to another government shutdown that affected 260,000 federal employees and lasted nearly three weeks.

Public opinion polls over this period decisively favoured Clinton. As their shutdown strategy turned into a political debacle, Republicans abandoned their attempt to return domestic spending policy to pre-Great Society levels and settled for largely symbolic cuts in domestic appropriations Bills. In 1997, with Clinton easily reelected and Republicans still in control of Congress, balanced-budget negotiations were renewed, and the deficit-reduction plan that finally emerged allowed both sides to claim some modest victories.

The Balanced Budget Act of 1997 extended discretionary spending caps through 2002, providing deficit savings of approximately $90 billion (Ippolito, 2003, p. 280). Mandatory programme reductions added net savings of more than $100 billion, primarily through lower Medicare payments for healthcare providers. The Taxpayer Relief Act of 1997, the second part of the balanced-budget accord, contained net revenue costs of $80 billion over five years, with a new child tax credit, lower capital gains tax rates and tax credits for education expenses. The child tax credits and education tax credits, however, were phasedout at high income levels, and earned-income tax credits were increased for low-income earners. The top marginal rate on individual income remained at 39.6 per cent.

When action was completed on the 1997 spending and tax reconciliation Bills, the projected date for an actual balanced budget was 2002. The fiscal outlook, however, was shifting towards balance much more quickly and decisively than expected. During the 1980s and early 1990s, revenue growth had lagged behind estimates. By the late 1990s, the opposite had occurred. Revenue-GDP levels had soared to 20 per cent in 1998, and by 2000 they had reached nearly 21 per cent. And these higher levels were almost entirely the result of individual income tax increases. With outlay-GDP levels unexpectedly falling below 19 per cent for the first time in a quarter-century, projected deficits were turning into large and growing surpluses.

Despite these surpluses, Republicans were stymied in their efforts to reverse the 1993 tax increases. Clinton blocked both targeted and broad-based tax cuts after 1997, insisting that surpluses be used instead for additional domestic spending and debt reduction. Moreover, Clinton's impeachment by the House of Representatives in 1998 did virtually nothing to lessen his leverage on budget policy. Indeed, he was able to press Congress for entitlement expansions as well as additional domestic discretionary spending in 1999 and 2000.

By the time Clinton left office, his impact on budget policy was comparable to Reagan's, albeit with very different priorities. Clinton had managed to raise marginal rates significantly, to shift income tax burdens and effective tax rates sharply upward for high-income taxpayers, and to balance the budget, while accommodating continued high levels of domestic spending. In addition, the increased revenue levels and higher marginal rates of the 1990s did no apparent damage to the economy. Instead, the economy grew strongly and steadily as tax rates and revenue levels climbed.

The budget policy battles of the 1990s reinforced the linkage between tax policy and domestic spending. When Republicans had advocated a constitutional balanced-budget amendment during the 1980s, and again in 1995, they had assumed the inevitable result would be massive domestic spending cuts. Most Democrats had shared that assumption, which is why they opposed a constitutional amendment and were notably unenthusiastic about deficit reduction generally. With the surpluses of the late 1990s, however, these assumptions no longer held. Republicans realised that without tax cuts to reduce these surpluses, they could not possibly force retrenchments in domestic spending. As Democrats recognised that balanced-budget discipline could protect domestic spending programmes, their fiscal strategy focused on maintaining high revenue levels, and particularly high individual income taxation. In the 2000 elections, not surprisingly, the most contentious budget policy issue was tax cuts.

The Bush Tax Cuts

Republican frustration over tax cuts came to an end with the presidency of George W. Bush. From 2001–06, Bush signed more than a dozen tax cuts with an estimated cost of approximately $2.1 trillion over 10 years (Brill, 2007, p. 347). The largest and most controversial of these were the Economic Growth and Tax Relief Reconciliation Act of 2001 (EGTRRA) and the Jobs and Growth Tax Reconciliation Act of 2003 (JGTRRA). The first reduced marginal tax rates for individuals, provided additional relief for married couples and families with children and repealed estate taxes. The 2003 tax cut accelerated the phase-in of some provisions enacted in 2001, while reducing tax rates for dividends and capital gains.

During his 2000 presidential campaign, Bush had advocated a massive tax cut — $1.3 trillion over 10 years, with lower marginal rates for all income groups (*Congressional Quarterly*, 2006, p. 91). With large and growing budget surpluses being projected at the time, Bush argued that broad-based tax relief was a deserved reward for taxpayers. But Bush and congressional Republican leaders were also anxious to lower long-term revenue levels in order to reduce surpluses that would otherwise support new or expanded domestic programmes. Indeed, by the time that Bush signed the 2001 tax cut, the economy was weakening and surplus projections were starting to shrink. When the 2003 tax cut was enacted, the budget had fallen into deficit, and future surplus projections had evaporated. The Bush administration, however, never wavered in its belief that low tax levels were more important than balanced budgets. For Bush and most congressional Republicans, balancing the budget at high revenue levels — as Clinton had done — threatened long-term economic growth and advanced the Democratic domestic agenda.

The 2001 Tax Cut

When Bush took office in 2001, Republicans controlled the House and, narrowly, the Senate. Indeed, a Republican senator's defection in May switched Senate control to the Democrats, but by that time Republicans had used the special reconciliation rules of the congressional budget process to move Bush's tax-cut programme through Congress. During congressional deliberations, especially on the Senate side, the size of the tax cut was scaled back and its distributional impact modified, but the final version of the 2001 tax Bill embodied the major policy changes Bush had advocated. Since the reconciliation process had been needed to ease its legislative path, however, the tax cut was not permanent. Republicans assumed that the 10-year limitation on the 2001 tax cuts would eventually be repealed, but repeated efforts over the next several years to make the tax cuts permanent failed.

According to Congress's Joint Committee on Taxation, the tax-cut package Bush initially proposed totaled $1.8 trillion (*Congressional Quarterly*, 2006, 91). The budget resolution that Congress adopted, however, imposed a $1.4 trillion ceiling on any tax cut, and the tax reconciliation Bill Congress then passed was kept within that ceiling. The largest revenue reductions in the 2001 EGTRRA came from lower marginal rates for all income groups, but distributional effects were complicated by other provisions regarding phase-ins, child tax credits and standard deductions (see Table 9.3).

Table 9.3: Major Provisions of the 2001 Economic Growth and Tax Relief Reconciliation Act

Marginal Rates:
- 10-15-25-28-33-35
  (replaces 15-28-31-36-39.6)
- 10 per cent bracket retroactive (tax rebate)
- 15 per cent bracket effective immediately
- 25, 28, 33, 35 per cent brackets phased in throughout 2006

Child Tax Credit:
- Increased from $500 to $1,000 (phased in through 2010)
- Refundability expanded

Earned Income Tax Credit:
- Eligibility expanded

Marriage Penalty:
- Increased standard deduction (phased in through 2009)
- Expanded 15 per cent bracket

Estate and Gift Tax:
- Reduced tax rate to 45 per cent (from 55 per cent), phased in through 2007
- Increased exemption to $3.5 million (from $1 million), phased in through 2009
- Repealed estate tax in 2010

Other:
- Increased IRA (retirement accounts) limits
- Temporary credits for retirement savings
- Deductions for college tuition expenses
- Tax preference for education savings accounts
- Repealed income restrictions on itemised deductions and personal exemptions

Source: Congressional Quarterly (2006, pp. 95–100).

In terms of percentage reductions, the marginal rate cuts in 2001 were greater for low- and middle-income groups. Actual dollar reductions in tax liabilities, however, necessarily rose with income. The phase-in of lower rates for upper-income groups made this disparity somewhat less pronounced, at least immediately. Moreover, by 2001 many low-income earners had no income tax liability (because of increased standard deductions and personal exemptions under the 1986, 1990 and 1993 tax laws). In order to extend tax benefits to these individuals, expanded child tax credits and earned-income tax credits were made refundable for payroll as well as income taxes.

The progressivity effects of the 2001 tax cuts, then, were more complicated than the rate cut provisions alone might suggest (Steuerle, 2004, pp. 212–16). There were additional complications with respect to tax benefits for upper-income groups. For high-income taxpayers (adjusted gross income between $100,000 and $500,000), effective net tax cuts were greatly reduced by the alternative minimum tax that remained in effect. For very high-income taxpayers, the alternative minimum tax had a much smaller impact, while the estate tax benefits were substantial. These estate tax changes were decidedly non-progressive, particularly if they were made permanent after 2010 (Steuerle, 2004, p. 217).

Distributional effects aside, the revenue impact of the 2001 tax cut was much greater than expected. The economy had begun to weaken early in the year, and the terrorist attacks of September 11 helped to trigger a full-blown recession. The combined impact of recession and tax cuts on revenue levels was dramatic. In 2000, the revenue-GDP level was 20.9 per cent. During FY2002, the level fell to 17.9 per cent, and by 2004 revenue-GDP was 16.3 per cent. With spending moving up as a result of defence and domestic programme increases after 9/11, the FY2004 deficit exceeded $400 billion.

The 2003 Tax Cut

During 2002, congressional Democrats rejected Bush's pleas to make the 2001 cuts permanent. In the November mid-term elections, however, Republicans regained control of the Senate and increased their majority in the House, paving the way for another significant tax cut in 2003. Once again, Bush asked for a much larger reduction than Congress ultimately approved. The Bush request was estimated at $725 billion over 11 years, with more than half of this tied to the elimination of individual income taxes on corporate dividends (*Congressional Quarterly*, 2006, 105).

The estimated total cost of the Jobs and Growth Tax Relief Reconciliation Act of 2003 was $350 billion, less than half of what Bush had requested. Bush's dividend tax repeal was dropped, but Congress lowered dividend and capital gains tax rates to 15 per cent. In addition, the phase-in of lower marginal rate brackets under the 2001 tax law was accelerated by three years. A similar acceleration was applied to the child tax credit.

The 2003 tax Bill did not, however, make the 2001 tax cut permanent. Indeed, a new array of 'sunsets' (or automatic expirations) was needed to keep the cost of the 2003 tax Bill within the $350 billion ceiling. The new capital gains and dividend tax rates, for example, expired at the end of 2008. The increased income exemption under the alternative minimum tax was effective for only two years, as was the accelerated child tax credit. While some of these sunsets were subsequently extended over the next three years, none of the key tax-cut provisions in the 2001 and 2003 laws was made permanent. Repeated efforts to make permanent the estate tax repeal failed, and even the alternative minimum tax received only temporary fixes. In sum, the Bush administration and Republican-controlled Congresses could not redirect long-term tax policy; between 2007 and 2010, more than six dozen tax law provisions are scheduled to expire, and baseline revenue projections will rise accordingly (Congressional Budget Office, 2007a, pp. 102–07).

Taxes, Deficits, Tax Burdens

In 2005 and 2006, revenue growth rates picked up sharply, and the rise in individual income taxes was especially pronounced. By 2006, the revenue-GDP level was 18.4 per cent, slightly above the average revenue over the preceding four decades. With spending above 20 per cent of GDP, the budget remained in deficit, but the deficit-GDP level was less than 2 per cent, again roughly comparable to long-term averages. Finally, the publicly held debt-GDP level remained well below 40 per cent, despite the Bush deficits.

The tax cuts that were enacted from 2001–04 would have lowered revenue-GDP levels if the economy had remained healthy. But the stock market decline and recession that took hold in 2001 sharply depressed taxable income and greatly amplified the revenue impact of legislated tax cuts. By the time that the major provisions of the 2001 and 2003 tax cuts became fully effective, taxable income growth was surging, and revenue levels were rising accordingly. The deficit record under Bush, then, shows the enormous impact that the economy has on revenue levels. In terms of structural deficits — that is, the imbalance between revenues and spending with business cycle effects removed — the Bush tax cuts look much more moderate.

In addition, the Bush administration's tax programme has had very little impact on long-term revenue trends in social insurance taxes, corporate income taxes and excise taxes (see Figure 9.1). Social insurance taxes (Social Security and Medicare) account for more than 35 per cent of federal revenues, and social insurance tax-GDP levels have remained fairly stable for the past two decades. Corporate income taxes, which account for about 10 per cent of total revenues,

Figure 9.1: Revenues by Source, as a Share of Gross Domestic Product, 1966–2017

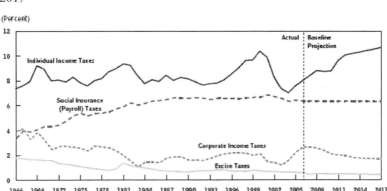

Source: Congressional Budget Office (2007a, p. 52).

Figure 9.2: Share of Individual Income Tax Liabilities, 1979–2005

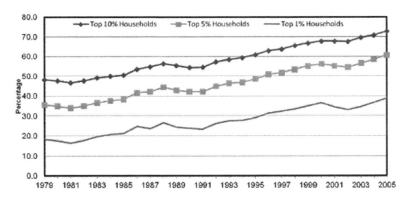

Source: Congressional Budget Office (2007b, Appendix).

are now at their highest GDP level since the late 1970s. Excise taxes, a minor revenue source, have stayed in the same GDP range for the last 15 years.

The individual income tax, by comparison, is where the Bush administration has attempted to make major changes. Individual income tax-GDP levels are now well below those of the late 1990s and roughly on a par with those of the Reagan era. But the Bush tax cuts for individuals will expire in 2010, after which Clinton-era tax policy and individual income tax-GDP levels will be restored.

Finally, with regard to equity, long-term trends in progressivity have remained largely in place despite the Bush tax cuts. The share of individual income tax liabilities for high-income earners has been climbing steadily for the past 25 years (see Figure 9.2). The top 1 per cent of households, for example, accounts for about 40 per cent of individual income taxes, roughly double the share in 1980.

Looking at income tax burdens across the income spectrum underscores this trend. The share of income tax liabilities for the first through fourth income quintiles has declined significantly over the past quarter-century, and that decline has continued under Bush (Congressional Budget Office, 2007b, Appendix). The share for the highest quintile has risen from 65 per cent to over 86 per cent over this period, and that upward trend has continued under Bush as well.

The Congressional Budget Office has also estimated the level of progressivity in total federal tax liabilities — individual income taxes, payroll taxes, corporate income taxes (based on shares of capital income) and excise taxes (based on consumption). The shares of total federal tax liabilities for all but the highest income quintile have declined steadily over the past 25 years (Congressional

Figure 9.3: Share of Total Federal Tax Liabilities, 1979–2005

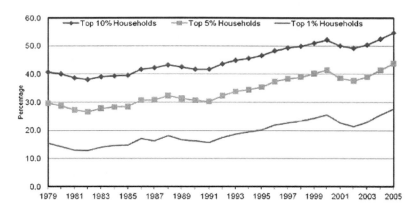

Source: Congressional Budget Office (2007b, Appendix).

Budget Office, 2007b, Appendix). And, as shown in Figure 9.3, high-income households now account for more than half of all federal tax liabilities, with the top 1 per cent at nearly 30 per cent.

Of course, these high-income groups have also increased their share of total income. Between 1979 and 2005, for example, the share of pre-tax income for the top 1 per cent of households nearly doubled — from 9.3 to 18.1 per cent (Congressional Budget Office, 2007b, Appendix). Shares of income (pre- and post-tax) for all but the highest income quintiles fell over this same period. These long-term trends in income inequality, however, have been largely unaffected by tax policy changes. The after-tax income shares for low- and middle-income groups declined during the Clinton presidency, and that decline has continued under Bush. Whether more aggressively distributive tax policy can reverse these long-term patterns is unclear. What is clear is that the problem of growing income inequality long predates the Bush tax cuts.

Conclusion

The politics of tax policy in the United States are a bit unusual. Compared with other advanced democracies, revenue-GDP levels are extremely low. According to the OECD, for example, tax-GDP levels for industrial democracies now exceed 36 per cent, an increase of 20 per cent over the past three decades (Johnston, 2007, p. C3). In the United States, federal revenue-GDP levels have averaged slightly over 18 per cent over this period; combined federal and state government tax-GDP remains under 30 per cent.

Balancing the federal budget, then, would appear to be relatively simple, since it could be accomplished with revenue levels that would be well below

— in some cases, far below — revenue levels elsewhere. Nevertheless, balanced budgets have been rarities since the 1950s, which suggests that tax policy is part of a broader debate over budget policy. Republicans and Democrats may support balanced budgets in principle, but they sharply differ over whether budgets should be balanced at high or low revenue levels. During the 1970s and 1980s, Democrats were unwilling to sacrifice their social welfare agenda in order to balance the budget. Under Reagan and George W. Bush, Republicans have accepted deficits as an acceptable price for protecting their low-tax programme.

It is not surprising, then, that critics of the Bush tax cuts have revived their critiques of Reagan. There are, of course, obvious parallels with respect to deficits. In Bush's case, the deficit record is seen as even worse, given the balanced budgets he inherited. Tax policy under both administrations has also been attacked as unfair, since the marginal rate cuts under Reagan and Bush have provided significant benefits to high-income taxpayers.

But the Bush record, like Reagan's, is more complicated than critics are willing to acknowledge. Revenue levels for both administrations have been in line with long-term revenue trends, despite tax cuts. Progressivity has increased significantly for most income groups, again despite tax cuts. The tradeoff between the economic benefits of lower taxes and the economic costs of deficits has been deliberate, and it is not at all certain that this tradeoff has been misguided or foolish. Indeed, the economic rationale for lower marginal tax rates goes back to the Kennedy–Johnson tax cut of 1964. But the Reagan and Bush tax programmes have also attempted, albeit unsuccessfully, to force retrenchments in large and costly domestic programmes. The budget policy battles of the past several decades make very clear the debate over the size of government is a serious one in the United States, and we can expect tax policy to remain at the heart of that debate for a very long time.

References

A.M. Brill (2007) 'Individual Income Taxes After 2010: Post-Permanence-ism', *National Tax Journal*, vol. LX (September), pp. 347–69.

Congress and the Nation, 2001–2004 (2006) (Washington, DC: *Congressional Quarterly*).

Congressional Budget Office (1983) *Revising the Individual Income Tax* (Washington, DC: CBO).

Congressional Budget Office (1990a) *An Analysis of the President's Budgetary Proposals for Fiscal Year 1991* (Washington, DC: CBO).

Congressional Budget Office (1990b) *The Economic and Budget Outlook: An Update* (Washington, DC: CBO).

Congressional Budget Office (1993) *The Economic and Budget Outlook: An Update* (Washington, DC: CBO).

Congressional Budget Office (2001) *The Budget and Economic Outlook: An Update* (Washington, DC: CBO).

Congressional Budget Office (2007a) *The Budget and Economic Outlook: Fiscal Years 2008 to 2017* (Washington, DC: CBO).

Congressional Budget Office (2007b) *Historical Effective Tax Rates: 1979 to 2005* (Washington, DC: CBO).

Congressional Quarterly Almanac 1984 (1985) (Washington, DC: *Congressional Quarterly*).

Congressional Quarterly Almanac 1986 (1987) (Washington, DC: *Congressional Quarterly*).

Congressional Quarterly Almanac 1990 (1991) Washington, DC: *Congressional Quarterly*).

Congressional Quarterly Almanac 1993 (1994) (Washington, DC: *Congressional Quarterly*).

Congressional Quarterly Almanac 1995 (1996) (Washington, DC: *Congressional Quarterly*).

Internal Revenue Service (1985) *Statistics of Income Bulletin 4* (Washington, DC: Internal Revenue Service).

D.S. Ippolito (1981) *Congressional Spending* (Ithaca, NY: Cornell University Press).

D.S. Ippolito (1990) *Uncertain Legacies: Federal Budget Policy from Roosevelt Through Reagan* (Charlottesville, VA: University Press of Virginia).

D.S. Ippolito (2003) *Why Budgets Matter* (University Park, PA: Pennsylvania State University Press).

D.C. Johnston (2007) 'Taxes in Developed Nations Reach 36% of Gross Domestic Product', *New York Times*, 18 October, p. C3.

B.D. Jones and W. Williams (2008) *The Politics of Bad Ideas* (New York: Pearson Longman).

C.E. Steuerle (2004) *Contemporary U.S. Tax Policy* (Washington, DC: Urban Institute Press).

J. Tobin and M. Weidenbaum (1988) *Two Revolutions in Economic Policy: The First Economic Reports of Presidents Kennedy and Reagan* (Cambridge, MA: MIT Press).

US Government (1960) *Historical Tables, Budget of the United States Government, Fiscal Year 1961* (Washington, DC: Government Printing Office).

US Government (1963) *Budget of the United States Government, Fiscal Year 1964* (Washington, DC: Government Printing Office).

US Government (1990) *Budget of the United States Government, Fiscal Year 1991* (Washington, DC: Government Printing Office).

US Government (2007) *Historical Tables, Budget of the United States Government, Fiscal Year 2008* (Washington, DC: Government Printing Office).

J.F. Witte (1985) *The Politics and Development of the Federal Income Tax* (Madison, WI: University of Wisconsin Press).

Notes

[1] Congressional budget process rules limited the 2001 tax cuts to 10 years. Subsequently, the Bush administration has failed to make these cuts permanent. At the end of calendar year 2010, the 2001 tax law changes will automatically expire, and pre-2001 tax law will be reinstated.

[2] The Bush deficits have, of course, increased the publicly held debt, from 33% of GDP to approximately 37%. Current debt-GDP levels, however, are well below those of the early and mid-1990s, and projected baseline levels are even lower.

[3] Budget surpluses were registered in fiscal years 1956, 1957, 1960, 1969 and 1998–2001.

[4] Revenue-GDP levels rose from 14.4% in 1950 to 19.0 per cent two years later.

[5] In FY1969, outlays were 19.4% of GDP, compared with 20.6 in 1968. Revenues moved in the opposite direction, from 17.7% in 1968 to 19.7% in 1969.

10

PUBLIC BUDGETS AND INCOME INEQUALITY IN LATIN AMERICA: A COMPARATIVE PERSPECTIVE

Diego Sánchez-Ancochea

Introduction

Latin America is the most unequal continent in the world. It has the highest aggregate Gini coefficient and, according to 2006 World Bank statistics, 14 of the 20 more unequal countries are there. The Latin American distribution is particularly skewed at the top, with the richest decile receiving a larger share of total income than in any other region of the world. Income inequality has created social and political tensions, harming the prospects for long-term growth. It has also made poverty reduction harder than under more equal economic structures.

Reducing income inequality should thus be at the heart of the economic strategy of Latin American countries. Achieving success in this area will depend on many factors, ranging from the type of insertion in the global economy to the structure of the labour market and the influence of different actors in the process of production. While the state has some responsibility in all these areas, its role in the redistribution of income through social spending and taxation is particularly important.

This chapter focuses on the use of both of these instruments to create more equal economic structures in Latin America. Focusing on the extensive literature on inequality and welfare regimes in developed countries, I argue that moving towards more universal social systems may be the only way to improve the secondary distribution of income. While the type of conditional cash transfers (CCTs) and other targeted programmes that are currently proliferating in Latin America can play a complementary role, they are unlikely to significantly reduce the large share of income at the top. They may also be less successful in building more integrated societies than a more universal approach.

Universal social programmes by themselves, however, may not be sufficient to resolve a particularly pervasive feature of inequality in Latin America: the concentration of income and other resources in the top decile (and, even more, in the richest 1 per cent of the population). Unless Latin American governments devise new ways to tax the very rich, there are few reasons to expect a substantial reduction of their income share, at least in the short and middle run. Redistribution between the middle class and the poor in Latin America may be important, but it is unlikely to resolve some of the most perverse effects of inequality in the region.

After presenting evidence on the importance of universal social policies and discussing the need for a more progressive tax regime, the chapter analyses the main constraints on the implementation of a more redistributive management of the budget: globalisation and domestic weaknesses. These are both real obstacles, but may be overcome through gradual reforms that link social spending with the deepening of democracy.

The remainder of the chapter is divided into four sections. The next section discusses the extent of income inequality in Latin America in comparative perspective, and evaluates the impact of the neoliberal economic model. The following section relies on insights from the welfare literature in OECD countries to argue for universal social policies. The chapter then focuses on the tax system, arguing that the skewed nature of income distribution in Latin America can only be resolved if the rich pay more taxes. Finally, I evaluate two key obstacles that may challenge the type of policies recommended in this chapter. The conclusion highlights the importance of integrating the management of the public budget within the overall economic strategy.

The Extent of the Problem: Income Inequality in Latin America

While one should always be sceptical about any measure of income inequality, there is convincing evidence that Latin America is the most unequal continent in the world (Machinea and Hopenhayn, 2005; Mann and Riley, 2007).[1] This is evident in Table 10.1, which relies on World Bank data to rank countries based on the Gini coefficient. While the data are not strictly comparable because of differences in measurement and in the year of the observation, the table still gives a suggestive picture of the extent of the problem. With a Gini coefficient of 60, Bolivia is the third most unequal country in the world and is followed by four other Latin American countries. According to this particular ranking, seven of the 10 most unequal countries and 14 of the 20 are from Latin America. Uruguay, the least unequal economy in the region, has a Gini coefficient of over 43. UNDP (2006) places more African countries at the bottom of the income distribution ranking, but still 10 of the 20 most unequal countries in its ranking are Latin American.

Table 10.1: The 20 Most Unequal Countries in the World, 1995–2003

Rank	Country	Gini
1	Lesotho	63.13
2	Swaziland	60.65
3	Bolivia	60.05
4	Haiti	59.21
5	Colombia	58.62
6	Brazil	57.96
7	Paraguay	57.77
8	South Africa	57.77
9	Chile	57.61
10	Panama	56.45
11	Guatemala	55.13
12	Peru	54.57
13	Honduras	53.84
14	Ecuador	53.53
15	Argentina	52.79
16	El Salvador	52.36
17	Dominican Republic	51.69
18	Niger	50.61
19	Malawi	50.31
20	Gambia. The	50.23

Note: Most recent year available for each country. Data are not strictly comparable.

Source: World Development Indicators database (accessed 1 April 2007).

The most striking characteristic of inequality in Latin America is how much of the country's resources are controlled by the very rich. This is clearly reflected in Table 10.2, which describes the distribution by decile in 1992. The richest decile in Latin America received 48 per cent of total income in that year, 1.7 times more than in OECD countries and even higher than in Sub-Saharan Africa. According to data from Mann and Riley (2007, p. 96), 'the top 5 per cent of the income distribution in Latin America remains double that of the North and 60 per cent than that of East Asia'.

The specific nature of inequality in the region becomes even clearer in Table 10.3, which compares the pattern of distribution in each region with that of OECD countries.[2] Each observation represents the income share of a specific decile in relation to the share that the same decile receives in OECD countries. For example, the poorest decile in Latin America receives in relative terms just 64 per cent of what the poorest decile in OECD countries receives.

Table 10.2: Various Regions of the World — Income Distribution by Decile, 1992

Decile	LA	Africa	Asia	Eastern Europe	Developed Countries
1	1.6	2.1	2.6	2.2	2.5
2	2.4	3.0	3.5	3.8	3.4
3	3.0	3.7	4.8	5.1	5.3
4	3.4	4.6	5.8	5.7	6.3
5	5.0	5.5	6.5	7.5	7.3
6	6.0	6.5	7.5	8.2	8.6
7	7.6	8.6	9.0	9.4	10.5
8	9.0	10.5	10.5	10.8	12.2
9	14.0	13.3	12.4	12.8	14.8
10	48.8	42.2	37.4	34.7	29.1

Source: World Bank (2004).

Table 10.3: Various Regions of the World — Income Shared Compared with that of the OECD, 1992

Decile	LA	Africa	Asia	Eastern Europe	Developed Countries
1	0.64	0.84	1.04	0.88	1.00
2	0.71	0.88	1.03	1.12	1.00
3	0.57	0.70	0.91	0.96	1.00
4	0.54	0.73	0.92	0.90	1.00
5	0.68	0.75	0.89	1.03	1.00
6	0.70	0.76	0.87	0.95	1.00
7	0.72	0.82	0.86	0.90	1.00
8	0.74	0.86	0.86	0.89	1.00
9	0.95	0.90	0.84	0.86	1.00
10	1.68	1.45	1.29	1.19	1.00

Source: Own calculations based on data from Table 10.2.

This exercise is useful to compare distributional patterns across the whole population in different regions. The real problem in Latin America is the difference between the richest 20 per cent and the rest of the population. In Latin America, all deciles but the top one receive a lower share of real income than in any other part of the world. The situation is particularly dramatic at the bottom of the distributional structure, but the lower middle class is also affected. Latin Americans in the fifth decile, for example, receive just 68 per cent

Table 10.4: Number of High Net Wealth Individuals — Total Wealth and Average Wealth per Person, 2006

Region	Number[1]	Total Wealth[2]	Wealth per Person[3]
Europe	2.8	9.4	3.4
North America	2.9	10.2	3.5
Asia-Pacific	2.4	7.6	3.2
Latin America	0.3	4.2	14.0
Middle East	0.3	1.2	4.0
Africa	0.1	0.8	8.0
World	8.7	33.3	3.8

Notes: High net wealth individuals are defined as those with at least one million in financial assets.

(1) Millions of people.

(2) Trillions of US$.

(3) Millions of US$.

Source: Merrill Lynch (2006).

of what those in OECD countries do (in relative terms). At the same time, the share of the richest 10 per cent is 168 per cent of that of their counterparts in the OECD and significantly higher than in Africa, Asia and Eastern Europe.

The extent of the concentration at the top is also evident when taking into consideration the distribution of wealth. Merrill Lynch, in collaboration with Capgemini, elaborates a yearly estimation of the number of high net wealth individuals (HNWI) — people who hold at least US$1 million in financial assets (Merrill Lynch, 2006). Latin America has 300,000 HNWI (3.6 per cent of the world total), each of which has an average of US$14 million in financial assets, more than four times that of rich individuals in North America or Europe (Table 10.4).[3]

What these data clearly illustrate is that the policy challenge in Latin America is twofold. Latin America must increase the relative income of the very poor, who receive a lower share of total GDP than in any other part of the world. This process, however, cannot be undertaken at the expense of the middle class, which is substantially worse off in relative terms in Latin America than in the rest of the world. This conclusion is also evident when comparing the patterns of distribution among Latin American countries. A similar exercise to that of Table 10.3 appears in Table 10.5, but in this case the Uruguayan pattern of distribution (the least unequal in the region) is taken as the reference. This comparison reveals that differences between countries in the region concentrate at the top and bottom of the distributional structure. The income share that the middle class (understood as quintile four to eight) receives is relatively similar

Table 10.5: Latin America and the Caribbean — Income Shared Compared with that of Uruguay, c.2000

					Deciles					
	1	2	3	4	5	6	7	8	9	10
Uruguay	1.00	1.00	1.00	1.00	1.00	1.00	1.00	1.00	1.00	1.00
Costa Rica	0.78	0.92	0.96	0.96	0.96	0.97	1.00	1.01	1.01	1.04
Venezuela	0.71	0.89	0.92 ˙	0.94	0.96	0.98	0.99	0.99	1.01	1.06
Dominican R.	0.77	0.85	0.88	0.89	0.91	0.92	0.94	0.95	0.96	1.15
Peru	0.42	0.71	0.85	0.92	0.98	1.00	1.00	0.99	0.97	1.11
Jamaica	0.64	0.75	0.80	0.83	0.85	0.89	0.94	0.95	0.97	1.20
Argentina	0.56	0.70	0.76	0.79	0.84	0.88	0.94	1.00	1.06	1.16
El Salvador	0.48	0.67	0.77	0.81	0.86	0.89	0.92	0.94	1.00	1.21
Mexico	0.54	0.69	0.76	0.78	0.81	0.83	0.87	0.89	0.96	1.29
Honduras	0.48	0.62	0.69	0.75	0.80	0.86	0.89	0.94	1.01	1.26
Nicaragua	0.44	0.62	0.72	0.77	0.81	0.84	0.88	0.91	0.94	1.30
Ecuador	0.39	0.63	0.72	0.75	0.78	0.82	0.87	0.89	0.96	1.32
Panama	0.39	0.58	0.67	0.72	0.77	0.81	0.87	0.93	1.03	1.29
Paraguay	0.35	0.52	0.66	0.74	0.78	0.83	0.88	0.92	0.99	1.31
Chile	0.65	0.72	0.71	0.71	0.73	0.74	0.78	0.82	0.92	1.40
Colombia	0.45	0.62	0.70	0.72	0.75	0.78	0.81	0.85	0.93	1.39
Bolivia	0.17	0.34	0.56	0.69	0.79	0.87	0.94	0.98	1.07	1.26
Brazil	0.49	0.57	0.62	0.65	0.70	0.74	0.79	0.86	0.97	1.41
Guatemala	0.40	0.54	0.61	0.66	0.70	0.74	0.79	0.83	0.93	1.44

Source: Own calculations with data from World Bank (2004).

in all countries. In Guatemala, for example, the share of the poorest decile is only 40 per cent of that in Uruguay, while the share of the richest decile is 148 per cent. Differences in the middle deciles, while still significant, are lower.

The unequal character of inequality in Latin America in comparative perspective is not a new phenomenon. Yet the neoliberal policy model implemented in Latin America since the mid-1980s has done little to improve the situation. Most evidence indicates that inequality has remained stable or even increased in the last two decades. Taylor and Vos (2003) found that inequality increased during 17 of 24 episodes of reform identified in 16 different Latin American countries. According to a World Bank study of 16 Latin American countries published in 2004, inequality only decreased in Brazil and Honduras during the 1990s. Berry's review (2005) of a large number of studies on income distribution during the neoliberal era also concludes that inequality increased in a significant number of cases.

The negative evolution of income inequality in the 1990s— and in many countries in the 2000s — has been the result of a complex combination of factors, many connected with the neoliberal policy model. Some of the most relevant are:

- growing asymmetries between wages received by skilled and unskilled labour and expansion of the informal market (Portes and Hoffman, 2003; Taylor and Vos, 2003);

- the advantages enjoyed by large firms over small and medium firms in adapting to the increasing level of competition created by trade openness (Pizarro, 2001);

- the weakening effect of privatisation on trade unions in many countries and the substituting of many well-paid jobs in the public sector with badly paid jobs in the informal economy;

- the transition from import substitution to export promotion, resulting in a transformation of the role of real wages in many countries, from drivers of effective demand to costs of production.

Public expenditures and taxes could not reverse the negative trend in the primary distribution of income. The evolution of total social spending can be divided into two different stages in most countries: retrenchment during the 1980s and slow expansion based on liberal principles during the 1990s. While the latter growth resulted in growing transfers to the poor, it also deepened economic segmentation and social fragmentation (Filgueira et al., 2006).

The debt crisis and the inflationary process that followed forced Latin American countries to implement stabilisation measures. Sooner or later, most countries opted for orthodox structural adjustment programmes that reduced public spending significantly. Both public investment and social programmes suffered reductions, even in countries with social-democratic traditions and stable democracies. In Costa Rica, for example, public social spending fell from 20.7 per cent to 15.2 per cent as a proportion of GDP between 1980 and 1982 — decreasing also as a proportion of public spending. Governments did not pay attention to income inequality during this period, and concentrated instead on designing compensatory social programmes for the poor. So-called 'emergency funds' were implemented to transfer resources to the poor, thus dealing with the social costs of adjustment and securing social stability in the new democracies (Filgueira, 2005).

These programmes were front-runners for the New Social Policy that emerged in Latin America in the late 1990s. Mistrust in the government and in previous welfare models dominated the design of these new policies. Given the new accent on macroeconomic stability and fiscal conservatism, poverty reduction through programmes that targeted the poor became a central policy objective. Conditional cash transfers (CCTs) like Progresa (now Oportunidades) in Mexico or Bolsa Familia in Brazil were introduced to improve the income levels of the poor, while simultaneously promoting their participation in new educational programmes. The reduction of personal insecurity and the promotion of high-quality social services for the rest of society became less important. As Lo Vuolo (2005, p. 2) puts it, 'the security of the "non-poor" should no longer be "social" and should be resolved by private insurance mechanisms'.

CCTs have brought some positive innovations (Filgueira et al., 2006; Molyneux, 2006; World Bank, 2004). The best-run programmes have succeeded in targeting the poor, reducing clientelism and administrative waste. According to Veras Soares et al. (2006), for example, 80 per cent of the resources spent by Bolsa Familia went to households below the poverty line. In the case of Chile's Subsidio Unico Familiar, more than two-thirds of the beneficiaries were in the bottom quintile. By conditioning transfers to participation in educational and other social programmes, CCTs can facilitate the accumulation of human capital by the poor. Many of these programmes have also introduced rigorous evaluation schemes that help to gradually improve the quality of provision.

CCTs have thus played a useful role in poverty reduction, but their contribution to income inequality is bound to be minimal. These programmes have so far been small, accounting for less than 0.5 per cent of GDP in all countries (World Bank, 2004). Due to their cost-efficiency concerns and concentration on temporal income support, they are unlikely to constitute a major component of social spending in quantitative terms (Mkandawire, 2006a). CCTs could lead to segmentation in the provision of social services, as the middle class opts out of low-quality services in health and education. Probably the most problematic feature of CCTs is their lack of integration with a broader strategy of economic development that simultaneously secures competitiveness, political participation, economic growth and sustained improvements in equity (Molyneux, 2006).

The Use of Social Policy: Learning from the OECD Experience

Reducing income inequality requires a comprehensive strategy that modifies static comparative advantages, transforms the labour market, and reforms social policy and the tax regime. The public budget has an influence in all these areas, but it is particularly important in establishing the volume and characteristics of social programmes and defining the tax system. Both of these issues will be the subject of this section and the next.

The growing literature on varieties of capitalism and welfare regimes that emerged out of Esping-Andersen's (1990) seminal work constitutes an excellent starting point for the discussion of social policy, economic development and redistribution. Much of the literature takes the diversity of distributional structures and welfare regimes as its starting point. Table 10.6, which shows the

Table 10.6: Indicators of Income Inequality in Selected Developed Countries,
c.2000

	Level of income per share			Gini coefficient
	10% Poorest	10% Richest	Ratio	
Denmark	2.6	21.3	8.1	24.7
Finland	4.0	22.6	5.6	26.9
France	2.8	25.1	9.1	32.7
Germany	3.2	22.1	6.9	28.3
Japan	4.8	21.7	4.5	24.9
Norway	3.9	23.4	6.1	25.8
Sweden	3.6	22.2	6.2	25.0
United Kingdom	2.1	28.5	13.8	36.0
United States	1.9	29.9	15.9	40.8

Source: UNDP Human Development Report, 2005.

Gini coefficient and other indicators of inequality, gives some evidence in this regard. The United States and the United Kingdom are more unequal than all other developed countries, while the Scandinavian countries and Japan are the most equal countries in the world. These differences in distributional outcomes are not new. According to Stephens (2002), during the early 1980s Sweden had a Gini coefficient (after taxes and transfers) of 0.2 compared with 0.25 in Germany and 0.31 in the United States. Poverty at all ages was also substantially lower in the Scandinavian countries than in the rest of the world.

The literature identifies a combination of interrelated factors to explain the variance in distributional outcomes.[4] The character of the welfare regimes is one of the most important ones, as argued by Esping-Andersen (1990, 1996) and more recently by Huber and Stephens (2001) and Pontusson (2005). In his analysis, Pontusson divides a selected number of developed countries into three different groups: Nordic social market economies (SMEs); Continental SMEs; and liberal market economies (LMEs).[5] Table 10.7 reflects the Gini coefficient before and after taxes and transfers (market income and disposable income) in each of these three groups. The data show that differences in inequality, while significant in market income, widen even more when taking into consideration the effects of public budgets. In Sweden, for example, state intervention reduces inequality by 36 per cent, while in the United States it does so by only 16 per cent.[6]

According to this evidence, governments in Nordic SMEs have succeeded in promoting equality. LMEs, on the other hand, are relative failures, having a more unequal distribution of market income and a less redistributive state. A look at the structure of the welfare state explains the root of these comparative

Table 10.7: Selected Number of OECD Countries — Distribution of Market and Disposable (After-tax and After-transfer) Income, Gini Coefficient, Late 1990s

Country	Market Income	Disposable Income	Degree of Redistribution*
Nordic SMEs		.	
Denmark	34.5	23.7	31.3
Finland	35.2	23.3	33.8
Norway	33.7	23.6	30.0
Sweden	37.5	23.8	36.5
Continental SMEs			
Belgium	37.8	23.7	37.3
Germany	34.2	24.0	29.8
Netherlands	33.9	25.1	26.0
Switzerland	33.2	29.7	10.5
LMEs			
Australia	39.6	29.3	26.0
Canada	39.0	29.8	23.6
United Kingdom	45.0	34.1	24.2
United States	43.6	36.3	16.7

* Percentage difference between Gini coefficients in market income and disposable income.

Source: Pontusson (2005).

differences. In particular, welfare states in Nordic SMEs have three characteristics that are important to understand their positive performance and can be useful for any discussion on Latin America: high social spending, specialisation in universal public services and a significant effort in promoting high-quality public education. Let us discuss each of them in some detail.

High Social Spending

The first basic explanation for the redistributive power of Nordic SMEs is that they devote more resources to social spending than other societies. In fact, Sweden and Denmark are the two countries in the OECD that spend more on public social services (in relation to GDP), while the United States and Ireland are two of the countries that spend less (Table 10.8). On average, Nordic SMEs spent nine percentage points more than LMEs in 2001, a difference that has remained stable since 1980.

Table 10.8: Selected Number of OECD Countries — Social Spending as a Percentage of GDP, 1980 and 2001

Country	1980	2001
Nordic SMEs	23.6	26.7
Denmark	29.1	29.2
Finland	18.5	24.8
Norway	17.9	23.9
Sweden	28.8	28.9
Continental SMEs	22.1	25.8
Austria	22.5	26.0
Belgium	24.1	27.2
Germany	23.0	27.4
Netherlands	26.9	21.8
Switzerland	14.2	26.4
LMEs	15.2	17.5
Australia	11.3	18.0
Canada	14.3	17.8
Ireland	17.0	13.8
New Zealand	17.2	18.5
UK	17.9	21.8
US	13.3	14.8
Others	–	
France		28.5
Italy		24.4
Japan		16.9

Source: OECD social spending database.

High social spending has a redistributive effect, even if taxes are neutral and spending is not targeted to the poor. In the hypothetical case that all citizens received an equal transfer, for example, the Gini coefficient would decrease because the income of the poor increases more than proportionally. The larger the transfer (and spending in other social services), the larger will be the government's redistributive effect. This positive relationship among 13 OECD countries is reflected in Figure 10.1.

Figure 10.1: Selected OECD Countries — Social Spending and Degree of Redistribution, mid 1990s

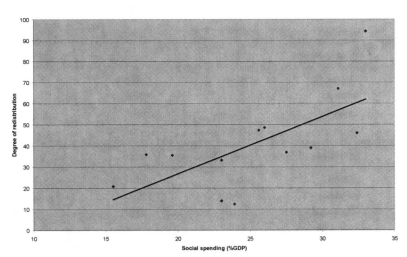

Sources: See Tables 10.8 and 10.9.

Universalism in Social Provision

The volume of social spending, however, is not sufficient to explain the Northern European success in building a redistributive welfare state. This is particularly evident when Sweden and Finland are compared with countries like Germany or Switzerland. The share of social spending in GDP was similar in all countries, but the Nordic SMEs reduced inequality more. Finland, for example, spent 25 per cent of GDP and had a degree of redistribution of 34 per cent, while Germany spent 27 per cent but its degree of redistribution was just 30 per cent. The differences between Nordic SMEs and Continental SMEs would be even larger if the provision of services were taken into consideration.

The importance of the structure of the welfare state has long been recognised by social policy experts. Total social spending is an incomplete measure of the commitment to equality and redistribution. Researchers have long 'move[d] away from the black box of expenditures and towards the content of welfare states' (Esping-Andersen, 1989, p. 20).

The comparative analysis of the content of welfare states has revealed the differences between regimes and highlighted the particularities of the Northern European model. Nordic SMEs were unique in the promotion of publicly provided universal services for all citizens. The public sector directly produced a large range of services, including 'health care ... day care, elder care, job training programmes, temporary employment programmes in the public

Table 10.9: Selected Number of OECD Countries — Structural Characteristics of the Welfare Regimes, c.1980

	Transfer Spending	Welfare-related Public Employment	Mean-tested Social Assistance	Population Coverage	Benefit Differentiation
Nordic SMEs	62.7	16	2.8	90	81
Continental SMEs	87.2	5	5.7	79	58
LMEs	75.2	7	35.3	71	53

Source: Pontusson (2005) from various original sources.

services, and after school programmes ... along with improvement of maternal and parental leave' (Stephens, 2002, p. 310).

These unique characteristics of Nordic SMEs are clearly reflected in Table 10.9. While the data are from 1980, we can regard the table's contents as stylised facts that have not changed significantly. Major differences emerge between the different groups. Means-tested programmes (like food stamps in the United States) targeted to specific segments of the population are more important in LMEs than in SMEs. In the Nordic SMEs, the direct provision of services through public employment is larger than in Continental SMEs and LMEs, and transfers less important.[7] Finally, both transfers and services are more generous in Nordic SMEs, and target a larger share of the population. In Northern Europe, 90 per cent of the working population (aged 16–64) was eligible for sickness, unemployment and pension benefits in 1980. And benefit differentiation between receivers was low, as the average transfer was 81 per cent of the maximum established by law.

Having a large public sector that provides universal social services to all citizens has multiple positive effects on distribution that go beyond the redistributive power of the budget. The existence of affordable child care and generous pensions for the elderly, for example, has allowed Sweden, Finland, Norway and Denmark to achieve the highest participation rates in the world. It has also facilitated the massive access of women to the labour market. Lower income families particularly benefit from the programmes because they do not have resources to pay for private provision of child care and attention to their elderly. Public provided social services also contribute to securing the accumulation of specialised skills (Mares, 2001) and reduce personal insecurity.

The existence of a large public sector has also strengthened trade unions, thus shifting power away from powerful business interests. Pontusson and colleagues (2002) found that a large share of public employment in the total contributes to wage compression and thus to equity in OECD countries.

Wages in the public sector are usually more equal than in private firms, with unskilled workers gaining more than any other group. Moreover, trade unions in the public sector are more inclined to support wage solidarity, as the Swedish experience clearly demonstrates.

High-quality Public Education

The Northern European accent on the public provision of universal services also extends to education. In 2002, Nordic SMEs devoted an average of 6.5 per cent of GDP to public spending compared with 5.3 per cent in Continental

Table 10.10: Selected Number of OECD Countries — Expenditure on Educational Institutions as a Percentage of GDP, 2002

Country	Total	Public	Private
Nordic SMEs	6.7	6.5	0.2
Denmark	7.1	6.8	0.3
Finland	6.0	5.9	0.1
Norway	6.9	6.7	0.3
Sweden	6.9	6.7	0.2
Continental SMEs	5.7	5.3	0.5
Austria	5.7	5.4	0.3
Belgium	6.4	6.1	0.3
Germany	5.3	4.4	0.9
Netherlands	5.1	4.6	0.5
Switzerland	6.2	5.7	0.5
LMEs	5.6	4.4	1.2
Australia	6.0	4.4	1.5
Canada	3.1	1.9	1.2
Ireland	4.4	4.1	0.3
New Zealand	6.8	5.6	1.2
UK	5.9	5.0	0.9
US	7.2	5.3	1.9
Others			
France	6.1	5.7	0.4
Italy	4.9	4.6	0.3
Japan	4.7	3.5	1.2

Source: OECD (2007).

SMEs and 4.4 per cent in LMEs (Table 10.10). Countries like Sweden, which emphasised the importance of comprehensive knowledge for all children, paid less attention to the type of vocational programmes dominant in Germany and other Continental SMEs (Pontusson, 2005).

To be sure, higher public spending on education does not mean that Nordic countries are investing more in human capital than others. In fact, in 2002 the United States ranked first in spending in education as percentage of GDP (7.2 per cent compared with 7.1 per cent in Denmark, 6.9 per cent in Sweden and 5.3 per cent in Germany). Yet the United States' remarkable achievement, which constitutes a major force behind technological innovation and productivity growth in the 1990s, is mainly the result of a large private university system. Around 60 per cent of total spending in tertiary education in the United States is privately financed, compared with 10 per cent or less in Denmark, Finland, Norway and Sweden. A large, privately financed university system has deepened inequality in the United States and strengthened economic elitism (Cook and Frank, 1995).

In Scandinavia, higher public spending has most likely contributed to promoting equality of opportunities and reducing asymmetries in educational attainment. Pontusson (2005, Table 6.6) offers some evidence in this regard, based on test results from the International Adult Literacy Survey implemented between 1994 and 1998. The literacy test results of the best students (those in the 95th percentile) in Northern Europe are 1.76 times better than those of the worse students (those in the 5th percentile). Both in Continental SMEs (2.00 times more) and the LMEs (2.49), the differences are significantly higher.[8]

Lessons for Latin America: Towards Universal Social Policy

There are profound differences between OECD countries and Latin America. Income per capita is substantially larger, public institutions are more effective and the political system is less prompted to clientelism. Their place in the global economy is also very different, and Latin America faces a more unstable and vulnerable environment.

This does not mean, however, that we should not try to draw lessons from the experience of developed countries. Stylised facts from developed countries have always informed the debate on economic development. The Washington Consensus, for example, is to a large extent the reflection of an idealised version of the LME model. Latin American countries were advised to emulate the United States in many regards, notably making their central banks independent, promoting stock markets and reducing the role of the state. The accent on targeting in social policy was one more example of this process (Filgueira and Filgueira, 2002).

LMEs are particularly bad models to follow if economic equality constitutes a primary policy goal. LMEs, particularly the United States, are the most unequal countries in the developed world. Their social policy is also less effective in redistributing income than that of other economies. Nordic SMEs, on the other hand, have been extremely successful in building the institutions and policies required to achieve equitable economic growth since the beginning of the twentieth century.

Nordic SMEs offer a central lesson to Latin America with regard to public expenditure: the creation of generous and universal public transfers and services is the best instrument to secure redistribution of income. In particular, and following Huber (2002, 2005), Latin America should pay attention to the Nordic policy approach to public health and education. Given Latin America's high levels of informality, the region should also implement benefits that are not dependent on participation in formal employment — including universal pensions and child allowances.

Following the Nordic countries would have numerous advantages for Latin America. First, it would likely increase political support for social spending, thus creating a redistributive virtuous circle (Huber, 2002; Mkandawire, 2006a). The middle classes are more likely to support an expansion of the state if they are benefiting from it. The resulting expansion of transfers and high-quality services in health and education would have a substantial redistributive effect. In Mkandawire's words (2006b, p. 13), 'institutions of welfare also act as intervening variables, shaping the political coalitions that eventually determine the size and redistributive nature of the national budget'.

Second, universal policies are likely to create long-term political constellations in support of a more equal economic model. The expansion of public services will strengthen the influence of trade unions in the public sector, which are likely to support wage compression and other progressive policies. This is clear in the experience of Scandinavian countries and, within the Latin American case, of Costa Rica during the period 1950–80. During these three decades, higher social spending led to an increase in the number of public employees who supported a social-democratic party that favoured economic equality (Sánchez-Ancochea, 2004).

Third, universal social spending may have lower management costs than targeted programmes, and can reduce clientelism. Targeting requires sophisticated institutional mechanisms to identify the deserving population, making sure that the benefits are properly allocated. In the case of CCTs, an institutional apparatus that enforces conditionality has to be created as well. Allocation to narrow segments of the population is also subject to political abuse and favouritism.

Fourth, a universal welfare regime will empower the poor and strengthen a citizen-based democracy. According to Solimano (2006), universalism can be considered part of the 'right-based approach'. Andrenacci and Repetto (2006) develop this idea further, placing universalism within a broader discussion of full citizenship. For them, social policy is a key component of a strategy that aims at 'the construction of societies that are economically integrated, socially cohesive and politically participatory, where differences do not create segmentation' (2006, p. 100). All these objectives are much harder to obtain when targeted programmes are dominant, partly because the poor will be stigmatised and will receive lower quality services.

Universal social policies are also likely to have a positive impact on sustainable economic growth and competitiveness. As Mkandawire (2006b) points out, social policy and economic development are interlinked. Social programmes should not simply compensate for the negative effects of external shocks and economic adjustment, but should also contribute to the generation of competitive assets. A universal social policy can assist in the accumulation of human capital, expand aggregate demand and improve social capital. The result will be higher economic growth and the creation of new competitive advantages.

The importance of the link between universal social programmes and economic development is clear when the Nordic countries are compared with Latin American ones. Valenzuela (2006a, 2006b), for example, tracks the evolution of social programmes and economic performance in Chile and Sweden. He demonstrates that the introduction of universal and generous pensions and other social programmes in Sweden triggered key socio-economic transformations at the beginning of the twentieth century. In particular, they facilitated the incorporation of women into the formal labour market, the reduction in demographic growth and the increase in productivity. Chile's failure to introduce a similar policy package resulted in a more rapid expansion of its population and a less dynamic economic path.

Reducing Inequality at the Top: The Need for a More Progressive Tax System

A significant number of researchers believe that government should only use social spending to redistribute income. In their view, taxation should only be used to increase public revenues but not to directly redistribute income from the rich to the poor. According to Chu and colleagues (2004, p. 250), for example, 'the major contribution of tax policy as a redistributive instrument should be to raise the revenues needed to finance efficient pro-poor and other essential governments expenditures'. The World Bank (2006, p. 12) concurs, arguing that 'the main aim of good tax policy is to mobilize sufficient funding, while distorting incentives and compromising growth as little as possible'.

Table 10.11: Selected OECD Countries — Total Taxes (% of GDP) and Tax Structure (% of total taxes), 2003

Country	Total taxes (% GDP)	Personal Income Tax	Corporate Income Tax	SS Contrib.	Taxes on Goods and Services	Other Taxes
Nordic SMEs	47.1	34.9	9.7	19.9	30.2	5.3
Denmark	48.9	53.2	5.8	3.4	33.1	4.5
Finland	45.9	31.2	9.3	24.7	30.2	4.6
Norway	43.5	24.8	18.9	21.4	31.2	3.7
Sweden	50.2	30.4	4.8	30.0	26.4	8.3
Continental SMEs	39.2	26.4	6.7	29.6	27.1	10.2
Austria	44.0	22.8	5.1	29.5	28.2	14.4
Belgium	46.4	31.7	7.6	28.9	24.6	7.1
Germany	36.0	25.1	2.9	37.4	29.2	5.5
Netherlands	39.2	18.3	8.8	28.3	30.8	13.8
Switzerland	30.3	34.4	8.8	23.8	22.6	10.4
LMEs	31.8	34.9	11.2	11.7	30.2	12.0
Australia	31.5	38.5	16.8	0.0	30.3	14.4
Canada	33.9	35.0	10.1	14.8	26.3	13.9
Ireland	28.4	26.2	13.1	14.1	39.5	7.1
New Zealand	34.9	42.3	12.1	0.0	35.2	10.4
United Kingdom	35.8	29.8	8.1	16.4	32.7	13.0
United States	26.4	37.7	6.7	24.7	17.6	13.2
Others						
France	44.0	17.3	6.6	34.6	25.4	16.2
Italy	42.6	25.5	7.6	26.0	26.9	14.0
Japan	25.8	18.4	12.2	34.0	20.1	15.4

Source: OECD (2007).

The argument that taxes have a small direct effect on the redistribution of income is partly supported by the comparison of tax structures in OECD countries. The main difference between the most equal countries and the most unequal is the level of taxes, not its structure. While the tax burden in Nordic SMEs is nearly 47 per cent of GDP, it is just 31 per cent in LMEs. Compared to the United States, Sweden collects twice as much money in taxes (in proportion to GDP, see Table 10.11). At the same time, the share of different taxes in total revenues is relatively similar in all countries. The contribution of income taxes

Figure 10.2: Various Regions of the World — Share of Income Taxes on Total Taxes, 1998–2005

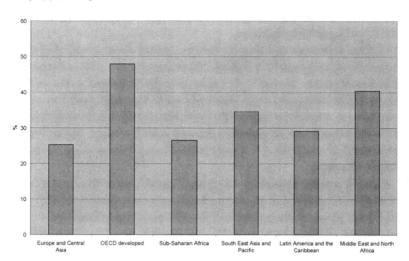

Sources: Own calculations with data from World Bank World Development Indicators database.

(arguably the most progressive of all types), for example, is the same in Nordic SMEs as in LMEs. In Continental SMEs, income taxes are less important, but only because of the central role that social security transfers (and thus contributions) play in their welfare regime.

The limited evidence available on the incidence of taxes in OECD countries indicates that they are only slightly progressive. A study published by the OECD in 1998 presents some evidence in this regard by comparing the distribution of market income and disposable income in 13 countries (Burniaux et al., 1998). The study concluded that 'the effect of the direct taxes and social-security contributions paid by individuals was quite redistributive' (1998, p. 11). In the United States, taxes reduced inequality in disposable income by 44.4 per cent in 1995, while in Sweden they did it by 70 per cent. Yet Burniaux et al.'s data and those of other studies do not show major differences between countries in the redistributive impact of taxes (Wagstaff et al., 1999). Different studies are also unclear about which countries have more progressive tax regimes. Pontusson's numbers (2005) seem to indicate that LMEs are more successful in this regard than Nordic SMEs, but Alesina and Glaeser (2004) give opposite evidence in their comparison between Europe and the United States.

Building progressive tax regimes is particularly hard in developing countries, where governments prefer to raise revenues from consumption taxes and import tariffs (Tanzi and Zee, 2000). Increasing the amount and progressivity of income taxes is difficult because 'the economic and political power of rich taxpayers often allows them to prevent fiscal reforms that would increase their tax burdens' (2000, p. 1). In fact, the share of personal and corporate income taxes in the total is significantly lower in developing countries than in the OECD, as Figure 10.2 illustrates.

All these arguments demonstrate that the task of creating more progressive tax systems in Latin America is difficult. Yet at the same time, it is indispensable. As indicated above, inequality in Latin America is primarily the result of income concentration at the top. Moving towards more equity will thus require a reduction in the income share of the top decile, something that social services by themselves will not do. Increasing income taxes that target the rich will be fundamental to avoid the risk of only redistributing income from the middle classes to the poor.

A simple exercise may clarify this point. Let us assume that (a) we have a universal social system that consists on equal monetary transfers for all deciles, and (b) neither transfers nor taxes result in efficiency losses of any kind or affect the distribution of market income. We can now compare the effect of different

Table 10.12: Impact of Various Tax Regimes Based on Guatemala's Distribution of Income

Tax Regimes	Share of Income		10th/1th	Gini
	1st	10th		
Flat tax 10%	1.63	44.57	27.29	0.522
26% tax on the 10th	1.70	39.41	23.13	0.489
15% tax on the 10th	1.43	41.88	29.29	0.514
15% tax on the 10th and 5% on 6th to 9th	1.62	42.07	25.90	0.505
Initial distribution	0.70	48.41	68.79	0.58

Table 10.13: Impact of Various Tax Regimes Based on Uruguay's Distribution of Income

Tax Regimes	Share of Income		10th/1th	Gini
	1st	10th		
Flat tax 10%	2.60	31.16	12.00	0.394
26% tax on the 10th	2.77	24.51	8.84	0.348
15% tax on the 10th	2.28	28.99	12.73	0.392
15% tax on the 10th and 5% on 6th to 9th	2.51	29.22	11.66	0.381
Initial distribution	1.77	33.51	18.89	0.437

tax regimes in two different distributional structures, the Guatemalan and the Uruguayan ones.

Tables 10.12 and 10.13 reflect the impact of several tax regimes on inequality. The baseline is given by a flat tax of 10 per cent on every household. This kind of tax will have significant redistributive effects: in both Guatemala and Uruguay, the Gini coefficient decreases by 11 per cent. The improvement of the poor is particularly large in Guatemala because of lower initial income: the Guatemalan poor would double their share in total income with this programme.

This finding demonstrates the importance of social transfers for the poor. At the same time, however, notice that the income share of the top decile decreases relatively little and remains high in both countries. Redistributive taxation can in these circumstances be a good complement to social programmes. Imposing a high income tax will have a particularly redistributive impact in Uruguay, with the Gini coefficient going down an additional 13 per cent over the baseline scenario. In Guatemala, the effect of redistributive taxes on the overall distribution of income is relatively small, but its impact on the income share at the top of the distribution is substantial.

This is just a partial equilibrium exercise with unrealistic assumptions. It does not take into consideration the different uses of the transfers and the cost of administrating all these programmes. Yet it illustrates two important points about the combined effect of public taxation and expenditures. First, the current consensus on the importance of social spending is understandable. In unequal countries, transfers are more powerful than taxes to redistribute income because of their contribution to expand the income share of the poor. At the same time, however, social programmes by themselves will only have a moderate effect on the top deciles. Complementing them with progressive taxation will be useful to reduce both the economic and political power of the rich.

There is an even more important reason to expand the tax burden of the rich: it may be the only effective way to increase overall tax revenues. Latin America's problem is not only the regressive nature of its tax system, but also the low level of aggregate taxes (Aldunate and Martner, 2006). The region has a smaller tax-GDP ratio than not only OECD countries but also countries with similar levels of development. While the former factor is not surprising given the positive relationship between tax revenues as percentage of GDP and GDP per capita reflected in Figure 10.3, the latter is more problematic. As Table 10.14 indicates, Chile is the only country that collects the expected amount of taxes relative to income level. If we also consider social security contributions, Brazil would join Chile as another exception to the Latin American trend (Aldunate and Martner, 2006). The World Bank (2004) offers similar results

Figure 10.3: Various countries — Tax Revenues as Percentage of GDP and GDP per Capita, 1995–2005

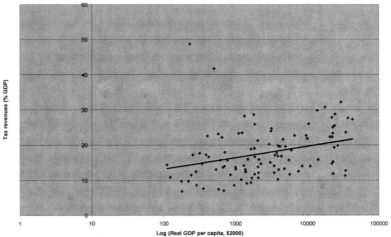

Source: Own calculations with data from the World Development Database.

Table 10.14: Latin America and the Caribbean — Expected and Real Tax Burden, 1995–2005

	Expected	*Real*	*Difference*
Argentina	19.23	12.52	–6.71
Bolivia	16.38	13.18	–3.20
Brazil	18.13	12.15	–5.98
Chile	18.65	19.59	0.94
Costa Rica	18.33	13.01	–5.32
Dominican Republic	17.52	14.67	–2.85
El Salvador	17.40	10.71	–6.69
Guatemala	17.11	10.63	–6.48
Mexico	18.83	11.66	–7.17
Nicaragua	16.00	15.7	–0.30
Paraguay	16.88	9.13	–7.75
Peru	17.41	12.1	–5.31
Uruguay	18.91	18.53	–0.38
Venezuela. RB	18.60	13.29	–5.31

Source: See Figure 10.3.

with regard to income taxes. According to its analysis, 'Latin American tax efforts tend to lie below the average even in relation to income levels, with the exception of Nicaragua and Uruguay (Brazil is also closed to the norm). This is particularly true with regard to personal income and property taxes collection, as well as social security contributions.' (2004, pp. 250–52)

The expansion of revenues from direct taxes may require a small increase of the top marginal rates, which were excessively reduced in the last two decades. According to data from Gómez (2006), the top marginal rate in the personal income tax went down from 50 per cent in 1986 to 29 per cent in 2004. The top marginal rate of the corporate income tax decreased from 44 per cent to 27 per cent during the same period. Any expansion of the tax rates should be accompanied by additional measures, including broadening the tax base (incorporating financial income and capital gains), eliminating tax incentives and enforcing compliance.

While the relative weakness of public institutions makes the fight against evasion complicated, gradual improvements are possible. In fact, the unequal distribution of income makes supervision technically easier. Since just 10 per cent of households receive between one-third and one-half of total income, targeting them for inspection constitutes the most efficient use of resources and could yield significant results. Enforcement should be accompanied by a more rigorous analysis of the distributive effects of tax subsidies and legal loopholes.

In order to improve the efficiency and progressivity of direct taxes, two additional changes should be adopted (CEPAL, 2006). First, countries should promote legislative changes to expand personal income taxes over corporate income taxes. The latter raised twice as much as the former in the period 1995–99 (1.7 per cent of GDP versus 0.9 per cent) in Latin America.[9] To promote this change, governments should maintain the top marginal rate of the personal income tax and the corporate income tax rate at similar levels.

Second, property taxes should receive more attention. Property taxes are not a large source of income in any country, but are particularly low in Latin America. They represent only 0.3 per cent for the region as a whole, and in five Latin American countries they generate no revenues at all (Gómez, 2006; World Bank, 2004). Yet, given the high concentration on land and the difficulties to tax mobile factors like capital, property taxes have a large potential as a redistributive source of income. Improving the information available on land property is a precondition to expanding property taxes. Governments should also be careful in the design of their property taxes, as their impact on distribution and economic efficiency can vary substantially (Bird and Slack, 2002).

None of these proposals is particularly innovative. Several studies on taxes and income distribution in Latin America have recently recommended the expansion of income taxes, the reduction of tax incentives, the simplification of the tax system and improvements in enforcement (see, e.g., Aldunate and Martner, 2006; CEPAL, 1998, 2006; World Bank, 2004). The World Bank (2004, p. 256) proposes a six-point agenda for 'equity-enhancing tax reform in Latin America' that includes broader tax bases together with low tax rates, more intense use of property taxes and greater compliance. Yet most studies fail to identify who must be the key contributors in the region. CEPAL (1998) recognises the need for a new 'fiscal pact', but pays insufficient attention to the central role of the elites. In the end, expanding tax revenues — particularly income and property taxes — will ultimately depend on the ability and political will of the government to impose new conditions on the rich.

Obstacles to Redistribution Through the Public Budget

The previous two sections have shown that the management of the public budget can have a major impact on the reduction of income inequality in Latin America. Focusing on social policy and taxes, I have argued that countries in the region should build universal social systems and promote more progressive taxation. While social spending is particularly important to improve welfare at the bottom of the distribution, progressive income taxes will help to reduce the income share of the rich.

Are these recommendations really useful for Latin America? Does the region have the external and internal conditions required to radically alter the structure of its public? In this last section, I will briefly address these key questions, insisting on the importance of politics and institutions to secure significant change. The section will explore two major obstacles for policy reform in this area: globalisation, and domestic political and institutional constraints.

Globalisation

By strengthening the role of transnational corporations (TNCs) and financial capital in economic development, globalisation may reduce the autonomy of the state to sustain generous, universal social policies financed by progressive taxes.[10] Competition for foreign investment, together with the liberalisation of the current and financial accounts, has reduced the ability of the state to raise taxes. Financial openness and deregulation have increased the scope of financial transactions, creating pressures for 'market-friendly' macroeconomic management — that is, fiscal conservatism. According to Rao (1999b, p. 357), the result of these negative trends is that 'the fiscal basis of constructive state action to promote human development and resolve the distributive conflict is now more limited than ever before'.

Globalisation creates downward pressure on tax revenues and has made tax expansion difficult in all countries, including those in Latin America. Four different factors are particularly important to explain this trend (Grunberg, 1998; Tanzi, 2003):

1. *Trade liberalisation.* The reduction of tariffs has given rise to a fall in revenues from taxes on foreign trade. In Latin America, taxes on foreign trade as a percentage of GDP decreased from 2 per cent in 1985–89 to 1.6 per cent in 2000–03. In countries like Chile, Costa Rica and Honduras, the reduction was more dramatic. In Chile, for example, they went down from 3.2 per cent in the second half of the 1980s to just 1 per cent at the beginning of the twenty-first century (Gómez, 2006).

2. *Globalisation of the tax base.* The increasing weight of TNCs in the world economy has rendered most tax systems obsolete. Adapting them to the new global conditions, however, is not easy because foreign income is very difficult to track, and companies are able to avoid taxes through transfer pricing and other tax planning techniques. In fact, empirical studies have shown that firms systematically post a higher rate of return on average in countries with low tax rates than in countries with high tax rates (Grunberg, 1998).

3. *Tax competition to attract foreign capital.* Many developing countries have created export processing zones, which produce a large share of the country's manufactures but have a marginal contribution to tax revenues.

4. *Expansion of the informal economy.* The elimination of all restrictions on the movement of capital has been particularly negative. By creating an 'exit' option for domestic and foreign firms, capital account liberalisation has increased capital's bargaining power vis-à-vis the public sector and other social actors. Increasing income taxes on individuals and corporations has thus become harder than ever before. Capital account liberalisation has particularly strengthened the financial class, increasing its influence in the process of economic decision-making (Amadeo and Baduri, 1991). Securing the approval of global financial markets has become a primary concern for all countries, forcing governments to run primary fiscal surpluses. More generally, according to Amadeo and Baduri (1991, p. 46), it has left most countries 'unable or unwilling to pursue such social objectives as income distribution ... whose urgency and need is not perceived as such by financial groups'.

The experience of developed countries confirms the negative influence of globalisation on welfare regimes (Pontusson, 2005). While we cannot talk about a systematic retrenchment of public social spending in any country, there have been some changes in the generosity of many services and in the way they are provided. Pressures to implement restrictive fiscal policies and difficulties to increase taxes may have constrained the growth of the welfare state. In the European Union, for example, the convergence requirements set in the Maastricht Treaty (particularly the upper bound of 3 per cent for the public deficit) constrain the growth of public spending, including social services.

Financial deregulation forced most governments to reduce corporate taxes, as well as marginal taxes on personal capital investments. According to Clift and Perraton (2004, p. 211), 'there is evidence that globalization has reduced the effective corporate tax rates (including amongst the Scandinavia countries) ... Arguably globalization constrained governments' ability to raise revenues to levels that they desired.'

There is thus little doubt that implanting redistributive policies in Latin America now may be harder than ever before. Yet the constraints on redistribution should not be over-estimated, as different evidence from developed and developing countries demonstrates. In particular, diversity in both the level and structure of public expenditures and revenues shows that governments still maintain significant degrees of freedom. Within developed countries, for example, sharp distinctions between the LMEs, Nordic SMEs and Continental SMEs remain, and no convergence to low spending levels is evident (Huber, 2002).

Latin American countries present significant differences in tax and welfare regimes as well. Tax revenues (including social security contributions) as a percentage of GDP range from 36 per cent in Brazil to 11 per cent in Guatemala and 9 per cent in Haiti. There are countries with similar income levels but significant differences in tax burdens. In Chile, for example, the share of taxes in GDP is 17 per cent, while in Mexico it is only 11 per cent. Martínez, in a recent set of studies on the role of states, markets and families in welfare provision, shows that there are sharp differences between some Latin American countries and others (see, e.g., Martinez, 2005, 2006, 2007).[1] In her own words, 'from the perspective of welfare production, we observe many types of states' involvement, both in the quantity of resources spent, and in the allocation criteria adopted' (Martinez, 2005, p. 23).

Two additional arguments should be taken into consideration when evaluating the effect of globalisation on social spending and taxes. First, all Latin American countries have some room to expand total taxes as a proportion of GDP. As Table 10.14 demonstrates, the region's tax burden is low when compared to other economies with similar income levels. Second, higher public spending can be compatible with an orthodox management of the budget and with macroeconomic stability. The experience of Northern European is particularly illustrative in this regard. According to data presented in Stephens (2002), fiscal policy in all these countries was quite conservative with public surpluses or small deficits for the period 1960–90.

Domestic Political and Institutional Constraints

Domestic obstacles to redistributive universalism may be even more difficult to overcome than those created by globalisation. Creating the type of institutions required to support a universal welfare regime has always been hard, and may be even more difficult after the neoliberal reforms implemented in recent times. High levels of income and political inequality also reduce the likelihood of creating powerful social coalitions in favour of redistribution.

When analysing the likelihood of the proposed agenda, one should not forget the difficulties that Latin America has historically faced to promote redistributive policies. Between 1950 and 1980, many Latin American countries implemented new policies with stated universal objectives. They expanded health and education services and some also created social security programmes. Yet in most countries the result was only a highly stratified welfare system with limited redistributive capacity. According to Molyneux (2006, p. 427), 'despite the expansion of social provision from the 1960s, most of the region still suffered from poor and skewed coverage and low quality services. Entitlements remained for the most part tied to formal employment.' Tax systems were also inefficient and not particularly progressive, with over-reliance on taxes on foreign trade and ineffective indirect taxes.

The truncated nature of industrial modernisation, which was unable to incorporate many workers into the formal labour market, was partly responsible for the failure of social policy. A welfare regime based on labour entitlements could not work adequately for economies with dual labour markets and high levels of informality. Yet the lack of accountable and efficient public institutions and economic and political inequality were even more important. As Filgueira and Filgueira (2002, p. 129) put it, problems in the region were the result of 'centralized authoritarianism, general inequality, rent-seeking political elites, and the bureaucratic weakness of the state in coordinating and distributing services'.

Weak bureaucracies and unequal class structures are still obstacles to universalistic redistribution funded by progressive taxation. Neoliberal policies of marketisation and state retrenchment weakened the bureaucracy in many countries, without improving the efficiency of the state and the quality of services. Both the middle class and the poor remain politically weak and economically vulnerable, while the elites maintain privileged access to the state (World Bank, 2004). Improving the quality of social services — a necessary condition to achieve real universalism (Filgueira et al., 2006) — and succeeding in expanding direct taxes, is thus complicated.

This pessimistic conclusion, however, should be qualified in at least three ways, as detailed below.

Historical Diversity Among Countries

Social policy in the post-World War II era was indeed generally been flawed, but performance has varied significantly among countries. Filgueira (1998,

2005) identifies three types of welfare regimes in Latin America up to 1970: stratified universalistic (Uruguay, Argentina, Chile and Costa Rica); dual (Brazil and Mexico); and exclusionary (Bolivia and Central America, with the exception of Costa Rica). While dual and exclusionary regimes concentrated social policy on a relatively small number of people, those with stratified, universalistic social systems expanded services and social security transfers to most citizens. Social spending in Uruguay, Argentina, Chile and Costa Rica — despite problems of segmented provision and sustainability — contributed to significant improvements in human development. The case of Costa Rica constitutes a good example: Costa Rica's expansion of spending in health and education during the period 1950–80 resulted in larger social progress than that of most other developing countries, as Table 10.15 illustrates. In 1987, only two developing countries (out of 96 analysed) had lower infant mortality, only four had lower illiteracy rates and none had a better life expectancy than Costa Rica. In all three areas, Costa Rica's comparative position improved between 1960 and 1987.

Higher success in those Latin American countries that adopted a more universalistic approach constitutes a new proof of the importance of universalism. It also signals that creating this type of welfare regime is not impossible in Latin America: a combination of mass support and democratic institutions can go a long way in instituting them (Filgueira, 2005). Yet the difficulties that Argentina, Uruguay and Costa Rica face in sustaining universalism in the

Table 10.15: CR Comparisons with 94 Other Developing Countries in Terms of Human Development, 1960–87

	Infant Mortality[1]		Life Expectancy		Adult Illiteracy	
	1960	*1987*	*1960*	*1987*	*1960*	*1987*
Number of countries with better indicators than CR	13	2	5	0	3	4
Low-income countries	0	0	0	0	0	0
in Latin America	0	0	0	0	0	0
Medium-income countries	3	0	1	0	0	1
in Latin America	1	0	1	0	0	1
Medium–high-income countries	10	2	4	0	3	3
in Latin America	6	1	3	0	3	3

Notes: (1) Refers to children younger than five years.

(2) This is the group where Costa Rica is included.

Source: Trejos (1991) with data from UNICEF and the World Bank.

long term, and complementing it with a successful economic model, are still worrying.

Diversity between countries also points to the importance of avoiding 'one size fits all' approaches when promoting universal programmes funded by progressive taxation. Each country should follow a different policy path that takes into account its own historical conditions, class relations and institutional capabilities.[12] While countries with a long tradition of social security transfers (e.g. Brazil) may consider how to redefine them in a more universalistic way, countries with very weak states and low social spending (e.g. Central America) should concentrate on increasing spending gradually while improving services.

Institutional Quality Must Improve Even Without Universal Policies

There is little doubt that most Latin American countries — including Uruguay and Costa Rica — must improve the institutional quality of the public sector in order to sustain an expansion of social services and taxes. According to Filgueira et al. (2006), the public sector must improve its systems of information, its management of services and the coordination between different institutions in charge of social provision. Also required is a Weberian civil service with high levels of professionalism and commitment.

Even countries opting for targeted social provision need to undertake such institutional improvements. In fact, CCTs and similar targeted programmes may require even greater institutional capacity to identify the right beneficiaries and enforce conditionality (Mkandawire, 2006a). CCTs also require sustained improvements in health and education services to minimise waste of resources and frustration. Inter-agency coordination and proper evaluation are also necessary conditions for the success of conditional cash transfers.

The Potential Positive Effect of Democratic Consolidation

Democratic consolidation (as flawed as it has so far been) can hopefully alter the terms of the political debate on social spending and taxes. The experience of Costa Rica and Uruguay — the two Latin American countries with the best social systems and income distributions — shows the importance of well functioning democracies. The expansion of social spending as a proportion of GDP during the 1990s further reinforces the optimistic view on the contribution of democracy to redistribution.[13]

In order to be effective in promoting better redistributive systems, however, democracy will have to be accompanied by different political reforms. Without finding institutional and political channels to strengthen those supporting a more redistributive management of the public budget, no real change is likely.

The modernisation and strengthening of left-wing parties would be particularly useful, given their contribution to secure redistribution (Huber et al., 2006). This will require, among other measures, changes in the party financing legislation to reverse traditional resource imbalances (Huber, 2005).

Trade unions have historically been strong supporters of universal redistributive policies. Yet they have been weakened in nearly all Latin American countries in the last two decades due to privatisation, the growth of informality and the lack of internal capacity. The unionisation of informal workers and the modernisation of the ideas of trade unions may be essential to strengthen trade unions. Huber (2005) also emphasises that other civic organisations — including women's, environmental and community-based non-profit organisations — have a major role to play in redistributive politics. In her view, they should be incorporated in 'consultation with public agencies … It is [also] crucial to link civil society organizations directly to the policy-making process via engagement with political parties' (2005, p. 19).

Conclusions

Reducing income inequality must become a primary policy objective if Latin America is to enjoy sustained social and economic development. High inequality is ethically undesirable, and can harm the prospects for economic development. It is also one of the factors behind the recurrent episodes of social and political instability that the region has faced since colonial times.

Any study of the public budgets in Latin America should thus consider how to manage public expenditures and revenues to improve the distribution of income. This chapter has argued that Latin American countries should follow the lessons from the Northern European countries and slowly build up universal welfare regimes. In order to finance more generous social programmes, countries in the region must also expand taxes and make the tax structure more progressive.

The promotion of universal programmes may not only reduce income inequality but also contribute to improving competitiveness. High spending on education and health can assist in the accumulation of human capital. Universalism and lower income inequality can thus contribute to improve social cohesion and promote an investment-friendly social environment.

Yet this virtuous circle between economic and social policy — high social spending leading to higher economic growth which in turn delivers more resources for social investment — is not automatic, particularly in the current era. Intense global competition and the emergence of China as the world's factory could still leave Latin American countries empty handed. The region would then face an unsustainable situation, with generous welfare regimes but stagnant economies. This may already have happened in countries like Argentina or even Costa Rica, where high social spending has not been accompanied by economic success.

Building more dynamic interactions between the social and economic sphere is thus the ultimate challenge for Latin America. While the approach to the public budget outline in this chapter can constitute a useful first step, it must be accompanied by a serious redefinition of the Latin American economic model.

References

E. Aldunate and R. Martner (2006) 'Política fiscal y protección social', *Revista de la CEPAL*, no. 90, pp. 87–104.

A. Alesina and E. Glaeser (2004) *Fighting Poverty in the US and Europe: A World of Difference* (Oxford: Oxford University Press).

L. Andrenacci and F. Repetto (2006) 'Un camino para reducir la desigualdad y construir ciudadanía', in C. Molina (ed.), *Universalismo básico: Una nueva política social para América Latina* (Washington: Inter-American Development Bank).

T. Banuri and E. Amadeo (1991) 'Policy, Governance, and the Management of Conflict', in T. Banuri (ed.), *Economic Liberalization: No Panacea. The Experience of Latin America and Asia* (Oxford: Clarendon Press).

A. Berry (2005) 'The Distributional Impacts of Economic Integration on Latin American Society, and the Institutional Response', paper prepared for the ESRC Seminar Series Social Policy, Stability and Exclusion in Latin America, London, 2–3 June.

R. Bird and E. Slack (2002) 'Land and Property Taxation: A Review', unpublished manuscript (Toronto: University of Toronto).

R. Boyer (2005) 'How and Why Capitalisms Differ', *Economy and Society*, vol. 34, no. 4, pp. 509–57.

J.-M. Burniaux et al. (1998) 'Income Distribution and Poverty in Selected OECD Countries', Economics Department Working Paper, no. 189 (Paris: Organization for Economic Cooperation and Development).

CEPAL (1998) *El Pacto Fiscal. Fortalezas, Debilidades y Desafíos* (Santiago: Economic Commission for Latin America and the Caribbean).

CEPAL (2002) *Globalization and Development* (Santiago: Economic Commission for Latin America and the Caribbean).

CEPAL (2006) *Tributacion en America Latina. En busca de una nueva agenda de reformas* (Santiago: Economic Commission for Latin America and the Caribbean).

K.-Y. Chu, H. Davoodi and S. Gupta (2004) 'Income Distribution and Tax and Government Social-Spending Policies in Developing Countries', in G. Cornia (ed.), *Inequality, Growth and Poverty in an Era of Liberalization and Globalization* (Oxford: Oxford University Press).

B. Clift and J. Perraton (ed.) (2004) *Where are National Capitalisms Now?* (New York: Palgrave Macmillan).

P. Cook and R. Frank (1995) *The Winner-Take-All Society. Why the Few at the Top Get So Much More Than the Rest of Us* (New York: Simon and Schuster).

G. Esping-Andersen (1989) 'The Three Political Economies of the Welfare State', *Canadian Review of Sociology and Anthropology*, vol. 26, no. 1, pp. 10–36.

G. Esping-Andersen (1990) *The Three Worlds of the Welfare State* (Princeton: Princeton University Press).

G. Esping-Andersen (ed.) (1996) *Welfare States in Transition. National Adaptation in Global Economies* (London: Sage).

M. Esteve-Abe, T. Iversen and D. Soskice (2001) 'Social Protection and the Formation of Skills: A Reinterpretation of the Welfare State', in P. Hall and D. Soskice (eds.), *Varieties of Capitalism: The Institutional Foundations of Competitiveness* (Oxford: Oxford University Press).

C. Filgueira and F. Filgueira (2002) 'Models of Welfare and Models of Capitalism: The Limits of Transferability', in E. Huber (ed.), *Models of Capitalism: Lessons for Latin America* (University Park, PA: Pennsylvania State University Press).

F. Filgueira (1998) 'El nuevo modelo de prestaciones sociales en América Latina: Residualismo y Ciudadanía Estratificada', in B. Roberts (ed.), *Ciudadanía y Política Social* (San José: FLACSO/SSRC).

F. Filgueira (2005) 'Welfare and Democracy in Latin America: The Development, Crises and Aftermath of Universal, Dual and Exclusionary Social States', paper prepared for the UNRISD Project on Social Policy and Democratization, Geneva.

F. Filgueira et al. (2006) 'Universalismo básico: Una alternativa posible y necesaria para mejorar las condiciones de vida en América Latina', in C.

Molina (ed.), *Universalismo básico: Una nueva política social para América Latina* (Washington: Inter-American Development Bank).

J. Gómez (2006) 'Evolución y situación tributaria actual en América Latina: una serie de temas para la discusión', in CEPAL, *Tributacion en America Latina. En busca de una nueva agenda de reformas* (Santiago: Economic Commission for Latin America and the Caribbean).

I. Grunberg (1998) 'Double Jeopardy: Globalization, Liberalization and the Fiscal Squeeze', *World Development*, no. 26, pp. 591–605.

P. Hall and D. Soskice (eds.) (2001) *Varieties of Capitalism: The Institutional Foundations of Competitiveness* (Oxford: Oxford University Press).

E. Huber (2002a) 'Conclusions: Actors, Institutions, and Policies' in E. Huber (ed.), *Models of Capitalism: Lessons for Latin America* (University Park, PA: Pennsylvania State University Press).

E. Huber (ed.) (2002b) *Models of Capitalism: Lessons for Latin America* (University Park, PA: Pennsylvania State University Press).

E. Huber (2005) 'Inequality and the State in Latin America', paper prepared for the Conference of the APSA Task Force on Difference and Inequality in the Developing World, University of Virginia, 22–23 April.

E. Huber et al. (2006) 'Politics and Inequality in Latin America and the Caribbean', *American Sociological Review*, no.71, pp. 943–63.

R. Kozul-Wright and R. Rowthorn (eds.) (1998) *Transnational Corporations and the Global Economy* (New York: Macmillan).

R. Lo Vuolo (2005) 'Social Protection in Latin America: Different Approaches to Managing Social Exclusion and their Outcomes', paper presented at the ESRC Seminar Series Social Policy, Stability and Exclusion in Latin America, London, 2–3 June.

J.L. Machinea and M. Hopenhayn (2005) 'La esquiva equidad en el desarrollo latinoamericano. Una visión estructural, una aproximación multifacética', in *Serie Informes y Estudios Especiales 14* (Santiago: Economic Comission for Latin America and the Caribbean).

T. Mkandawire (2006a) 'Targeting and Universalism in Poverty Reduction', UNRISD Social Policy and Development Programme Paper no. 23, Geneva

T. Mkandawire (ed.) (2006b) *Social Policy in a Development Context* (Geneva: United Nations Research Institution for Social Development).

M. Mann and D. Riley (2007) 'Explaining Macro-regional Trends in Global Income Inequality, 1950–2000', *Socio-economic Review*, no. 5, pp. 81–115.

I. Mares (2001) 'Firms and the Welfare State: When, Why, and How Does Social Policy Matter to Employers?' in P. Hall and D. Soskice (eds.), *Varieties of Capitalism: The Institutional Foundations of Competitiveness* (Oxford: Oxford University Press).

J. Martínez (2006a) 'Regímenes de bienestar en América Latina: consideraciones generales y trayectorias regionales', *Revista Centroamericana de Ciencias Sociales*, vol. II, no. 2, pp.45–79.

J. Martínez (2006b) 'Regímenes de bienestar en América Latina: ¿cuántos y cuáles son?' Avance de investigación, Fundacion Carolina, April, available from www.fundacioncarolina.es.

J. Martínez (2006c) 'What are Welfare Regimes in Latin America? Shared and Distinctive Features of Markets, States and Families', paper submitted to the XXVI Congress of the Latin American Studies Association, Puerto Rico, 15–18 March.

Merrill Lynch (2006) *World Wealth Report, 2006* (New York: Merrill Lynch and Capgemini).

W. Milberg (1998) 'Globalization and Its Limits', in R. Kozul-Wright and R. Rowthorn (eds.), *Transnational Corporations and the Global Economy* (New York: Macmillan).

C. Molina (ed.) (2006) *Universalismo básico: Una nueva política social para América Latina* (Washington: Inter-American Development Bank).

M. Molyneux (2006) 'Mothers at the Service of the New Poverty Agenda: Progresa/Oportunidades, Mexico's Conditional Transfer Programme', *Social Policy and Administration*, vol. 40, no. 4, pp. 425–49.

R. Pizarro (2001) 'La vulnerabilidad social y sus desafíos: una mirada desde América Latina', *Estudios estadísticos y prospectivos*, no. 6, Comisión Económica para América Latina y el Caribe.

J. Pontusson (2005) *Inequality and Prosperity: Social Europe vs. Liberal America*) (Ithaca, NY: Cornell University Press).

J. Pontusson, D. Rueda and C. Way (2002) 'Comparative Political Economy of Wage Distribution: The Role of Partisanship and Labour Market Institutions', *British Journal of Political Science*, no. 32, pp. 281–308.

A. Portes, A. and K. Hoffman (2003) 'Latin American Class Structures: Their Composition and Change during the Neoliberal Era', *Latin American Research Review*, vol. 38, no. 1, pp. 41–83.

M. Rao (1999) 'Openness, Poverty and Inequality', *Human Development Report 1999 Background Papers*, vol. 1 (New York: United Nations Development Program).

D. Sánchez-Ancochea (2004) 'Leading Coalitions' and Patterns of Accumulation and Distribution in Small Countries: A Comparative Study of Costa Rica and the Dominican Republic under Globalization, unpublished doctoral dissertation, New School University, New York.

A. Solimano (2005) 'Hacia nuevas políticas sociales en América Latina: crecimiento, clases medias y derechos sociales', *Revista de la CEPAL*, no. 87, pp. 45–60.

J. Stephens (2002) 'European Welfare State Regimes: Configurations, Outcomes, Transformations', in E. Huber (ed.), *Models of Capitalism: Lessons for Latin America* (University Park, PA: Pennsylvania State University Press).

V. Tanzi (2004) 'La globalización y la necesidad de una reforma fiscal en los países en desarrollo', *Documento de divulgación IECI*, 06, Instituto para la Integración de America Latina y el Caribe, Inter-American Development Bank.

V. Tanzi and H. Zee (2000) 'Tax Policy for Emerging Markets: Developing Countries', IMF Working Paper no. 35.

L. Taylor and R. Vos (2003) 'Balance of Payments Liberalization in Latin America: Effects on Growth, Distribution and Poverty', in R. Vos, L. Taylor and R. Paes de Barros (eds.), *Economic Liberalization, Distribution and Poverty: Latin America in the 1990s* (Cheltenham, UK: Edward Elgar).

J.D. Trejos (1991) 'La política social y la valorización de los recursos humanos', in J. Garnier et al. (eds.), *Costa Rica: entre la ilusión y la desesperanza* (San José, CR: Ediciones Guayacán).

UNDP (2006) *Human Development Report, 2006* (New York: United Nations Development Program).

J.S. Valenzuela (2006a) 'Demografía familiar y desarrollo. Chile y Suecia desde 1914', in J.S. Valenzuela, E. Tironi and T. Scully (eds.), *El eslabón perdido. Familia, modernización y bienestar en Chile* (Madrid: Taurus).

J.S. Valenzuela (2006b) 'Diseños dispares, resultados diferentes y convergencias tardías. Las instituciones de bienestar social en Chile y Suecia', in J. Valenzuela, J. Samuel, E. Tironi and T. Scully (eds.), *El eslabón perdido. Familia, modernización y bienestar en Chile* (Madrid: Taurus).

F. Veras Soares et al. (2006) 'Cash Transfer Programmes in Brazil: Impacts on Inequality and Poverty', International Poverty Centre Working Papers no. 21.

A. Wagstaff et al. (1999) 'Redistributive Effect, Progressivity and Differential Tax Treatment: Personal Income Taxes in Twelve OECD Countries', *Journal of Public Economics*, vol. 72, no. 1, pp. 73–98.

World Bank (2004) *Inequality in Latin America: Breaking with History?* (Washington, DC: World Bank).

World Bank (2006) *World Development Report 2006: Equity and Development* (New York: World Bank and Oxford University Press).

Notes

[1]   Measuring income inequality is costly and difficult because it requires complex household surveys. Inequality indicators vary significantly depending on the way these surveys are done. Nicaragua, for example, has a Gini coefficient of 0.42 when using consumption surveys and 0.53 when using income data (World Bank, 2006).

[2]   Although this comparable data is for the early 1990s, the analysis is still valid today. Income inequality has decreased slightly in Mexico and more significantly in Brazil in the last five years, but the pattern of distribution among deciles remains similar.

[3]   While these calculations are just crude approximations based on national account statistics and income distribution, the data are useful to illustrate the extent of concentration in Latin America when compared with other regions.

[4]   Unfortunately, we do not have enough space in this chapter to discuss this literature in any detail. Nevertheless, it is important to emphasise that the most important contribution of the varieties of capitalism approach is their systemic approach. The character of welfare regimes is directly linked to the way in which countries organise their economies and insert themselves in the global economy. See, for example, Hall and Soskice (2001).

[5]   Pontusson's classification is just one of many that appear in this literature. Esping-Andersen (1990), for example, distinguishes between three welfare states: liberal, social-democratic and conservative/corporativistic. This is also the starting point for Stephens' (2002) division between social democratic, Christian democratic,

liberal and 'wage earner' welfare states. Hall and Soskice (2001), in their study of varieties of capitalism, distinguish only between coordinated market economies and liberal market economies. The regulation school incorporates a longer classification with at least four categories: market-oriented capitalism, meso-corporatist capitalism, state-driven capitalism and social-democratic capitalism (Boyer, 2006). All these studies recognise the unequal nature of the liberal or Anglo-Saxon model and many emphasise the particularities of the Nordic countries in terms of social spending and equity.

[6] The post taxes-post transfer Gini coefficient does not incorporate the value of social services that people receive. Otherwise, we could probably see even larger differences in the redistributive power of different governments.

[7] The differences in the importance of public provision are also evident in health. While in the Nordic SMEs 81% of total spending in health was done by the public sector in the early 1980s, in Continental SMEs the share of the public sector was only 71% and in LMEs it was 68%.

[8] See similar evidence in Estevez-Ave et al. (2001).

[9] Data from World Bank (2004). Tanzi and Zee (2000) show that a similar problem exists in other developing countries. In the Middle East, corporate income taxes as a proportion of GDP were 3.2% during the period 1995–97, while personal income taxes were just 1.3%.

[10] Globalisation can be broadly understood as the 'economic interdependence between countries where cross-border linkages among markets and production and financial activities have reached such an extent that economic developments in any one country are influenced to a significant degree by policies and developments outside its boundaries' (Milberg, 1998, p. 71). For a detailed discussion of globalisation and its main forces, see CEPAL (2004).

[12] For an interesting presentation of this argument based on the notion of basic universalism ('universalismo basico'), see Molina (2006).

[13] This paragraph relies heavily on Filgueira (2005).

INSTITUTE FOR THE STUDY OF THE
AMERICAS
UNIVERSITY OF LONDON · SCHOOL OF ADVANCED STUDY

The Institute for the Study of the Americas (ISA) promotes, coordinates and provides a focus for research and postgraduate teaching on the Americas – Canada, the USA, Latin America and the Caribbean – in the University of London.

The Institute was officially established in August 2004 as a result of a merger between the Institute of Latin American Studies and the Institute of United States Studies, both of which were formed in 1965.

The Institute publishes in the disciplines of history, politics, economics, sociology, anthropology, geography and environment, development, culture and literature, and on the countries and regions of Latin America, the United States, Canada and the Caribbean.

ISA runs an active programme of events – conferences, seminars, lectures and workshops – in order to facilitate national research on the Americas in the humanities and social sciences. It also offers a range of taught master's and research degrees, allowing wide-ranging multi-disciplinary, multi-country study or a focus on disciplines such as politics or globalisation and development for specific countries or regions.

Full details about the Institute's publications, events, postgraduate courses and other activities are available on the web at www.americas.sas.ac.uk.

Institute for the Study of the Americas
School of Advanced Study, University of London
Senate House, Malet Street
London WC1E 7HU

Tel 020 7862 8870, Fax 020 7862 8886, Email americas@sas.ac.uk
Web www.americas.sas.ac.uk

Recent and forthcoming titles in the ISA series:

Democracy after Pinochet: Politics, parties and elections in Chile (2007)
by Alan Angell

Mexican Soundings: Essays in Honour of David A. Brading (2007)
edited by Susan Deans-Smith and Eric Van Young

America's Americans: Population Issues in U.S. Society and Politics (2007)
edited by Philip Davies and Iwan Morgan

Football in the Americas: Fútbol, Futebol, Soccer (2007)
edited by Rory Miller

Bolivia: Revolution and the Power of History in the Present. Essays (2007)
James Dunkerley

American Civilization (2007)
Charles A. Jones

Caribbean Literature After Independence: The Case of Earl Lovelace (2008)
edited by Bill Schwarz

Joaquim Nabuco, British Abolitionists and the End of Slavery in Brazil: Correspondence 1880–1905 (forthcoming)
edited by Leslie Bethell and Jose Murilo de Carvalho

Contesting Clio's Craft: New Directions and Debates in Canadian History (forthcoming)
edited by Christopher Dummitt & Michael Dawson

The Contemporary Canadian Metropolis (forthcoming)
edited by Richard Dennis, Ceri Morgan and Stephen Shaw

Latin London: The Lives of Latin American Migrants in the Capital (forthcoming)
by Cathy McIlwaine

Printed in the United Kingdom
by Lightning Source UK Ltd.
135109UK00002B/55-99/P

9 781900 039949